Field Guide to

Developing, Operating and

Restoring Your Nonprofit Board

Third Edition

By Carter McNamara, MBA, PhD

AUTHENTICITY CONSULTING, LLC
MINNEAPOLIS, MN USA

For reprint permission, more information on Authenticity Consulting, LLC, or to order additional copies of this or any of our other publications, please contact:

> Authenticity Consulting, LLC
> 4008 Lake Drive Avenue North
> Minneapolis, MN 55422-1508 USA
>
> 800.971.2250 toll-free
> 763.971.8890 direct
> http://www.authenticityconsulting.com

Trademarks

"Authenticity Circles," "Free Management Library," "Free Nonprofit Micro-eMBA" and "Free Micro-eMBA" are service marks of Authenticity Consulting, LLC, Minneapolis, Minnesota. "Leveraging the Power of Peers" is a registered mark of Authenticity Consulting, LLC, Minneapolis, Minnesota. "Policy Governance" is a registered trademark of Carver Governance Design, Inc.

Credits

Cover design and illustrations by Erin Scott/Wylde Hare Creative, Woodbury, Minnesota.
Photographs © 2005 JupiterImages Corporation/Photos.com, primary cover photo;
  © Teri McNamara/Impressions & Expressions and © Erin Scott/Wylde Hare Creative,
  secondary cover photos.
Clip art by Nova Development Corporation Art Explosion 750,000 Images.
Printed by Graphic & Printing Services, Big Lake, Minnesota.

Manufactured in the United States of America
First Edition April 2002
Second Edition June 2003
Third Edition July 2008

Waivers of Responsibility

1. Various Web addresses are referenced in this book. The author and publisher have no legal responsibility or liability for the currency or accuracy of these Web addresses or their content.
2. Information in this book is not to be considered as legal, tax and/or financial advice as if from an expert specifically in those areas. In-depth and technical advice needed in those areas should be obtained from professionals in those areas.

Publisher's Cataloging in Publication Data

McNamara, Carter, 1953 -

   Field Guide to Developing, Operating and Restoring Your Nonprofit Board
/ by Carter McNamara

   Includes bibliographical references and index.

   ISBN 10 1-933719-06-1 (paperback)

   ISBN 13 978-1-933719-06-0 (paperback)

   1. Board of Directors. 2. Nonprofits. 3. Governance. 4. Leadership
I. Author   II. Title

FSC
Mixed Sources
Product group from well-managed
forests and other controlled sources

Cert no. SW-COC-004306
www.fsc.org
©1996 Forest Stewardship Council

Table of Contents

Table of Tables

Introduction

Audiences – New, Established and Struggling Nonprofits

This guide will be extremely useful to you if you are starting a new Board, rejuvenating a current Board, or restoring a struggling Board. The guide is written especially for audiences in the United States of America and Canada, including for:

- Founders of nonprofits
- Current Board members
- Potential Board members
- Chief Executive Officers (Executive Directors) or other staff members
- Nonprofit consultants
- Nonprofit service organizations
- Funders

In a guide about Boards, different audiences might want different types of content. Experts on Boards might want inclusion of state-of-the-art concepts about Boards. Visionary people might want descriptions of Boards in terms of grand outcomes, such as visionary, transformational and community-changing. This guide focuses primarily on practical tips and tools, rather than the latest research, although emerging Board models are mentioned. These tips and tools can bring about transformational change in Boards, nonprofits and even their communities. Government agencies and funders might want information about cultivating transparent and accountable Boards. The guide includes plenty of guidelines to accomplish those traits in Boards. Management support organizations, Board members and staff members probably prefer comprehensive, easy-to-reference information, especially with focus on practical tips and tools. They will love this book.

Guide Recognizes Diversity of Board Models

There are a variety of structures or designs (models) of nonprofit governing Boards of Directors. Some Boards might choose not to use committees and to use temporary task forces instead. Members of a "working Board" might choose to be highly involved in the day-to-day matters of an organization, possibly because the organization is just getting started or does not have any staff members. Likewise, members of a "collective" Board might choose to be involved in the day-to-day activities because they do not differentiate between Board and staff, and instead prefer to work together as one "team." Members of a Policy Governance® Board often choose not to use any committees. ("Policy Governance" is a registered trademark of Carver Governance Design, Inc.) The most important function of the model is to guide Board members to ensure that the nonprofit is successfully meeting the needs of the community.

Many experts on nonprofit governance assert that the traditional policy Board, with its seemingly top-down, rigid roles and hierarchy of committees, is becoming obsolete – or at least should be increasingly questioned – as demands for Board effectiveness and accountability continue to grow, especially among highly diverse groups. (Actually, few Boards adopt the top-down, rigid-roles and instead most modify the design to suit the nature and needs of their nonprofits.) This guide provides guidelines and tools primarily – but not exclusively – from the perspective of the traditional policy Board because, despite its drawbacks, it remains the most frequently used model. It also is the most well-known model and, therefore, the most useful to reference when suggesting various Board practices and policies. It also can be useful to compare against the variety of other types of Board models. You should develop your own Board model or structure as necessary to suit the nature and needs of the nonprofit. For example, if you prefer not to utilize traditional Board committees, then you might prefer instead to utilize temporary task forces wherever the guide mentions committees.

Step-by-Step, Easy-to-Reference Content

The nature of this guide is to be as highly practical as possible. Guidelines are written in a "how to" style to be readily understandable and useful. The90

guide focuses on all of the basic activities required for you to build and restore a nonprofit Board of Directors in the United States of America or Canada. People in other countries can also benefit from this guide; however, they should seek additional assistance regarding legal filings to start a nonprofit, laws and regulations regarding nonprofit financial and tax matters, and employment laws (employments laws are very similar between nonprofit and for-profit organizations). Additional sources of assistance in these areas are mentioned throughout this guide.

Content of Guide

- In PART I, you learn how to start a nonprofit organization and a Board of Directors. The section describes nonprofit organizations – an understanding that Board members often do not have, but really should have. The major parts of nonprofits are described, especially its programs and how to differentiate programs from activities that really are not programs at all – this is very important for Board members to understand. Board members from for-profit organizations often come to nonprofits, expecting them to perform as if they have extensive resources, which they do not. So this guide also describes the culture of the typical small nonprofit. The roles of the Board and staff are made clearer with several organization charts of typical nonprofits. An extensive checklist is included to ensure that you take all of the necessary steps to successfully start a nonprofit. (It is not really "your" nonprofit, as nonprofits are owned by the public.)

- In PART II, you gain a solid understanding of the basic building blocks to further build the Board. It explains the roles of Boards, including fiduciary and legal responsibilities, primary governance documents, and types of committees. This section also describes the role of the Chief Executive Officer (if the nonprofit decides to have a CEO role in the organization). Many nonprofits use the job title "Executive Director" instead of "Chief Executive Officer." The section describes the diversity of ways that Board members structure their Boards and how they sometimes involve themselves in management activities (many experts assert that Board members should focus only on top-level policy-making, but many times that delineation is not practical for certain types of nonprofits).

- In PART III, you learn all about how to successfully build and operate the Board. You learn about typical Board operations, or how Board members get their job done. One of the most important jobs of the Board is to make sure that constituents are heard and that their needs are reflected in the mission, or purpose, of the nonprofit. The purpose and goals for a nonprofit, including for its Board, result from good strategic planning. Consequently, this section on Board operations starts with a basic overview of strategic planning and provides guidelines to help you develop a basic, short-term strategic plan. Strategic planning can also point to what expertise is needed on the Board and how members might be organized into various Board committees, or task forces, associated with achieving each of the strategic goals. All of the most common types of committees are described in this section, for those Boards that decide to use committees. Boards members conduct their important deliberations and decisions in Board meetings, so the quality of Board meetings is extremely important. This section includes many guidelines for how to improve those meetings. The section also includes an extensive listing of guidelines to help Board members provide effective oversight in a wide range of important Board functions. The section ends with description of how a Board can ensure that it remains high-quality.

▪ PART IV describes how the Board and CEO can work together in a manner that is highly cooperative and productive. It includes a rather detailed procedure for hiring, or replacing, a Chief Executive Officer (CEO) for the organization. It also explains how the Board supervises the CEO (depending on the particular Board model used by the nonprofit) and establishes a successful working relationship – sometimes a "strategic partnership" – with the CEO.

▪ PART V provides guidelines and one example of a step-by-step procedure to restore a struggling Board. Important principles for changing a Board are explained in preparation for using the procedure that follows. Guidelines in this section also help Boards to avoid Founder's Syndrome, a condition where the Board and staff follow the direction of a powerful and persuasive personality, rather than the direction set by the organization's mission.

▪ APPENDICES include a variety of highly practical information.

  ❑ Appendix A provides a Glossary that defines key terms used throughout the guide and in nonprofits.

  ❑ Appendix B provides directions to a vast amount of resources – many of them free – for nonprofits.

  ❑ Appendix C provides guidelines for forming Advisory Boards, which is an increasing trend in nonprofits.

  ❑ Appendix D provides guidelines for hiring consultants, an activity which Board members often should be involved in, or at least aware of.

  ❑ Appendix E provides references to a large number of free, online tools that can be used to measure the health or effectiveness of nonprofits – an activity that Board members should be very concerned about.

  ❑ Appendix F describes the "best practice" goals and associated objectives that are assigned to a Board Development (or Board Governance) Committee – the Committee charged to ensure high-quality operations of the Board (the Committee that would have the most use for this book).

  ❑ Appendix G lists the typical contents of a Board manual, which is the document that each Board member should have, and includes all of the most important resources that a Board member needs in order to do his/her job well.

❑   Appendix H includes samples of 20 of the most commonly used Board policies.
These can be downloaded for use within the organization that purchased this book.

The guide focuses on starting, operating and restoring Boards of Directors in nonprofits. The guide does not include detailed information about each of the major management functions in a nonprofit, for example, in strategic planning, programs, staffing, marketing, finances and fundraising.

 The Bibliography on page 281 suggests resources in each of these functions.

Guide's Focus on Human and Structural Aspects of Boards

Today, there is strong emphasis on humanistic values – as there should be – when guiding change in organizations, including in Boards. Accordingly, there is strong emphasis on considering peoples' feelings, beliefs and perceptions during change. Sometimes this is to the detriment of other important – although seemingly impersonal – matters, such as structures, processes and operations in organizations. In this guide, the author strives to maintain focus on humanistic values, yet also on the very important aspects of organizations that do not always seem so human in nature. Thus, there are many guidelines in this guide regarding structures, processes and operations, along with management functions, such as planning, organizing and coordinating resources in nonprofits.

Because of today's strong focus on humanistic values and the balance aimed for in this guide, some readers might find the guide lacking in discussions about warm matters of human development and dynamics. Hopefully, these readers will recognize that the guide contains many guidelines about aspects that make us so human during change, including intra-personal, interpersonal, intra-group and inter-group aspects.

The primary emphasis of this guide is on practical guidelines, tips and tools to start, operate and restore nonprofit Board of Directors. This emphasis is sometimes at the expense of extended discussions about broad topics, such as philosophies, values and paradigms about Boards. Certainly, there are many people who thrive on the creativity, insight and inspiration generated from those topics. Those readers might find the guide lacking in these highly inspirational discussions. Hopefully, they are compensated by the excitement of actually applying the book's tips and tools proven to be so successful in improving nonprofit Boards of Directors.

There is a recent explosion in the amount of books about corporate (especially for-profit) governance. These books suggest many new theories and models, replete with new names and packaging. Their authors explain what they believe to be wrong with traditional approaches to governance and Boards. Their explanations sometimes reference traditional terms, such as "plans," "policies" and "procedures," as somehow being too traditional, mechanistic and constraining. As a result, some readers might react that those terms in the guide are somehow no longer valid and useful. Those readers will benefit most from the guide if they focus on the intent of the terms, rather than on the terms themselves.

How to Use This Guide

To Start a Nonprofit and Board

1.   If you are just getting started with a new nonprofit, then you will want to carefully understand and follow guidelines in PARTs I, II and III. Go through these PARTs in sequence, one after the other. They will lead you to start a nonprofit, conduct basic organizational planning, and get your Board started with the most appropriate structure and roles for now.

2.   The resources in Appendix B, G and H will be particularly useful to you by suggesting a vast array of free resources for you to use as you start a nonprofit and Board. Be sure to download and begin to customize the numerous Board policies in Appendix H. They will help you to structure and effectively operate your Board.

3.   If it is clear to you that you will be hiring a Chief Executive Officer (Executive Director), then follow the guidelines in PART IV to do so.

4.   If you already want to learn about what problems can occur as a result of the founder's maybe taking too strong of a role, then review the guidelines in PART V about how to evolve a Board from being led by personalities to instead being led by plans and policies.

To Refine and Improve Current Operations of the Board

1.   If your Board is already somewhat established (members have been recruited, trained, and participating in deliberations and decisions about important matters), then you might skip PARTs I and II, and focus particularly on PART III about how Boards work.

2.   Guidelines in PART III will help you to continually refine and improve the operations of your Board, especially to regularly recruit and develop the most useful Board members, conduct the most useful Board meetings, and make the most judicious decisions.

3.   Consider use of the organizational assessments in Appendix E in order to identify which Board and management functions might need to be improved to continue to grow and/or improve a nonprofit and Board.

4.   You might even conduct brief, practical trainings for your Board members by training them about the contents of one of the sections of the book, for example, about decision making or guidelines for successful governance as included in PART III.

If Your Board Has Chronic Problems

1.   If the nonprofit and its Board have continued to experience chronic problems, then go to PART V and follow the guidelines in that section. Examples of chronic problems might be low attendance and participation of Board members, sustained and damaging conflicts among members, ineffective decision-making, and high turnover among Board members and the Chief Executive Officer.

2.   Consider using the organizational assessment resources in Appendix E to carefully identify the "root causes" of the nonprofit's issues and what you might do to resolve them.

3.   If you decide to hire outside help, then follow the guidelines in Appendix D to hire the most appropriate consultant and work with that person to ensure successful results.

4.   Guidelines for restoring your Board might suggest that you revisit some of the basics described in PART II and PART III about how to structure the Board, determine the best roles, and use the structure and roles to accomplish a high-performing Board.

5.   You might be faced with taking strong action about the role of Chief Executive. In that situation, follow the guidelines in IV.

In many of the topics in the guide, there are frequent cross-references to other related topics in the guide. Follow those to learn more about the topic.

As Preparation, Learn to Contact These Government Agencies

State- or Provincial-Level Agencies that Govern Corporations and Nonprofits

Laws and regulations governing nonprofit corporations can vary by state, province and/or federal levels. It is useful now to identify the Website of the state or provincial government agency that governs corporations and charities in your state or province. In several places in the guide, it mentions where you should contact that agency, for example, to incorporate your new nonprofit. Also, a brief scan of the agency's Website can quickly inform you of any laws or regulations and any other useful information about governing nonprofits in your state or province.

In the USA, the Website of the Secretary of State of Minnesota is http://www.sos.state.mn.us . Other states have a similar format, where "mn" is replaced by the abbreviation for the state.

Provinces in Canada each have their own unique Website – the following site lists Websites for many provinces: http://www.charityvillage.com/cv/guides/guide4.asp#Incorporation . Note that in Canada, you can incorporate at the provincial or federal level.

Federal-Level Agency That Governs Tax-Exempt Organizations

In the USA, one of the responsibilities of the Internal Revenue Service is to enact laws and regulations affecting tax-exempt and charitable organizations. Thus, its Website has an extensive amount of information. Go to http://www.irs.gov/charities/topic/index.html .

In Canada, the Canada Revenue Agency is responsible to enact laws and regulations affecting tax-exempt and charitable organizations. Go to http://www.cra-arc.gc.ca/tax/charities/menu-e.html .

Also, the Index on page 289 includes many relevant terms that you can find in the guide.

Frequently Used Terms in Guidebook

The following terms are used frequently in this guide and with the following definitions:

Clients

Clients are people or groups of people who directly benefit from the programs and services of a nonprofit.

Board of Directors

This is the group of people who are legally charged to govern the corporation, whether for-profit or nonprofit.

The term "Director" is not used in this guide as it is in many other books about Boards. The term can be confusing because it can apply to members of a Board of Directors or to the Executive Director. The guide instead refers to "Board members" or "members of the Board."

Chief Executive Officer (or CEO, Chief Executive or Executive Director)

Traditionally, the CEO is the singular, organization-wide, staff position that is primarily responsible to carry out the strategic plans and policies established by the Board of Directors. The CEO (in nonprofits, commonly referred to as the Executive Director) reports to the Board of Directors. This arrangement depends on the Board model preferred by the nonprofit. Sometimes the Board and CEO work in a "strategic partnership" in which the Board does not direct the CEO in such a top-down, hierarchical manner. Not all nonprofits have staff members, including a CEO. This guide uses the phrases Chief Executive Officer (or Chief Executive), Executive Director and CEO interchangeably.

Governance

Governance is the Board of Director's activities to ensure that the nonprofit operates effectively and efficiently according to its mission and strategic priorities. Governance is not only looking inward on nonprofit activities, but outward to ensure the nonprofit is meeting the needs of constituents. (Some new perspectives on governance consider governance to include stakeholders affiliated with the nonprofit.) Board members might conduct governance activities in a very hands-on approach, by delegating to staff members, or by some combination of these approaches. Gill defines governance as "the exercise of authority, direction, and control of an organization in order to ensure that its purpose is achieved" (Trafford Publishing, 2005, p. 15). New perspectives on governance consider the nonprofit's stakeholders to also be involved in governance.

Nonprofit

A nonprofit organization is formed to meet a public need – and should be held accountable to prove that it is meeting that need (ensuring accountability is one of the Board's most important jobs). A nonprofit organization often is a corporation, that is, an organization that is chartered with the appropriate government agency to be a legal entity apart from its members, and requiring a Board of Directors. The nonprofit also can also be tax-exempt and/or charitable in status. The guide often refers to "nonprofit" to mean the overall organization, including members of its Board and staff.

Stakeholders

These are people or groups of people who "have a stake," or strong, vested interest in the operations of the organization, for example: Board members, staff members, clients, funders, collaborators, community leaders and government agencies. The most important stakeholder of the nonprofit is the group of clients whose needs the nonprofit is aiming to meet.

 This guidebook also includes a Glossary on page 203 that provides definitions of these and other key terms.

Frequent References to Free, Useful Resources

The guide includes numerous references to useful resources, internal and external to the book. Each reference is marked with a handy symbol for ease of recognition. The following symbols are used.

 References to other sections of the guide that you may want to look at more closely.

 References to other content in external resources, such as other books.

 References to content available on the Web, such as tools and sample documents.

1.   Numbered lists suggest guidelines and the order in which they should be applied. They also indicate that there are a specific number of items in the list.

■   Bulleted lists provide information that can be considered in any order and may not be all-inclusive.

Sample Board Policies for Use by Owner of This Book

This guide includes various Board policies that the owner of this book, or the organization of which the owner is a member, can modify to suit the nature and needs of the organization. The policies should not be modified for re-sale.

 To download a copy of the policies, point your Web browser to: http://www.authenticityconsulting.com/pubs/BD_gdes/board-policies.doc and then save the document(s) to your computer's disk, for example, use the "Save As" command in your browser and name the file "policies".

About the Author

Carter McNamara, MBA, PhD, is a partner in Authenticity Consulting, LLC. He started working with nonprofit Boards in 1978 and has worked with and for a variety of organizations since then – for-profit, nonprofit, government, small and large. He has strong experience in leadership and supervision from working his way along the "ladder" from individual contributor to director. He has consulted in a wide array of services to for-profit and nonprofit organizations. He is founder and developer of the Authenticity Circles[SM] peer coaching group models, Free Management Library[SM], and Free Micro-eMBA[SM] and Nonprofit Micro-eMBA[SM]. He has extensive training and experience in training and coaching, including Action Learning and peer coaching. He is confident of the ability of learners to recognize their own development needs and direct their own learning. Dr. McNamara holds a BA in Social and Behavioral Sciences, a BS in Computer Science, an MBA from the University of St. Thomas, and a PhD in Human and Organization Development from The Union Institute in Cincinnati, Ohio.

About Authenticity Consulting, LLC

Authenticity Consulting, LLC, publisher of this guidebook, is a Minneapolis-based consulting firm specializing in development of nonprofit organizations, management and programs. While many firms specialize in one or a few specific services to nonprofits, Authenticity brings a highly comprehensive and integrated approach with focus on building the capacity of the entire organization, including its governance, management and staffing, programs, marketing, finances, fundraising and evaluation. We provide services in nonprofit:

- Board development and governance
- Strategic planning and strategic management
- Leadership and management development
- Program development and evaluation
- Overall organizational change

We also provide powerful, practical peer learning programs for networking, training, problem solving and support – either freestanding or to enrich other programs – through Authenticity Circles peer coaching group model. Our unique Action Learning-based group coaching process ensures ongoing support and accountability among participants during the organizational change process – few change models recognize and build in processes to ensure these two critical elements of any change process. We also include ongoing, frequent one-on-one coaching sessions with key leaders in client organizations.

We can be reached by phone at 800.971.2250 or +1.763.971.8890.
You can see our Website at http://www.authenticityconsulting.com .

PART I:

STARTING A

NONPROFIT AND BOARD

To Govern Nonprofits, First Understand Them

The activities associated with starting a Board are highly integrated with the activities for starting a nonprofit. The guidelines in this section are meant to guide you through the basic stages of starting nonprofit organizations and their Boards. Before you begin these steps, it will help a great deal to understand the basic nature and forms of nonprofit organizations.

The guidelines in this book should not be interpreted as legal advice regarding specific rules and regulations from federal, state or provincial, and local agencies.

How Nonprofits Differ From For-Profits – and How They Are the Same

Nonprofits that have governing Boards of Directors (the focus of this book) are corporations. Perhaps the best way to explain the purpose and designs of nonprofit corporations is to compare them to for-profit corporations, a form with which most of us are quite familiar. Table I:1 depicts differences between both types of organizations.

Table I:1 – Comparison between For-profit and Nonprofit Corporations

For-Profit Corporations	Nonprofit Corporations
Owned by stockholders	Owned by the public
Generate money for the owners	Serve the public
Success is making sizeable profit	Success is meeting needs of public
Board members are usually paid	Board members are usually unpaid volunteers
Members can make very sizeable income	Members should make reasonable, not excessive, income
Money earned over and above that needed to pay expenses is kept as profit and distributed to owners	Money earned over and above that needed to pay expenses is retained as surplus and should be spent soon on meeting the public need (the nonprofit can earn profit from activities not directly related to the nonprofit's mission; however the nonprofit often has to pay taxes over a certain amount)
Chief Executive Officer is often on the Board of Directors, and sometimes is the President of the Board	Conventional wisdom suggests that the Chief Executive Officer (often called the "Executive Director") not be on the Board
Usually not exempt from paying federal, state/provincial, and local taxes	Can often be exempt from federal taxes, and some state/provincial and local taxes, if the nonprofit was granted tax-exempt status from the appropriate governmental agency
Money invested in the for-profit usually cannot be deducted from the investor's personal tax liability	Money donated to the nonprofit can be deducted from the donor's personal tax liability if the nonprofit was granted charitable status from the appropriate government agency

Although Table I:1 depicts distinct differences between for-profit and nonprofit corporations, there is much more similarity between them than many people often realize. Both types of organizations must have effective governance, leadership, robust planning, quality services to constituents, competent and committed personnel, and cost-effective operations.

Also, the types of issues that can occur in small nonprofits are very similar to the types of issues that can occur in small for-profits, including the constant struggle to obtain funding and good people, reacting to the changing day-to-day demands in the workplace, ensuring that customers are always satisfied, and managing time and stress to avoid burnout. In many ways, a small nonprofit is much more like a small for-profit in nature than a large nonprofit. Similarly, a large nonprofit is much more like a large for-profit in nature than a small nonprofit.

(The Board of a for-profit corporation often is referred to as a "corporate" Board – an insufficient distinction because the Board of a nonprofit corporation also is a corporate Board.)

Different Types of Public Needs Met by Nonprofits

Nonprofit corporations get special tax benefits from their governmental agencies (for example, tax-exempt and/or charitable status from the Internal Revenue Service in the USA) for providing services primarily to meet certain kinds of public needs, usually including:

- Arts
- Charitable needs
- Civic affairs
- Education
- Environment

- Health
- Literary
- Religion
- Scientific
- Social services (or human services)

There Is More Than One Type of Nonprofit Organization

As you form a nonprofit organization, you need to decide what form you want to use. A later section, "Starting a Nonprofit Corporation," includes more specific information and materials about actually starting a nonprofit.

1. **Informal nonprofits**
    If the purpose of your effort is to address an occasional need in your community, then perhaps you can start an informal nonprofit, rather than a formal ("chartered" or incorporated) nonprofit organization? For example, if you want to gather some people together for a short time in order to clean up your neighborhood, then you probably do not need to file to be a nonprofit corporation. Instead, you can form a rather informal nonprofit just by getting together with some neighbors for a seasonal project.

2. **Formal nonprofit corporations ("chartered" and incorporated)**
    If the purpose of your effort is to meet a current, major, ongoing need in your community, then you probably want to incorporate the nonprofit organization as a separate legal entity. In the United States of America (USA), you form a corporation by filing papers (usually Articles of Incorporation) in your state, usually by contacting your Secretary of State's office. In Canada, you can form a nonprofit corporation either at the provincial or federal

levels, and you might be able to form under a variety of regulations, for example, a provincial Societies Act or Companies Act, or the federal Canada Corporations Act. In Canada, it is necessary to be incorporated in order to become a charity. That is not always true in the USA.

Depending on the country in which you live, benefits of incorporation might be that the nonprofit corporation can:

a. Own property and its own bank account.

b. Enter into contracts.

c. Continue operations as a legal entity after you are gone.

d. Be eligible to conduct tax-exempt activities (see below).

e. Be eligible for tax-deductible donations (see below).

f. Conduct operations for which you are personally not liable (in most cases).

For examples of Articles of Incorporation, go to
http://www.managementhelp.org/boards/boards.htm#anchor13357 .

3. **Tax-exempt nonprofits**
    If you want the nonprofit to be exempt (and if you think the nonprofit deserves to be exempt) from paying federal and possibly other taxes, then you should file with the appropriate government agency to gain tax-exempt status. For example, in Canada, you can get tax-exempt status at the provincial or federal level. In the USA, you would to file with the Internal Revenue Service (IRS) to get tax-exempt status, almost always after first gaining corporate status. To qualify for tax-exempt status in the USA, the nonprofit must serve a need that is religious, educational, charitable, scientific or literary in nature. If the IRS grants 501(c)(3) status (often referred to as "charitable" status) to the nonprofit, it will send you a determination letter. Be sure to keep and safely protect this letter. Tax-exempt nonprofits sometimes do not have to pay certain state and local property taxes. Note that all nonprofits still must pay employment taxes. Contact the appropriate government agency to find out more about which taxes that nonprofits must pay in your region.

For guidance to apply for 501(c)(3) status in the USA, go to
http://www.managementhelp.org/tax/np_tax.htm#anchor648922 .

4. **Tax-deductible (charitable nonprofits, or charities)**
    Depending on the nature of the mission of the nonprofit corporation, it might also be granted tax-deductible (or charitable) status, for example, from the IRS in the USA or the Canada Revenue Agency in Canada. Being tax-exempt is not the same as being tax-deductible. Tax-deductible means that donors can deduct their contributions to your organization during their federal and (sometimes) state, or provincial, tax computations. Tax-deductible status is granted usually to nonprofits that serve needs in regard to: the arts, charitable, civic affairs, education, the environment, health and social services, literary, scientific and religious matters.

In the USA, the IRS does not grant tax-deductible status to all nonprofits, nor does the Canada Revenue Agency in Canada. For example, the IRS does not grant tax-deductible status to social welfare nonprofits, 501(c)(4)'s, that exist primarily to lobby, or to associations, 501(c)(6)'s, that exist primarily to support networking and development of their members. IRS Publication 526 lists the types of organizations to which donations are deductible.

> For more information about charitable status, go to
> http://www.drcharity.com/publicat.html or do a Web search from
> http://www.irs.ustreas.gov/ .

Three Most Important Levels Within Nonprofits

Boards and Governance

Because the nonprofit organization is incorporated, it requires a Board of Directors. The Board is responsible to provide governance in the form of overall strategic direction, guidance and controls. This does not mean that Board members only focus inward – they are responsible to ensure, even to verify, that the nonprofit is indeed meeting the needs of the community. Many people are coming to consider governance as a function carried out by the Board, top management and even by affiliated organizations. Effective governance depends to a great extent on the working relationship between Board and top management (if the nonprofit has staff members as management – not all of them do).

Central Administration

Central administration includes the staff and facilities that are common to running all programs and services. This usually includes at least the Chief Executive Officer (Executive Director) and office personnel, such as finance staff or executive assistants. If there are no paid staff members, then Board members might conduct the central administrative duties themselves. Nonprofits usually strive to keep costs of central administration low in proportion to the cost of running programs.

Programs

Nonprofit programs are services conducted to meet community needs by achieving outcomes among clients in that community. Evaluations ensure that the outcomes are achieved and that the program is a good investment. People often confuse programs with a random set of activities aimed to help people. Instead, programs are much more organized than that. Board members must recognize the difference between programs and activities.

> There is more information about programs versus activities on page 8.

Most Important Roles People Play in Nonprofits

Clients

Everything in a nonprofit is ultimately directed to serving clients. Clients are the "consumers" or "customers" of the nonprofit. Services can be in the form of tangible or intangible products, and are often provided in the form of nonprofit programs. Some people refer to "primary clients" as those who directly benefit from the program and "secondary clients" as those who indirectly benefit. This guide refers to clients as being the primary clients.

Board Members

Law and theory dictate that the Board is in charge and that its members are directly accountable for the overall direction and policies of the organization. Powers are given to the Board by its governing documents, for example, Articles of Incorporation, Articles of Association or its Constitution. The Board can configure itself and the nonprofit in whatever structure it prefers to best work toward the organization's mission, and usually does so via specifications in the By Laws (more information about By Laws is provided in the next section about starting a nonprofit). Members of nonprofit Boards are generally motivated by a desire to serve the community, their own professional development, and personal satisfaction of volunteering. Usually, nonprofit Board members do not receive direct monetary compensation for serving on the Board. Board members have authority only when acting as a body of all members – each member cannot officially act for the entire Board.

Board Chair

The Board Chair's role is central to facilitating and coordinating the work of the Board and Board committees, if the nonprofit chooses to use committees. The Chair's role is specified in the By Laws, and usually includes authority to appoint Chairs and members of Board committees. Members of the Board do not work for the Board Chair, they work for the entire Board. The power of the Board Chair is through persuasion and general leadership ability.

Committees or Task Forces

The Board might choose to carry out its operations and oversight function by using a variety of Board committees or temporary task forces. Not all nonprofits choose to use committees. Committees often are matched to the strategic priorities of the nonprofit (for example, to expanding markets or building a facility) or to oversight of common management functions. Examples of common committees are the Executive Committee, Finance Committee, Fundraising Committee, Marketing Committee, Programs Committee and Personnel Committee.

Chief Executive Officer (CEO, Executive Director)

The Board might choose to retain a Chief Executive Officer role in the nonprofit organization. If so, the Board typically chooses to have this role be ultimately responsible to carry out the wishes of the Board. Usually, the Chief Executive Officer is directly accountable for the work of the staff and supports the work of the Board committees. As mentioned previously, the Board members and Chief Executive often work together in the nature of a "strategic partnership." The Chief Executive Officer is a member of the staff. This role might not be compensated in a small nonprofit.

Staff

Staff members (if the nonprofit has staff members) other than the Chief Executive usually report to the Chief Executive and may support the work of Board committees at the request of the CEO (if the nonprofit chooses to use committees). As mentioned above, the role of Chief Executive is a staff role. Staff, in this context, might refer to program directors / managers, accountants, executive or administrative assistants, or people who provide direct services to clients. Some nonprofits might not have any paid staff; they might only have volunteers.

Volunteers

Volunteers are unpaid personnel who serve as staff members or assist staff members. In many nonprofits, the volunteers are every bit as valuable to the organization as paid staff members. In well-managed nonprofits, volunteers are supervised as carefully as staff members, including careful selection, orienting and training, organizing and evaluation. Board members of nonprofits are themselves volunteers.

Nonprofit Programs – What They Are, What They Are Not

True Programs Versus Random Activities

Activities

Activities are not the same as programs – Board and staff members need to understand this. Activities are a set of events that, although they are or seem beneficial to the community, are so loosely or informally conducted that it is difficult to readily ascertain if the events are truly needed by the community and/or are making any substantive difference in the community.

There are many types of activities that can be useful to a community, even someone standing on a corner and handing out food to whomever happens to walk by. On first impression, that event might seem beneficial to the community. However, without knowing whether the food is safe, whether those walking by really need the food or not, whether handing out the food on the corner is the best means to provide the food, it is difficult to ascertain whether the event deserves the ongoing investment of resources from the community.

Programs

The typical nonprofit organizational structure is built around programs. A nonprofit program is an integrated set of services conducted to meet specific, verified community needs by achieving certain specific benefits and changes (outcomes) among specific groups of clients in that community. Services include ongoing systematic evaluations, as much as possible, to ensure that the specific outcomes are indeed being achieved and that the community's resources are best invested in that particular program. Board members should always be asking if those outcomes are being achieved.

Community needs are verified to exist by some means of market research (formal or informal). The programs or services to meet those needs are researched to be sure they are likely to meet the community needs. During delivery of the programs, program activities are evaluated to ensure they remain high-quality. Outcomes from programs are evaluated, with strong feedback from clients, to be sure the program is indeed meeting the needs in the community.

In essence, a well-designed program is similar to a well-designed research project from which a community can benefit and a great deal can be learned. Common examples of nonprofit programs are food-shelf programs, transportation programs, training programs, health services programs and arts programs.

Nonprofits often define their programs during strategic planning. Programs become major methods, or strategies, to reach strategic goals. For example, a nonprofit might have a mission to "Enhance the quality of life for young adults by promoting literacy." Major strategies, or programs, to work toward that mission might be a High School Equivalency Training Program and a Transportation Program to get the young adults to the Training Program.

To clearly understand the nature of well-developed programs, it helps to think of them in terms of inputs, processes, outputs and outcomes.

- Inputs are the various resources needed to run the program, such as money, facilities, clients and program staff.

- Processes are how the program is carried out, for example, clients are counseled, children are cared for, art is created, and association members are supported.

- Outputs are the units of service, for example, number of clients counseled, children cared for, artistic pieces produced, or members in the association.

- Outcomes are the impacts on the clients from participating in the nonprofit's services, for example, increased mental health, safe and secure development, richer artistic appreciation and perspectives in life, and increased effectiveness among members.

Different Designs of Nonprofits

An organization chart is a handy tool for depicting the structure of an organization, including its various roles and programs and also how those roles and programs relate to each other. The charts on the following pages depict the typical designs of new and small nonprofit organizations. Keep in mind that, although there are distinct lines between the boxes (the roles) on the following images, there are seldom such distinct and rigid differences in application. Instead, people in various roles often share responsibilities and their responsibilities are often changing.

Organization Chart of Typical Start-Up Nonprofit Organization

It is common that a startup nonprofit organization has one major program that is carried out by a hands-on group of volunteers, some of whom act as the Board of Directors and perhaps others who act as staff. Both groups might be involved in providing services to clients. A new nonprofit often does not include the role of Chief Executive. It is important to remember that the Board of Directors, regardless of the Board model preferred by the nonprofit, works for the public.

Table I:2 – Organization Chart of Typical Start-Up Nonprofit

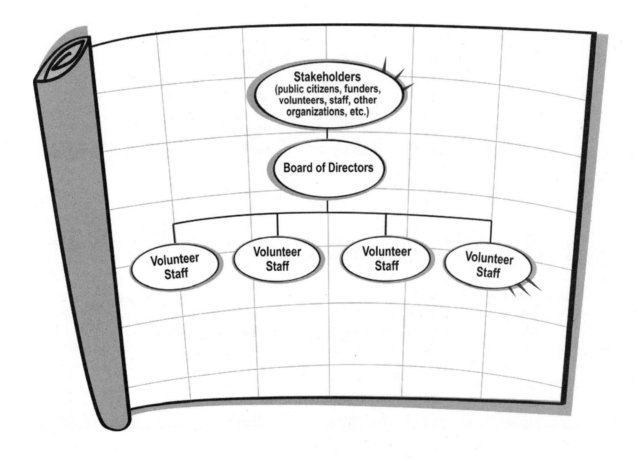

Organization Chart of Typical Small Nonprofit with CEO

A small nonprofit might have a part-time or full-time Chief Executive Officer (CEO) in a paid or volunteer position. Officially, the Chief Executive Officer reports to a Board of Directors (who are themselves volunteers). The Board members are expected to supervise the CEO, including selection, delegation and evaluation.

If the nonprofit has staff other than the CEO, then the CEO usually is expected to supervise the other staff members, who also might be part-time or full-time and in paid or volunteer positions.

The degree of formality of supervision between Board and CEO and between CEO and staff depends on the nonprofit's culture. Some nonprofits prefer a top-down, formal level of supervision, while others prefer a more team-based, egalitarian approach.

Table I:3 – Organization Chart of Typical Small Nonprofit

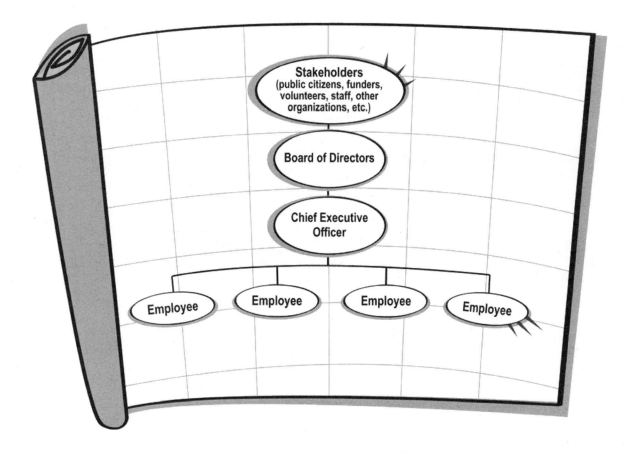

Organization Chart of Typical Medium-Sized Nonprofit

This design might be called a medium-sized nonprofit, although there really is no standard delineation of size for nonprofits. An organization like this usually has a paid Chief Executive, often on a full-time basis, who supervises various staff members. Staff members might be paid on a full-time or part-time basis, and can include volunteers. The Chief Executive reports to a Board of Directors (comprised of volunteers).

This size of nonprofit often has more than one program, each of which has a manager and is staffed by employees or volunteers.

Again, the degree of formality of supervision between Board and CEO and between CEO and staff depends on the nonprofit's culture. Supervision can range from a top-down, formal approach to more of a team-based, egalitarian approach.

Table I:4 – Organization Chart for a Typical Medium-Sized Nonprofit

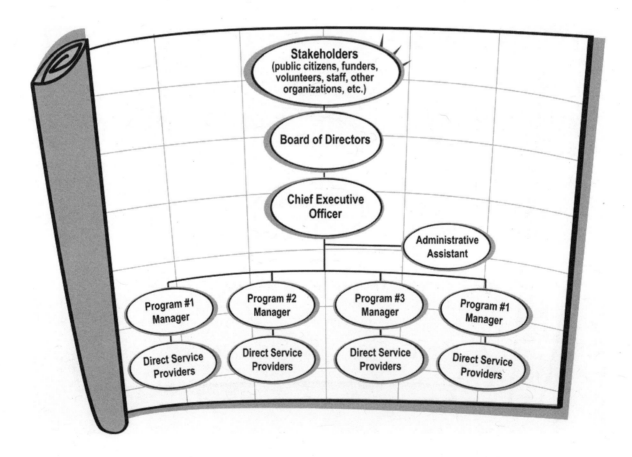

What A Small Nonprofit Typically Feels Like

It is very important for Board members to really understand the nature of a small nonprofit, especially so they have realistic expectations and do not become overly frustrated when things do not always get done on time for them. The culture of a small nonprofit tends to be a rather tight-knit group of people, each of whom is very dedicated to the mission of the organization. They will chip in to help wherever and whenever they can. Often, they are like a small family. This tends to change as the organization goes through various life cycles.

(Adapted with permission from Sandra Larson, previous Executive Director of The Management Assistance Program for Nonprofits, St. Paul.)

- **The heart of the matter is leadership and management.**
  At the heart of any successful nonprofit is an effective Chief Executive and Board of Directors, assuming the organization is big enough to warrant having a Chief Executive. These leaders must work as a team with vision, skill and sufficient resources to accomplish the organization's mission. While leadership is shared, critical management skills must rest with the Chief Executive. However, the Board must be sufficiently skilled in management to assess the work of this Chief Executive and assist in strategic decision-making.

- **Values are the bottom line.**
  Values are the driving force in a nonprofit. The bottom line is the realization of a social mission, not profits. This poses complex problems for the leadership team. How are programs agreed upon, progress monitored and success measured? How are priorities set and consensus reached? How is staff rewarded and what control systems are applicable? Skilled consultants may be needed from time to time to assist the team in answering these qualitative, value-laden questions and focusing on appropriate management systems.

- **Nonprofit personnel are often highly diverse.**
  Diversity is reflected, not only by different races and ethnic groups, but also by different values and perspectives. This strong diversity is a major benefit to the nonprofit because input from a wide variety of perspectives usually ensures complete consideration of situations and new ideas. However, nonprofit personnel must ensure they cultivate and remain open to the various values and perspectives.

- **Problems are especially complex for the small nonprofit.**
  The majority of nonprofits have small staffs and small budgets (less than $500,000) which compounds the leadership and management problems they face, especially given their charters and the magnitude of community needs with which they deal. Those new to nonprofits may assume that, because nonprofits tend to be small in size, issues in nonprofits should be simple in nature. On the contrary, the vast majority of organizations (regardless of size) experience similar issues: challenges in planning, organizing, motivating and guiding. However, when these issues are focused in a small organization, the nature of the organization becomes very dynamic and complex.

- **Sufficient resources to pay leadership may be lacking.**
  With lack of sufficient money, attracting and retaining paid management also can be problematic. Hard work with little career development opportunity encourages turnover of Chief Executives and staff. This can stall the organization's work. Expertise that is brought in to advise the management may be lost once that leadership leaves.

- **Lack of managerial training is problematic for the small nonprofit**.
  Many nonprofit managers have been promoted primarily for their technical or program expertise and may not have the managerial skills that are needed to run a nonprofit organization. Training and consultation can do much to help these new leaders and managers to gain the skills they seek and help them up the myriad of learning curves that rainbow out in front of them.

- **Chief Executives wear too many hats.**
  A nonprofit Chief Executive has to be a current expert in planning, marketing, information management, telecommunications, property management, personnel, finance, systems design, fundraising and program evaluation. Obviously this is not possible, regardless of the size of the organization. A larger organization may be able to hire some internal experts, but this is certainly not the case for the smaller organization. Furthermore, the technology of management today progresses too rapidly for the non-specialist to keep abreast of new thinking and expertise, whatever the size. Outside expertise therefore is often a must for both the large and small organization.

- **Nonprofit is too small to justify or pay for expensive outside advice.**
  Most nonprofits, even larger ones, often hesitate to spend money on administrative "overhead" such as consultants or other outside experts. This is seen as diverting valuable dollars from direct service. Of course, most nonprofits have no choice. They do not have enough money to even consider hiring consultants at for-profit rates. Low-cost, volunteer-based assistance often is an appropriate solution.

- **One-shot assistance often is not enough**.
  While most consultant organizations want to teach managers "how to fish," rather than give them a "fish," "fishing" (management skills) is not something that often can be learned in one consultation. Especially in more technical arenas such as computerization, learning comes while grappling with an issue or management problem over a period of time. Building internal management capacity takes more time than a one-shot consultation. Repeat help therefore is not a sign of failure but of growth – a new need to know has surfaced.

- **Networks are lacking.**
  Many people outside the nonprofit sector observe, "Why don't those Chief Executives get together more often and help each other?" There are many reasons. First of all, running a successful organization (delivering the quality service that fulfills the organization's mission) is not enough. Most nonprofit Chief Executives run a second business – raising money to support the first. Both are complex and very time-consuming activities, especially when the Chief Executive wears all the management hats. Second, developing networks or researching joint ventures is time-consuming, expensive and risky.

- **Nonprofits usually have little time and money.**
  Funders do not seem to think research and development activity justifies new expenditures; at least many are hesitant to fund what might not succeed. While nonprofits may be more entrepreneurial than funders, they have little capital to risk. Collaborative planning will be enhanced by computerization and telecommunications, but these investments also are difficult to fund. In some ways, affordable consultants can substitute for expensive, up-front research and development costs, at least at the feasibility level. In many cases, they can carry an organization through the needed planning to actually develop a new system of collaboration, merger, or automation.

14

■ **Nonprofits need low-cost management and technical assistance.**
Nonprofits are valuable community assets that must be effectively managed. The need to provide affordable, accessible management and technical assistance to these organizations is clear for all the reasons stated above: the complexity of the task, the lack of Board and internal expertise, the lack of time and money, changing needs, the learning curve, and the importance of the results to the community. What is well done is based on what is well run.

■ **Typical nature of planning in nonprofits is on current issues.**
Many nonprofits do not have a lot of time, money, or resources for sophisticated, comprehensive strategic planning. The focus is usually on the major issues facing the nonprofit and quickly addressing them. Typical major challenges for the facilitator are: basic training of personnel concerning planning concepts and processes, helping the nonprofit to focus and sustain its limited resources on planning, ensuring that strategies really are strategic rather than operational or efficiency measures, and helping design small and focused planning meetings which produce realistic plans that be implemented.

How to Start a Nonprofit

Successful leaders have learned not to undertake major projects, like starting a nonprofit, on their own. They have learned to trust the expertise and commitments of others, to share responsibilities. If you have already resolved that you alone are going to do all of the tasks necessary to start the nonprofit, then you probably have some important lessons to learn in leadership. If the nonprofit is to be successful, it will need more than one person – one "hero" – who does everything. Now is the time to start recruiting and accepting help to start the nonprofit. Use a team of people to do the tasks suggested in this section of the guide. These steps are depicted in Table I:5 at the end of this section.

What is the Purpose, or Mission, of the Nonprofit?

Now that you have a basic understanding of nonprofit organizations, you can get started in starting one. Begin by really clarifying what the purpose of the nonprofit is – what its mission is. The mission is all about meeting a need in the community – it is the most important reference point for Board members when doing their jobs. For now, when starting your nonprofit, write an initial, basic mission statement.

At this point, the mission statement needs to be generally descriptive. Note that later on, during strategic planning, the mission statement should be refined so that all key stakeholders have input to, and complete understanding of, the mission.

More information about strategic planning is included in this guide on page 56.

The following guidelines may be helpful to your team when writing the first, basic mission statement.

1. **The mission statement describes the overall purpose of the organization.**
   It addresses the question "Why does the organization exist?" If it is primarily to meet a public need in your community, then starting a nonprofit is indeed a good idea.

2. **The statement can be in a wide variety of formats and lengths.**
   It can range from a few sentences to a few pages. At this stage in the development of the nonprofit, it might be best to keep your mission statement to at most about a quarter page.

3. **Write a brief mission statement.**
   Consider at least these specific aspects of the mission:

   a. The primary benefits and services to clients – the difference in the community that the nonprofit aims to make.

   b. The groups of clients who will benefit from those services.

   c. The values that will guide how the nonprofit will operate.

   d. How you would like others to view the nonprofit.

4. **It is often useful to refine the first, basic mission statement.**
    Add or delete a sentence or a word from the mission statement until your team feels that the wording accurately describes the purpose of the new nonprofit organization. If you have any people in mind to serve as your initial group of Board members, then have them review the wording of the mission statement. (Usually, your first group of Board members was listed as officers when you filed your Articles of Incorporation – more about Articles later on in this guide.)

Are You Sure Potential Clients Really Need Your Services?

This may sound like a trite question. However, often someone feels that a particular group of clients has a strong, unmet need – only to find out later, after a lot of struggle to get a nonprofit started, that the clients really did not have that need at all.

If no other nonprofit has been started yet to serve what you think are the unmet needs of your client groups, then that might be a very good reason to start a nonprofit – or it might be good reason to believe that the needs among clients truly do not exist at all.

Clients will come to a program based on what they want. They will stay based on what they need. Therefore, do some upfront homework to learn about your clients. That is the purpose of basic market research. It is beyond the scope of this book to fully guide you through careful market research. For now, make some calls to leaders in each of the groups of clients that you intend to serve. Share your ideas for a new nonprofit. Get their opinions.

Consider the guidebook, *Field Guide to Nonprofit Program Design, Marketing and Evaluation,* from Authenticity Consulting, LLC. Go to the "publications" link at http://www.authenticityconsulting.com .

Are Current Nonprofits Already Addressing the Public Need?

It is not uncommon for people who want to start a nonprofit to also want to be the founder of "their own nonprofit." However, if you are starting a nonprofit to meet a need that is already being addressed by other existing organizations, then do not ignore those organizations. If you do, then you will end up competing with them for clients and funds. You and your clients will be much better off if you at least make an initial effort to contact local nonprofits with similar missions to see how you might collaborate with them. So when doing your basic market research, find out if there are other nonprofits doing what you intend to do.

To begin identifying nonprofits in your area, contact the National Council of Nonprofit Associations at http://www.ncna.org/ .
In Canada, it might be helpful to contact your local chapter of the United Way of Canada, available from http://www.unitedway.ca .

Consider Fiscal Sponsorship to Jump Start Nonprofit?

You might not have to do all of the necessary paperwork now (such as filing Articles of Incorporation, starting a bank account, getting sales permits, etc.) if you get a fiscal sponsor. In the case of a fiscal sponsor, your new "program" essentially can operate as a program of another sponsoring nonprofit corporation.

In effect, a fiscal sponsor shares its tax-exempt and tax-deductible status with the program that it sponsors. The nature of the program's services should be somewhat in accordance with the nature of the sponsoring organization's mission. The sponsor might also assist in financial management for your organization.

A fiscal sponsor might be useful to your team if your organization or program:

- Does not have sufficient resources to handle startup costs and filing fees as a nonprofit corporation. (These costs can range from $500 to $5,000, especially depending on legal costs to complete the necessary forms for tax-exemption and charitable status, for example, the Form 1023 in the USA.)

- Does not have sufficient skills to plan, organize and begin managing a new organization.

In the USA, the sponsoring organization becomes responsible to the Internal Revenue Service and any funders of the program, especially regarding how the program collects and spends its money. In return, the sponsor gets a fee, often a percentage (usually from 5%-15%) of the revenues associated with the sponsored activities.

For more information about fiscal sponsorship, go to http://www.managementhelp.org/finance/np_fnce/np_fnce.htm#anchor18 24012 .

What Help Might You Need?

Lawyer?

You can do much of the work yourself to incorporate (for example, completing Articles of Incorporation). Applying for tax-exempt and/or tax-deductible status is more complicated, and your team would benefit from the advice of a lawyer who understands nonprofit matters (for example, knows how to complete Form 1023 in the USA). It is very important that your filing for tax-exempt and/or charitable status be very accurate about the purpose and program of the new organization. Otherwise, the new organization might not get special tax status at all, or it might get only tax-exempt status and not charitable status. To get references for a good lawyer, ask nonprofits in your area, or call the local bar association. You might be able to find very low-cost legal fees from a Legal Aid chapter in your area, or from pro bono services of law firms in your area.

Accountant?

It is as likely that you will need an accountant as a lawyer. You can struggle through much of the legal filings and forms. However, if you do not have at least a basic understanding of bookkeeping and accounting, then you should get some help. Ideally, you can recruit a volunteer who has financial management skills, and even becomes your Board Treasurer.

Call the local volunteer organization to see if they can recommend someone. Call several local corporations to see if they have a volunteer center to help their employees find useful volunteer positions in the community. Look through the Yellow Pages to find accountant organizations.

Consider the book, *Bookkeeping Basics: What Every Nonprofit Bookkeeper Needs to Know* (Amherst H. Wilder Foundation, 2003). Click on "Publications" at http://www.authenticityconsulting.com .

Free Online Resources

Fortunately, there is a vast amount of resources available for nonprofit Board and staff members working to start a nonprofit.

In the USA, the Internal Revenue Service in the USA has an extensive amount of information at http://www.irs.gov/charities/topic/index.html . In Canada, the Canada Revenue Agency has extensive information at http://www.cra-arc.gc.ca/tax/charities/menu-e.html .

Appendix B on page 211 lists many of these resources. The Nonprofit Free Micro-eMBA^{SM} in that Appendix includes 13 on-line, self-directed training modules for the learner to progress through the initial stages of starting a nonprofit to go on to govern and manage the nonprofit.

Although they are not free, the CharityChannel discussion forums about nonprofit matters are a great source of low-cost information. At the time of this writing, the yearly fee is $37 to join one or more of the forums. Go to http://www.charitychannel.com .

What Should You Name the Nonprofit?

This requires some careful thought on the part of your team now. Consider the following:

- The name should designate what services will be provided and to whom.

- Do not pick a name that is very similar to other organizations in your area.

- Remember you can change the name later on if you want to do so.

- Pick several names and then discuss them with your Board members and several potential clients of your organization.

Recruit Your Initial Board Members ("First Board")

You will need at least a small number of Board members to help you start the new nonprofit. Sometimes this is your "first Board" of Board members because, as the organization grows, you might end up doubling or tripling the size of your Board, depending on your needs. There are different bases for staffing a Board, but for now you probably want to use a functional basis, which is recruiting Board members because of their unique expertise. For your first Board, select members who: 1) are very interested in the mission of your new nonprofit; 2) can provide the time and energy to help you start the organization, maybe 5-8 hours per month; and 3) have useful expertise, for example, in planning, Boards, finances and perhaps fundraising. Do not select Board members because they have passion only – that usually only results in passionate meetings.

Do not waste your time trying to recruit "big name" Board members, under the illusion that they will attract huge donations – that is rarely the result. Ideally, the first members of your Board have been on Boards before, have strong understanding of the needs of your clients, and how those needs could be met. Ideally, too, they are independent Board members, that is, members who are not on the staff (if the new nonprofit has staff members yet), will have no business affiliation with the new nonprofit, and are not very close and personal friends of the founder, especially of a CEO or Board Chair.

For additional information about recruiting and training Board members, see Part III, especially the sections "How to Staff and Fully Equip Your Board" on page 65 and "How to Ensure a High-Quality Board" on page 130.

Hire Chief Executive Officer (Executive Director) Yet?

It is very common that the person who starts a nonprofit goes on to become the first Chief Executive. Not all nonprofits have a Chief Executive. The Board may decide that it wants to continue completely as a volunteer organization, with members of the Board providing the day-to-day completion of tasks. If that is the case with the new nonprofit, then the Board members must decide how they will provide the ongoing leadership and energy to really do that. This type of Board is often considered to be a "working" or "Administrative" Board. If the culture of the people on your team is highly egalitarian and participative – you all want to be viewed as equals – then you might be using a Board model that is referred to as a "collective" Board.

If Board members are considering whether to hire a Chief Executive, then the guidelines in PART IV of this guide will be useful.

See "How to Hire Your Chief Executive Officer" on page 147.

Draft Your Articles of Incorporation and Initial By Laws

Articles of Incorporation

If you have decided to create (or "charter") a formal nonprofit organization, or corporation, then you will need to file the documents with the appropriate local government agency. For example, in the USA, you will probably need to file Articles of Incorporation with the Secretary of State's office in your state.

As mentioned previously in this guide, in Canada you can form a nonprofit corporation either at the provincial or federal levels. You might also be able to form under a variety of regulations, for example, a provincial Societies Act or Companies Act, or the federal Canada Corporations Act. In Canada, it is necessary to be incorporated in order to become a charity. It might be much quicker if you file in your province. You should contact officials in your province to identify the most suitable means to charter the nonprofit corporation.

There is more about Articles of Incorporation, including about its typical contents, on page 38.

By Laws

By Laws are the Board's internal specifications regarding how the organization will be configured and managed, and how the Board will operate. Consequently, it is one of the most important Board policies and usually the Board adopts it first. In the USA and Canada, some states or provinces require By Laws in order to file for incorporation.

Read more about By Laws, including typical contents, on page 39.

Conduct Basic Strategic Planning for Now

At this point, it is appropriate for your team to conduct some very simple strategic planning to produce a basic strategic plan document. The plan will likely prove useful to provide initial direction to Board members and key staff when applying for any start-up funding, and for recruiting new Board members. The plan should be updated by conducting more complete strategic planning later on, probably in three to six months. This round of planning will likely be short-term and primarily internally focused. The next round of planning will include much strategic thinking and analyses, especially with stakeholders input. For now, the plan need not be very comprehensive and detailed, for example, it might be three to five pages in length.

1.   On the first page, write down the 5- to 8-sentence mission statement that you crafted earlier.

2.   Then list 5-8 goals that must be achieved over the next year in order to get the nonprofit started. For example, goals might include getting and developing Board members, getting facilities, getting and developing staff to provide services, advertising to groups of clients, serving clients and doing fundraising.

3.   For each goal, write down 4-5 objectives, or smaller goals, that must be accomplished in order to achieve the overall goal.

4.   For each objective, write down what resources might be needed, who will achieve the objective and by when. Do not worry that this information has to be accurate throughout. You can change it later as needed.

5.   Finally, estimate how much money will be needed to obtain and support the resources to achieve the objectives over the next 12 months.

6.   Put that information in a document and refer to it as a basic "Strategic Plan."

For more information about strategic planning, see the section "Strategic Planning: Direction for Nonprofit and Your Board" on page 56.

Conduct Your Initial Board Meeting to Do Approvals

In the Board's first, official meeting, members should at least:

1.   Review and approve the draft of the mission statement.

2.   Review and approve Articles of Incorporation.

3.   Review and approve the By Laws.

4.   Review and approve the initial Strategic Plan document.

5.   Select Board officers (President or Chair, Vice Chair, Secretary and Treasurer).

Do All Necessary Filings

If you have not yet done so, you will probably need to attend to the following activities, depending on the requirements of your state, or provincial, and federal government agencies.

1.   **Get the necessary government identification numbers.**
In the USA, file to get an employer identification number (EIN). You will need this number to file for tax exemption from the IRS. Go to http://www.irs.ustreas.gov/ and search for "Form SS-4". In Canada, when you file to be a charity, you will get a "charitable taxation number" from the Canada Revenue Agency that you will need in order to administrate tax receipts activity with the government.

2.   **File for incorporation.**
(See the upcoming section, "Your Board's Most Important Documents," on page 38.)

3.   **After you get designation that the nonprofit is a corporation, file for tax-exemption?**
The nature of this filing depends on the requirements of the government agency in your state or province, and at the federal level. For example, in the USA, you will file Form 1023 to the Internal Revenue Service (this is true at the time of this writing). You might need your Articles of Incorporation, employer identification number and a strategic plan. You might need your By Laws, as well. Ask the IRS to return a determination of your tax status and provide you a "determination letter." It might take up to six months to get this letter. During this period, you can conduct operations including solicitations from funders. Tell other organizations that you have filed for exemption. When you get your letter of determination from the IRS, keep this form! You will need it to show funders that you are tax-exempt and/or tax-deductible.

4.   **Once you get tax exemption, file for any state, province and property tax exemptions.**
The nature of this filing depends on the requirements of the government agency in your state or province and at the federal level.

5.   **Get a bulk mail permit.**
This will come in handy when you do bulk mailings to clients, funders, etc. Contact your local post office to see if the nonprofit qualifies for this permit or other discounts.

Table I:5 – Checklist for Starting a New Nonprofit

	Activity	Comment
1.	Draft initial mission statement	Draft a brief mission statement that describes the purpose of the new organization; your Board should approve it in their first official Board meeting.
2.	Recruit initial Board members	If you plan to incorporate, recruit at least enough Board members to meet state/province/federal requirements for a corporate Board; if you do not plan to incorporate, consider an informal Advisory Board to help guide you.
3.	Get a lawyer	Lawyer can help file Articles (if you plan to incorporate) or you can do them yourself. Apply for tax-exemption (if you plan to seek exemption from certain taxes in USA). You can probably do the Articles yourself, but it is helpful to get a lawyer to file for tax status.
4.	Get banker and bank account	Get a bank account; seek a bank that understands the needs of new, small nonprofits. Get a reference from a similar nonprofit.
5.	Get accountant	Get an accountant or other finance expert to help you set up a basic bookkeeping system for the nonprofit corporation. When you get a Board Treasurer, he/she can be very helpful in this regard.
6.	Get insurance agent	You may need liability insurance, property insurance, and other insurance when you hire staff, including Worker's Compensation, health and life insurance benefits, etc. Get a reference from a similar nonprofit.
7.	Draft Articles and get Board approval	You will need to draft these only if you plan to file for incorporation with your state/province/federal level; the Board should approve the Articles before submission; the boilerplate / framework for the Articles is usually provided by the government agency where you file.
8.	Draft By Laws and get Board approval	Some states/provinces/federal levels require these; the Board should approve the By Laws. Get samples from a similar nonprofit.
9.	File incorporation with state	Submit your final, approved Articles; you may need to submit By Laws, too, depending on your state/provincial/federal requirements.
10.	Get government identification number	For example, in the USA, get a federal employer identification number. Do this once you start to hire employees in order to withhold income and FICA. Go to http://www.irs.ustreas.gov/ and search for "Form SS-4".
11.	Conduct basic strategic planning	Sketch out your mission statement, 5-8 goals that need to be achieved over the next year, 4-5 objectives to achieve each goal, resources needed for each method, and resulting budget of monies needed to achieve and support those resources.
12.	File for tax-exemption	After you get your corporate status, apply for tax-exempt status depending on state/province/federal requirements.
13.	Get local tax exemption	After you get your corporate status, apply for tax-exempt status depending on local agency requirements.
14.	Get solicitation license	If you plan to solicit funds, you might need a solicitation license.
15.	Get mail permit	If available, this permit gives you a discount on bulk mailings

For more information about starting a nonprofit in the USA, go to
http://www.managementhelp.org/strt_org/strt_np/strt_np.htm .
In Canada, go to http://www.charityvillage.com/guides/guide4.asp .

PART II:

BOARD ROLES

AND

RESPONSIBILITIES

Variety of Board Models for You

Some Boards members prefer to focus exclusively on policy-making almost as if there is a distinct wall between them and the Chief Executive (typical to a Policy Governance Board®, or a "pure" policy governing Board). Other Board members prefer to be involved in management (typical of a "working" or a collective Board) – members might have to be that involved if their nonprofit is to be successful, especially when starting the nonprofit or if their nonprofit does not have sufficient funds to pay any staff. The Board structure, or model, used by Board members can be chosen carefully or it can emerge naturally from how members work amongst themselves and with the Chief Executive (if the nonprofit has any staff). Information in this section is intended to provide Board members and the Chief Executive enough information to think about how the Board might be structured.

More information in the section "How to Work With Your Chief Executive" on page 160 will help Board members and the Chief Executive to be even clearer about how they want to work together.

What is a Board of Directors?

Before you review the various kinds of Boards, you should first understand what a Board of Directors is.

All incorporated organizations (nonprofit or for-profit) must have a Board.
An incorporated organization is an organization that has filed with the appropriate government agency to formally organize as its own official, legal entity (or corporation). This is usually done by filing a legal description, for example, Articles of Incorporation, with the appropriate government agency. (Note that not all nonprofits are incorporated. Some nonprofits are less formal, for example, a group of citizens gathered to address a community need, such as picking up garbage.)

Board of Directors is legally charged to govern a corporation, nonprofit or for-profit.
In a for-profit corporation, the Board of Directors is responsible to the stockholders. A more progressive perspective is that the Board is responsible to the stakeholders, that is, to everyone who is interested and/or can be affected by the corporation. A for-profit corporation is owned by its stockholders. In a nonprofit corporation, the Board is responsible to the stakeholders, particularly the communities which the nonprofit serves. The nonprofit is owned by the public.

The power of a Board is vested in all Board members, not individual Board members.
Individual Board members do not have formal authority. The Board as a body of members must approve the nonprofit's plans and procedures. Boards have policies and procedures (By Laws and Board policies) that determine how the Board acts as a body to make plans and procedures.

In theory, Board establishes top-level policies, staff implements. (Reality might be different.)
Boards are responsible to establish top-level plans and policies that define the purpose and direction for a nonprofit. The Chief Executive (if the Board chooses to have a CEO in the organization) is responsible to manage the nonprofit's resources in an effective and efficient manner according to the plans and policies of the nonprofit. Staff, or personnel who work for the Chief Executive, (if the nonprofit has a CEO) are responsible to implement the plans according to the policies of the nonprofit and the management practices of the CEO. How this all occurs in a nonprofit depends very much on the structure of the Board (more on this later). In some nonprofits, there is no CEO and the Board members do much of the work that staff members typically would do. In other

nonprofits, Board and staff members prefer that they work much more in an egalitarian fashion where Board members are involved in governance and management. (See the section immediately below.)

It is very important for founders of nonprofits to realize that they do not own the nonprofit; the public owns the nonprofit. It also is very important for founders to realize that, ultimately, they work for the Board of Directors, not the other way around.

How Much Should Your Board Be Involved in Management?

Policy-Making Versus Management Activities?

Experts often frame the question in terms of how much Board members should be attending to establishing top-level plans and policies versus how much Board members should be involved in management, that is, in actually implementing those plans and policies.

First, it is helpful to recognize that there are different levels of policy in organizations, as listed below. A policy is a set of guidelines that can guide the behaviors of others in a certain area or practice, including for them to generate more detailed policies or procedures.

1. **Strategic (top-level) policies**
   These affect the entire organization and how it is integrated with other organizations, for example, the organization's mission, vision, values and strategic goals. Strategic policies direct and guide the management activities in the organization.

2. **Management / functional policies**
   These guide the activities in major functions and operations, for example, Boards, strategic planning, staffing, programs, finances, fundraising and evaluations.

3. **Program policies**
   These guide how programs operate, for example, how clients first come into the program, how they receive services and how services are evaluated.

4. **Day-to-day policies and procedures**
   These are detailed sets of directions, for example, what to do in case of fire, how to ensure that there is always a sufficient amount of office supplies, etc.

Factors That Influence Focus of Board Members' Involvement

Experts on nonprofits often have very strong beliefs and feelings about what should be the extent of involvement of Board members in top-level policy making versus implementing those policies in the day-to-day affairs of the nonprofit. They usually assert that Board members should attend primarily to top-level policies. However, various factors influence how involved Board members are in policy making versus "management," that is, in implementing the policies.

- New and small nonprofits often have hands-on Board members who are heavily involved in day-to-day activities because the nonprofits have no staff or very little in staff resources.

To understand Board priorities for each life cycle of the nonprofit, see "How to Match Board's Priorities to Life Cycle of Nonprofit" on page 140.

- Larger, established nonprofits usually have members who attend primarily to top-level planning and policies because those nonprofits have adequate resources in staffing to effectively implement top-level policies.

- If Board members have little confidence in the CEO, there have been frequent operational problems, or the CEO is leaving the organization, then Board members often are highly involved in management affairs, at least temporarily.

- Very autocratic cultures usually place strong value on respecting the role of top-level leaders, in which case Board members would be perceived as being on a rather superior level and probably not involved in management affairs.

- Very egalitarian cultures that value equal treatment, value and participation of people might perceive Board members and the clients of the nonprofit to have equal influence in the affairs of the nonprofit, in which case members and others would have similar roles.

- If a nonprofit has been struggling to work toward clear mission and priorities, then Board members (who had previously been focused primarily on the activities of management) should probably focus much more on policy making – thereby ensuring more clear mission and priorities that can be conveyed to all members of the organization.

Regardless of the model chosen by the Board, the nonprofit has to be sure that certain strategic decisions are always made and certain questions are always addressed.

See "Typical Types of Decisions Your Board Should Make" on page 91 and "Questions Your Board Members Should Always Ask" on page 124.

For Board and staff members who prefer that Board members have some involvement in management (for example, in nonprofits that are new, small or have cultures of egalitarian participation), perhaps that level of involvement is successful as long as the Board is "healthy". (See the following section about what "healthy" might look like.)

For more information, see "Sample Comparison of Board and Staff Roles" on page 258.

What Does a Healthy Board Look Like?

There has been an extensive amount of research and sharing of opinions about what makes for a highly effective Board. Asking what a healthy Board looks like is akin to asking what a healthy person looks like or how much a car costs. It all depends. Yet for the sake of furthering your understanding of Boards, it might be useful to consider at least one description. One of the most useful, yet not constricting descriptions, is offered in the book *The Executive Director's Survival*

Guide (Mim Carlson and Margaret Donohoe, John Wiley and Sons, 2005, p. 95). The authors assert that the attributes of an effective Board include:

- Focus on, and passion for, the mission, and a commitment to setting and achieving vision. Board members realize that one of their most important jobs is to verify that their nonprofit is indeed meeting the community need that the nonprofit was formed to meet.

- Clear responsibilities that refrain Board members from micro-managing. [Micro-managing is when members are so involved in the details of management that they 1) damage operations because staff are continually updating members with trivial information, and 2) do not sufficiently attend to strategic matters of top-level policies and plans.]

- Desire of Board members to work together, listen to diverse views and build consensus.

- Flexible structure that changes to fit the nonprofit's life cycle and priorities.

- An understanding of, and ability to shape, the organization's culture.

- An interest in knowing the good, bad and uncertain about the nonprofit, and commitment to resolving its issues.

- Commitment to self-reflection and evaluation, with clear expectations and each member's accountability to meet them.

Others mention overall features of a high-performing Board, for example, that it has:

- Governance – Board members employing very effective practices to establish the nonprofit's purpose and priorities in the community, and ensuring they are effectively and efficiently addressed for maximum benefit of stakeholders (clients, funders, collaborators, government agencies, etc.).

- Diligence – All Board members consistently attending to their duties of care and loyalty, with full attention, participation and responsibilities in all deliberations, decisions and interactions with stakeholders.

- Transparency – Board members always providing full disclosure and explanation of the nonprofit's governance, finances and affects on communities, and willingly supporting stakeholders' efforts to understand that information.

- Accountability – Board members continually making their nonprofits and themselves responsible to meet the expectations of stakeholders, and continually verifying with those stakeholders that their expectations are indeed being met.

Variety of Board Models to Consider for Your Board

Board members can proactively and planfully decide the model (the roles and structures) they use to work together, or that model can emerge over time as members conduct their business. The model also depicts, or directs, the level of members' involvement in policy-making and managerial affairs. Therefore, it is useful for you to have some basic understanding of some of the various models that your Board members might choose to operate. Common models are described later on in this section. The various models are differentiated from each other usually based on:

- ▪ ˙ Their structure, for example, a top-down, hierarchical and directive style of governance versus a more egalitarian and team-based approach.

- ▪ Whether they have governing powers or not, for example, an Advisory Board which does not have governing authority.

- ▪ Their primary focus, for example, a Fundraising Board (which can be a governing or Advisory Board, with members primarily responsible for fundraising).

- ▪ Commercial and proprietary design, for example, the Policy Governance® Board.

A Board can have features of several different types of models, for example, a governing Board that focuses on fundraising and uses committees. Keep in mind that there is no one perfect model that all Board members should use all of the time for every nonprofit everywhere. Three common different governing Board models (based on different structures) are described below, including the policy governing Board, the working governing Board and the collective governing Board.

Reference "Factors That Influence Focus of Board Members' Involvement" on page 28. Also see "How to Match Board's Priorities to Life Cycle of Nonprofit" on page 140.

Policy (Traditional) Governing Board

In this model, Board members attend primarily to strategic matters, such as developing top-level plans and policies, while staff members attend primarily to managerial matters (implementing those plans and policies). Often, the definitive characteristic of a policy Board is the presence of a variety of Board committees and a Chief Executive who reports to the Board. Many people refer to this structure as a "traditional" Board because of its rather top-down, committee-driven nature. (The policy governing Board is not to be confused with the Policy Governance® Board.)

The extent to which the structure is strictly implemented depends on the nature of the nonprofit (see the above reference to factors that influence members' involvement and to matching the Board's priorities to the life cycle of the nonprofit). Also, the distinction between the roles of the Board and Chief Executive depends on the nature of the nonprofit as well.

When the Board's structure, including its various committees, is designed to be in close accordance and involvement with common management functions (for example, with staffing, programs, marketing, finances and fundraising), this type of Board is sometimes referred to as a "management Board." This type of Board might have staff or none at all.

Working Governing Board (Administrative Governing Board)

In a "working" Board, Board members attend to the top-level strategic matters of the organization in addition to attending to day-to-day matters. This structure usually arises when the nonprofit is just getting started and so it has no paid staff members, or it prefers to operate completely on a volunteer basis. The nature of this Board structure is usually rather flexible and informal. A working Board might utilize committees or not. Many times there is no Chief Executive role in the organization.

A "policy" governing Board is often viewed as more "mature," having passed through the "working" Board stage. This view is not fair because many nonprofits prefer to remain as working Boards because they do not want to hire staff, or because they benefit from Board and staff members successfully working together.

Ideally, Board members remember that they are responsible for the governance of the organization, and so they ensure that top-level plans and policies are established in addition to attending to whatever day-to-day tasks need to be done. They might conduct Board operations in the form of Board committees.

Sometimes people mistakenly refer to a working Board as a Board where members are actively working. The distinction is what the members are working on, not whether members are active or no. In a working-Board model, members are working on strategic and managerial tasks.

Collective Governing Board Model

In a collective, or co-operative, Board, the Board and staff members always prefer to share equal responsibility in all matters. The collective Board is the epitome of a democratic and team effort. This type of Board is often popular among cultures that highly value equality and power sharing. A collective Board might utilize committees or not. In this type of Board structure, it could be difficult to discern who is a Board member or a staff member – all members are considered as Board members and staff members.

Corporate law requires that specific persons be in the official positions as Board members – the fiduciary, or legal, responsibilities cannot be continually shared, changed and ultimately diffused with others who are not themselves Board members. While this structure is highly flexible and adaptable, it could be very difficult to efficiently identify any ultimate, personal responsibilities and accountabilities for fiduciary responsibilities. So it is important in this model that Board members can individually be identified if necessary.

Focus of This Guide: Policy, Working and Collective Boards

While there is no definitive research that clearly specifies the percentage use of certain types of Boards in the USA and Canada, conventional wisdom suggests that the most popular governing Board structures are the policy, working and collective Boards. Thus, this guide references them throughout because of their distinctions, usefulness and likely application among the readers of the guide. Table II:1 depicts differences between these three types of governing Boards.

For another useful overview, go to Mel Gill's information at http://www.synergyassociates.ca/publications/OverviewGovernanceModels.htm .

Also see Nathan Garber's information at http://garberconsulting.com/governance%20models%20what's%20right.htm .

Finally, see David Renz's typology of Board types at http://www.nonprofitquarterly.org/content/view/69/28/ .

Table II:1 – Comparison of Common Board Models (Based on Structure)

Activity	Policy Governing [1]	Working Governing	Collective Governing
Has ultimate authority	Board	Board	Per law: Board members Per the Board: shared
Hires / fires Chief Executive	Board (usually has CEO role)	Board (if CEO role exists)	Joint (probably does not have CEO role)
Delegates to Chief Executive	Board (although Board and CEO might work as "strategic partners")	Board and CEO might share duties	Joint
Staffing	Board approves Personnel Policies; distinct Board-staff hierarchy	Board approves Personnel Policies; might not have staff; loosely defined hierarchy	One team
Drive strategic planning	Board	Board and / or joint	Joint
Strategic planning	Board does mission, vision, values, and overall goals	Joint	Joint
Approves strategic plan	Board	Board	Joint
Fundraising	Board approves Fundraising Plan (heavily engaged)	Board approves Fundraising Plan (joint fundraising)	Joint
Financial planning and controls	Board approves budget, fiscal policies and procedures (Treasurer and Finance Committee take lead role)	Board approves budget, fiscal policies and procedures (Board and staff share other responsibilities)	Joint
Financial reporting and decisions	Board reviews statements, makes decisions (Treasurer and Finance Committee take lead role)	(Board and staff share responsibilities)	Joint
Program delivery	Board approves programs	Joint	Joint
Public / community relations	Board heavily engaged	Joint	Joint

Note 1: A policy governing Board is not the same as a Policy Governance® Board, which is a commercial Board design and a registered trademark of Carver Governance Design, Inc.

Some New Board Models to Also Think About

As demands for Board effectiveness and accountability continue to grow, research and discussions about how Boards might operate differently, continue to grow, as well. There are a variety of new ideas for Board models.

Networked Governance

David Renz suggests that the effectiveness of governance could be enhanced when we realize that governance can include organizations and activities that go beyond the role of the Board in an organization. Nowadays, many nonprofit services to a community are often delivered across a network of organizations and, thus, the distributed governance of that network is a key point in the effectiveness of those services. Renz mentions the advantages of the perspective on networked governance and also mentions the difficult challenges inherent in that perspective, for example, how can individual nonprofits and Boards influence the overall network and how can we ensure that individual Boards are doing their fiduciary responsibilities.

See *Exploring the Puzzle of Board Design: What's Your Type?* by David Renz, http://www.nonprofitquarterly.org/content/view/69/28/ .

System-Wide Governance

Judy Freiwirth asserts that the traditional "top down," "command and control" paradigm of Boards actually gets in the way of the nonprofit's successfully working toward its mission. She suggests that the governance responsibility to be shared among constituents, including members, staff and Board. In System-Wide Governance, Board members are from the community and constituency. Although, governance is very democratic in nature, Board members do perform some legal and fiduciary responsibilities. She mentions the Whole Scale Change methodology as an example of how constituency-based planning and operations can be successful.

See *System-Wide Governance for Community Empowerment* by Judy Freiwirth and Maria Elena Letona at http://www.bsbpa.umkc.edu/mwcnl/Conferences/Governance2007/Papers/ Session%20A/System-Wide%20Governance%20Model%20Freiwirth.pdf .

Community-Driven Governance: Governing for What Matters

Community-Driven Governance is a framework that defines a Board's primary purpose as leadership towards making a significant, visionary difference in the community the organization serves. The Board's work centers around an annual plan that aims first and foremost at the difference the organization will make in the community. The plan then addresses the organizational infrastructure needed to implement that plans. The approach is intended to be simple enough for any Board to put into practice, while comprehensively addressing first the ends, and then the means for which a Board will hold itself accountable. The approach also aims to avoid a typical problem in Boards when they attend primarily to internal operations, rather than truly representing the needs of stakeholders.

See *Governing for What Matters* by Hildy Gottlieb at
http://www.help4nonprofits.com/NP_Bd_Governing_for_What_Matters1
-Art.htm .

Relationship Model

Steven Block proposes a model that, instead of having a rigid, top-down structure of roles and hierarchy of the traditional policy model, provides for Board and staff members to work together with great priority on generating relationships and value from those relationships. The Executive Director and staff play an important role in bringing matters to the group (a group of Board members and staff) and their opinions are greatly valued. Board and staff share experiences together, for example, rituals and meals, to develop relationships. Board members are not expected to take part in activities outside Board meetings. They can be there to assist staff. Committees are not used.

See *Nonprofit Board Governance: The Relationship Model* by Stephen R. Block at
http://www.bsbpa.umkc.edu/mwcnl/Conferences/Governance2007/Papers/Session%20A/Stephen%20Block%20Relationship%20MOdel.pdf .

Nested Boards

While it is not necessarily a new perspective on Boards, nonprofit leaders should understand this Board model because they might encounter it when collaborating with other nonprofits. Nested Boards exist in associations or "umbrella" organizations that have members, or subgroups, that also are organizations. An example is a national organization that has chapters in various regions or states. Advantages to this arrangement are that the members benefit from the guidance and resources of the umbrella organization. The umbrella organization benefits from the structured involvement and representation of the various subgroups. Members of the organization's Board of often are members of the Boards of the various subgroups. There can be a continual tension in the arrangement. Subgroups want the autonomy to serve their local constituents, yet want the benefits of their affiliation with the umbrella organization. Likewise, the umbrella organization wants the dedicated participation and contributions of the subgroups, yet wants the subgroups to effectively manage their own operations in their own locales.

See *The Dynamics of Nested Governance in Nonprofit Organizations: Preliminary Thoughts* by Patricia Bradshaw at
http://www.bsbpa.umkc.edu/mwcnl/Conferences/Governance2007/Papers/Session%20A/Nested%20Gov%20Nonprofit%20Conf.pdf .

Policy Governance® Model

Although it is not new, Carver's Policy Governance® Board is another prominent Board model. ("Policy Governance" is a commercial product and registered trademark of Carver Governance Design, Inc.) The model is designed to ensure that Board members always operate in a fashion that maintains strong, strategic focus for the organization. Board members enforce clear policies that determine the "ends" for the organization to achieve and they set very strict limits within which the Chief Executive operates. This structure is characterized by few, if any, distinct officer roles or Board committees. Nonprofits are encouraged to use trained consultants to implement this model.

Similar to other models, there are very strong critics and proponents. This model is not referenced throughout the guide because of its commercial and highly technical nature.

See *Carver Policy Governance Model* at
http://www.policygovernance.com .

Typical Phases of Developing Your Board

Here are two different views of the life cycles of development of a Board of Directors. Remember that all of the stages are still in regard to a governing Board. All Boards of corporations are governing Boards – they just display different "personalities" during different stages of their development.

One View on Life Stages of a Board

Many people view some of the above structures as stages along the continuum of development of a governing Board.

1. **Working Governing Board**
    This is often the first phase of the life of a Board of Directors. Board members are usually very "hands on." They help start the organization including, setting the first mission, policies, etc. But they also help fix the fax, send out mailings – whatever it takes to get the organization off the ground. (Note that a working Board is a type of governing Board.) There is often a misconception that a working Board is somehow an immature Board because members are attending to day-to-day tasks, in addition to top-level policy making. However, some organizations, for example, those with no paid staff, might have a governing Board that is a working Board in nature, but that also successfully attends to top-level strategic matters. In that situation, it is appropriate to have a working Board.

2. **Policy Governing Board**
    In this type of governing Board, members attend primarily to establishing top-level plans and policies, while staff members implement those plans and policies. Policy governing Boards are characterized usually by committees and a Chief Executive who reports to the Board. It is rare that a policy governing Board did not first operate as a working Board.

3. **Institutional Board**
    Some Board experts recognize a third phase of Board maturity, the Institutional Board. This phase occurs when the organization is very mature, with all the systems in place to run the organization in a highly effective and efficient manner. The Institutional Board is usually larger than the typical policy governing Board, and often includes rather prominent people in the community because the Institutional Board often exists primarily to raise funds for the organization. Usually, there is a subgroup, such as an Executive Committee, that does much of the Board work.

Another View on Life Stages of a Board

1. **Personalities Board**
    The personalities Board is driven by the nature of a few personalities on the Board. It is common that new Boards are personalities Boards. In this type of Board, a few Board

members seem to do all the work, primarily because of their natures, not because of their expertise. Board members talk about whatever topics are brought up by the "major players" on the Board. Members talk about the topic until everyone is tired or time runs out in the meeting and then members leave the meeting.

Members are recruited onto the Board based on their personalities and relationships, not on their expertise. Members who desire truly strategic discussions and want to really make a difference often leave the Board. Members are usually driven by reactions to crises, not by proactively following policies and plans.

2.   **Best Practices Board**
In this type of Board, members have decided they want to move away from being a "personalities Board" to become more professionalized in their Board operations. Usually, this occurs in response to a member or two having attended a Board training or to a crisis where one or more stakeholders have insisted that the Board members become more strategic in their operations.

Members learn "best practices" about Board operations, for example, policies regarding an annual calendar of operations, clarifying roles of a Board versus staff, staffing the Board, evaluating the Board, evaluating meetings, Board attendance, conflict-of-interest and making decisions. Board leadership ensures that Board policies are followed. Conversations among Board members are often about remembering what practices and policies they should be following in order to improve the Board operations.

3.   **Strategic Board**
In the strategic Board, the best practices have become second nature for members – they follow the practices without having to work hard at remembering those practices. The policies and practices have become deeply instilled in how members operate on the Board.

The Members ask strategic questions, for example: Are we on schedule in implementing our Strategic Plan? Are the committees on schedule with their objectives? Are our discussions focused on top-level policies that Boards should address or on day-to-day matters that staff can handle? Are our programs really making a difference in the community? How do we know? What is next on our Board's annual calendar?"

See "How to Match Board's Priorities to Life Cycle of Nonprofit" on page 140.

Other Types of "Boards" for You to Be Aware Of

1.   **Governing Board**
This is the type of Board described so far in this guide, a Board that is legally charged to oversee a corporation.

2.   **Board of Trustees**
Certain types of organizations such as hospitals, universities, certain state and local agencies, etc., use the phrase Board of Trustees as the name for their governing Board. These Boards are legally charged to govern their nonprofits.

3. **Executive Board**

    Recently, this name is used for the Executive Committee, a frequently used type of committee in a governing Board. The Executive Committee is often comprised of the Board officers and/or the Chairs of the various other committees. The Executive Committee is a special committee that, when empowered by the Board in total and per the terms of their By Laws, can carry out certain activities to represent the entire Board.

4. **Advisory Board**

    Members of Advisory Boards provide recommendations to members of the governing Board, Chief Executive and staff. These Boards are advisory in nature and do not have legal authority to govern the nonprofit as does a governing Board.

     See "Guidelines to Form Your Advisory Board" on page 217.

5. **Auxiliary Board**

    These Boards are sometimes used to officially organize people to plan and carry out specific events like annual events, fundraising campaigns, etc. These Boards do not have legal authority to govern the nonprofit.

6. **Emeritus Board**

    Members are moved from governing Boards to Emeritus Boards so they can retain some formal affiliation with the nonprofit. The nonprofit benefits from the status of the members of the Emeritus Board and also from direct access to members who know much of the history of the nonprofit.

Your Board's Most Important Documents

It helps to have basic understanding of the four key types of documents that Board members use to organize themselves and carry out their operations. They are Articles, By Laws, resolutions and policies and procedures.

Articles of Incorporation

Your Board of Directors gets its authority from the Articles. This governing document specifies the name, the purpose or mission of the organization, place of business, primary officers, etc. The format of the Articles document is usually determined by the appropriate local agency and they will provide the Articles form to you. You will file Articles (or other forms of description, such as charters, constitutions, articles of association, etc.) with the appropriate agency in order to officially create the nonprofit corporation. The Articles are a public document. Depending on where you file, the Articles will probably ask you to specify:

- Name of the nonprofit.

- The purpose, or mission, of the nonprofit (authorities will refer to this mission to discern if the nonprofit can be classified as tax-exempt or tax-deductible).

- Agent of the corporation (this is the main contact and address of the organization).

- Names of initial directors (the number of directors that you need depends on the requirements of the agency where you are filing, whether that be your state or province, or federal agency).

- Name and address of the incorporator (this is the person who is filing the Articles).

- Classifying membership (you specify if the nonprofit will have voting or non-voting members).

It may take anywhere from one to six months to receive official corporate status from the government agency. Usually the agency will send you a certified copy of your Articles with an official seal stamped on the Articles.

For examples of Articles of Incorporation, go to http://www.managementhelp.org/boards/boards.htm#anchor133574 .

By Laws

Unlike Articles, the By Laws are written by the organization and can be changed by a Board decision. For membership organizations – organizations that include a classification of people who are corporate "members" with the authority to add or modify terms of governance, structure and management – changes in By Laws require approval of that membership, for example, a majority of the members agree. (The term "members" can be quite confusing. In addition to corporate "members," there also are general members of which many of us are familiar, for example, association in which members pay annual dues, receive a newsletter, attend an annual conference, etc.)

It is important to keep the By Laws up-to-date, not only for the sake of the Board members themselves, but also because stakeholders (for example, funders, collaborators or competitors) might refer to them to understand, or to have justified to themselves, certain acts of the Board members. The diligence shown in the writing of the By Laws can convey the diligence and good faith by which Board members are governing the organization.

The scope and level of detail in By Laws tend to change over the years. For example, By Laws used to be very comprehensive, detailed documents that specified what the Board and nonprofit could – and sometimes could not – do. This often led to confusion and conflict on the part of Board members because they were continually constrained by the requirements of the By Laws, or were by having to continually change them. Nowadays, By Laws tend to specify generally what the nonprofit and Board can do. Table II:2 shows the typical contents for By Laws. Unless By Laws specifically specify that Board members and the nonprofit cannot do something, then they can.

To see examples of By Laws, go to http://www.managementhelp.org/boards/boards.htm#anchor314119 .

Table II:2 Typical Contents for By Laws

- Name of the nonprofit corporation
- Mission / purpose
- Offices of the corporation
- Classes (e.g., membership dues)
- Board of Directors (number, selection, term limits)
- Duties of the Board (including power and scope of power)
- Board officers (listing and brief description of each)
- Committees (listing, including advisory committee)

- Notice of meetings (official meetings, actions without meetings)
- Annual meeting (for election of officers, input from community)
- Voting (forms of consensus and voting)
- Quorum requirements (minimum number to constitute official Board actions)
- Fiscal year specification
- Liabilities and indemnification of Board members
- Records and retention
- Change of contents

Board Resolutions

Articles, charters, constitutions, etc., and By Laws are ongoing rules. In contrast, a Board resolution is a key decision made and recorded by the Board in order to bring attention to a major decision. Such decisions may include adopting or changing a set of rules, a new program, a contract, etc. The resolution is described on an internal memo. Enactment of the resolution should be included in the minutes for the Board meeting in which the resolution was adopted.

To see examples of Board resolutions, go to http://www.managementhelp.org/boards/boards.htm#anchor277551 .

Board Policies and Procedures

Board policies are guidelines for how the Board members want to work together. Although the range of Board policies seems to be increasing, some examples of common Board policies are regarding staffing the Board, conflicts-of-interest, attendance and ethics, They can also be about more specific operational matters, for example: when and where Board members will meet, how they will recruit and train new Board members, how they will ensure consistent attendance to Board meetings, how they will work with the Chief Executive, etc.

See "Sample Board Policies" on page 249.

Board Roles and Responsibilities

Fiduciary Duties (Legal Responsibilities) of Your Board

Board members have fiduciary, or legal, duties as established in corporate law. These are the duty of care and duty of loyalty. The nature of the two duties can overlap. Variations or new duties are increasingly discussed, including duty of good faith, duty of candor and duty of obedience. (A Board member's good-faith action is acting truthfully and honestly with the best of intentions to benefit the nonprofit.)

Examples of performing the duty of care include clearly making a reasonable and good-faith effort to, for example:

- Be aware of the nonprofit's mission, plans and policies, and be sure that they indeed serve the needs of the community that the Board members represent.

- Be sure that all nonprofit activities are in accordance with the mission, plans and policies, and are in accordance with rules and regulations of the society and community. (Some people refer to these activities as being in accordance with a duty of obedience.)

- Fully participate in Board meetings, deliberations and decisions.

- Read, evaluate and ensure accuracy of all reports, including minutes, financial and evaluations.

- Ensure the organization has sufficient resources, including people, funding and other assets.

Examples of performing the duty of loyalty include clearly making a reasonable and good-faith effort, when acting as a Board or staff member, to:

- Always be thinking about, and focusing on, priorities of the nonprofit, and not that of yourself or another organization.

- Share ideas, opinions and advice to forward the progress of the nonprofit.

- Represent the nonprofit in a favorable light.

More clarity will come from considering more specific types of activities conducted by Board members. There are many resources that suggest roles and responsibilities of nonprofit Boards. Therefore, more than one perspective is included in this guide.

BoardSource (formerly the National Center for Nonprofit Boards), in its booklet *Ten Basic Responsibilities of Nonprofit Boards*, itemizes the following 10 responsibilities for nonprofit Boards.

1. Determine the organization's mission and purpose.

2. Select the Chief Executive.

3. Support the Chief Executive and review his or her performance.

4.   Ensure effective organizational planning.

5.   Ensure adequate resources.

6.   Manage resources effectively. (This is often done by appointing a Chief Executive to manage the organization.)

7.   Determine and monitor the organization's programs and services.

8.   Enhance the organization's public image.

9.   Serve as a court of appeal.

10.   Assess its own performance.

Brenda Hanlon (2001, www.ncnb.org) suggests the following duties from *In Boards We Trust*.

1.   **Provide continuity for the organization**.
        This is done by setting up a corporation or legal existence, representing the organization's point of view through interpretation of its products and services, and establishing advocacy for them.

2.   **Select, appoint and evaluate a Chief Executive Officer.**
        The CEO is the person to whom responsibility for the administration of the organization is delegated. The Board's activities include:

        a.   To review and evaluate his/her performance regularly on the basis of a specific job description including the Chief Executive's relations with the Board and leadership in the organization, in program planning and implementation, and in management of the organization and its personnel.

        b.   To offer administrative guidance and determine whether to retain or dismiss the Chief Executive.

3.   **Govern the organization by broad policies and objectives**.
        These are formulated and agreed upon with the Chief Executive and employees. This includes assigning priorities and ensuring the organization's capacity to carry out programs by continually reviewing its work.

4.   **Acquire sufficient resources for the organization's operations.**
        This includes more than getting money. It includes ensuring sufficient personnel, expertise, facilities and other assets.

5.   **Account to the public for the products and services of the organization.**
        This is true especially for the organization's expenditures and conformance to rules and regulations, for example:

        a.   To provide for fiscal accountability, approve the budget, and formulate policies related to contracts from public or private resources.

        b.   To accept responsibility for all conditions and policies attached to new, innovative, or experimental programs.

How to Minimize Liabilities of Your Board Members

Each Board member is personally liable in his/her fiduciary role as a Board member. The "business judgment rule" protects Board members from liability as long as they can show that they are trying to act reasonably and in good faith – that they are performing their duties of care and loyalty. An exception would be if there was clear evidence of intent to break the law, for example, theft, fraud, forgery, burglary, misappropriation of funds, or obstruction of justice.

Liability can be significantly reduced if Board members undertake the activities listed below. (The following is not offered as legal advice.)

Board Practices

- ❏ Have Board meetings at least quarterly.
- ❏ Be sure that By Laws accurately reflect Board members' specifications of the structure of the nonprofit and how it is to be managed.
- ❏ Produce and approve Board minutes that include highlights of members' deliberations, decisions and actions from Board meetings and committee meetings.
- ❏ Include an indemnification paragraph in By Laws, which explains corporate protection of members.
- ❏ Be sure the personnel policies are up-to-date and approved by the Board, and staff are trained on the policies.
- ❏ The Treasurer should not also be the auditor.
- ❏ Be sure each member undergoes basic training on roles and responsibilities of governing Board of Director.
- ❏ Be sure that Board members are trained on their roles and the roles of staff.
- ❏ Conduct a Board self-evaluation once a year.
- ❏ Conduct an evaluation of the Executive Director at least once a year according to the personnel policies.
- ❏ Approve and train about Board policies, including By Laws and conflict-of-interest.
- ❏ Adhere to the Board policies, especially conflict-of-interest and ethics policies.
- ❏ As much as possible, staff the Board with independent members – those who are not staff members, have no business affiliation with the nonprofit, and are not friends of the CEO.
- ❏ As much as practical, ensure staff members are not involved in recruiting Board members.
- ❏ Train Board members how to analyze financial information.

Board Deliberations and Decisions

- ❏ Participate in all Board meetings or be excused beforehand.
- ❏ Participate in Board deliberations and Board decisions.
- ❏ Notify members if there is an apparent conflict of interest with any member.
- ❏ Be sure that highlights from deliberations, decisions and actions are included in Board-approved meeting minutes.
- ❏ Be sure all contracts with vendors specify them as independent contractors and also specify the scope of their liabilities in dealings with the nonprofit.

Financial and Tax Management

❑ Train Board members about how to analyze financial information.

❑ Have up-to-date, Board-approved fiscal policies and procedures and follow them.

❑ Regularly review cash flow and budget-versus-actual reports, and Statement of Financial Activities and Statement of Financial Condition at least quarterly.

❑ Have a yearly audit (audits range from reviews to comprehensive analysis and reporting).

❑ Institute cash controls so all funds are recorded, tracked and reviewed.

❑ Ensure all cash transaction require two different people to track invoices and payments.

❑ Ensure that payroll taxes are paid.

❑ Ensure annual tax filing is submitted (for example, the Form 990 in the USA).

❑ Ensure any revenue not related to the charitable purpose of the nonprofit is reported (for example, Form 990-T in the USA).

Insurance

❑ Have you incorporated the nonprofit? (Corporations enjoy a limited liability shield, whereby the corporation is sued before its members. Benefits of the shield are in effect, especially if Board members can show good faith in their Board activities.)

❑ Do you have general liability insurance in case someone sues because of workplace injury?

❑ Do you need property insurance in case property is damaged or lost?

❑ Should you have professional liability insurance, which covers you in case someone sues as a result of perceived malpractice?

❑ Would the Board members benefit from Directors and Officers Insurance to pay any lawsuits lost by Board members when someone sued the Board, alleging damage because of members' actions or inactions?

❑ Do you need workers' compensation insurance in case someone is injured on the job?

How to Ensure Ethical Behavior of Your Board Members

Another way to ensure that Board members' actions are in accordance with their fiduciary duties, minimize their liabilities, and treat others with respect and fairness is to institute guidelines for ethical behaviors. Ethics policies and codes of conduct to ensure highly ethical behaviors are used increasingly on Boards of Directors. Here are some practices that Board members could commit to in order to ensure ethical behaviors:

1. Know the roles and responsibilities of a member of the governing Board of Directors.

2. Do his/her best to be fully informed of the nonprofit's operations that can have significant effect on fellow Board members, staff members and other stakeholders of our organization.

3. Always strive to contribute best judgment in carrying out the Board role, including provision of opinions and information during Board deliberations and decisions.

4. Avoid conflict of interest in appearance or in application – actions as a Board member will always be first and foremost for the benefit of the nonprofit organization.

5. Adhere to all of the Board policies presented to the member during Board orientation and included in the Board Manual.

6.   Not directly assign tasks to staff members, rather to coordinate suggestions for those tasks through the Board as a body, which can, in turn, assign the CEO to carry out the tasks as he/she desires.

7.   Maintain confidentiality about all Board information that is deemed by members to be confidential, including that generated and decided during closed sessions of the Board.

8.   Follow the ground rules for Board meetings as formally agreed upon by fellow Board members.

9.   Respect the values and perspectives of fellow Board members and staff members with whom a Board member interacts.

10.   Represent the nonprofit in the most positive image when dealing with the nonprofit's stakeholders.

11.   Adhere to the decisions made by the Board – avoid public disagreement with decisions, recognizing that all Board members must "speak from one voice.

The above guidelines are included as a "Sample Board Ethics Policy" on page 267. Also see the "Sample Whistleblower Policy" on page 277.

What Board Committees Typically Do (If You Use Them)

Depending on the particular Board structure preferred by Board members, Boards often organize their members into various committees, or small working groups. If your structure does not highly value committees then your Board might instead use task forces, or small groups of people who work together to conduct some current activity and then disband when the activity has been carried out. This guide will use the term "committees" for all of these approaches.

When starting your Board, it is useful to have some basic sense about typical Board committees. You will get a good sense for what committees your Board will need after you have done some basic strategic planning. There is more about strategic planning later on in this guidebook.

About Committees

The following points are in reference to small, working groups of the overall number of Board members. Whether the Board chooses to call them "committees" or not is up to the Board members.

1.   **Committees are useful to take full advantage of Board members' resources.**
        This includes members' expertise, time, commitment and diversity of opinions. These resources are more fully utilized if focused into a small working group of members.

2.   **Establish committees when issues are too complex or numerous for quick response.**
        Each of the major functions required to manage a nonprofit requires a complicated range of activities, for example, planning and oversight of financial management, fundraising, personnel management, programs and marketing. All Board members cannot be deeply involved in the planning and oversight of each. Thus, Boards often choose to associate a committee with each function.

3. **Use standing (permanent) and ad hoc (temporary) committees.**
    One of the biggest frustrations of Board members is having a committee for the sake of having a committee. Members of those committees usually struggle to find any purpose in the organization. Have standing committees only for the most important, current priorities; otherwise, terminate the committee. Temporary priorities, such as building a facility or coordinating an event, might need an ad hoc committee.

4. **Committees recommend policy for approval by the entire Board.**
    Be clear that the role of a Board Committee is not to act for the entire Board. Committees should not be making decisions for all Board members. Committees should make recommendations to the full Board for full Board deliberation and approval. (The full Board might delegate to the Executive Committee the ability to make certain types of Board decisions when it is impractical to gather all Board members together. However, all Board members are still responsible for the decisions made by the Executive Committee.)

5. **Frequency of committee meetings depends on urgency and complexity of priorities.**
    The more urgent and complex the issues facing the organization, the more frequently committees might meet. For example, a Fundraising Committees might meet at least monthly if the planned amount of donations is down dramatically. Likewise, a Programs Committee might meet monthly if the nonprofit has the opportunity to add several new programs to meet the needs in the community.

6. **Minutes should be recorded and approved for all committee meetings.**
    Boards often forget to do this and, as a result, the full Board often is not aware of the activities and results of meetings of the committees. Minutes are documentation usually of the meeting attendance, discussions, decisions and results.

Potential Standing (Permanent) Committees

Table II:3 portrays the various functions often conducted by standing Board committees, or committees that exist year round. Note that this list is not intended to suggest that all of these committees should exist; it is ultimately up to the organization to determine which committees should exist and what they should do. You likely will need only three or four of these standing committees during your first years of operation.

Potential Ad Hoc (Temporary) Committees

Table II:4 describes the various functions often conducted by ad hoc Board committees, that is, committees that exist to accomplish a goal and then cease to exist. This list is not intended to suggest that all of these committees should exist or that these are the only ad hoc committees that might be used; it is ultimately up to the organization to determine which committees should exist and what they should do.

 See "What Each Committee Typically Does" on page 85 for a list of typical goals associated with each of the most common types of committees.

Table II:3 – Potential Standing Committees

Committee Name	Their Typical Roles
Board Development - sometimes called Governance, with Nominating Committee	Ensures effective Board processes, structures and roles, including retreat planning, committee development, and Board evaluation; sometimes includes role of Nominating Committee, such as keeping a list of potential Board members and conducting orientation and training.
Evaluation	Ensures sound evaluation of products/services/programs, including, for example, outcomes, goals, data, analysis and resulting adjustments.
Executive	Oversees operations of the Board; often acts on behalf of the Board during on-demand activities that occur between meetings, and these acts are later presented for full Board review; comprised of Board Chair, other officers and/or committee Chairs (or sometimes just the officers, although this might be too small); often performs evaluation of Chief Executive.
Finance	Oversees development of the budget; ensures accurate tracking/monitoring/accountability for funds; ensures adequate financial controls; often led by the Board Treasurer; reviews major grants and associated terms.
Fundraising	Oversees development and implementation of the Fundraising Plan; with all Board members, identifies and solicits funds from external sources of support, working with the Development Officer if available; sometimes called Development Committee.
Marketing	Oversees development and implementation of the Marketing Plan, including identification of potential markets, their needs, how to meet those needs with products/services/programs, and how to promote/sell the programs.
Personnel	Guides development, review and authorization of personnel policies and procedures; sometimes leads evaluation of the chief Executive; sometimes assists Chief Executive with leadership and management matters.
Programs	Guides development of service delivery mechanisms; may include evaluation of the services; link between the Board and the staff on program's activities.
Promotions and Sales	Promotes the organization's services to the community, including generating fees for those services.
Public Relations	Represents the organization to the community; enhances the organization's image, including communications with the press.

Table II:4 – Potential Ad Hoc Committees

Committee Names	Their Typical Roles
Audit	Plans and supports audit of major functions, for example, finances, programs or organization.
Campaign	Plans and coordinates major fundraising event; sometimes a subcommittee of the Fundraising Committee.
Compensation	Conducts analysis to determine and recommend appropriate compensation for staff, particularly the Chief Executive, to the Board for approval.
Ethics	Develops and applies guidelines for ensuring ethical behavior and resolving ethical conflicts.
Events	Plans and coordinates major events, such as fundraising, team-building or planning; sometimes a subcommittee of the Fundraising Committee.
Nominations	Identifies needed Board member skills, suggests potential members and orients new members; sometimes a subcommittee of the Board Development Committee.
Research	Conducts specific research and/or data gathering to make decisions about a current major function in the organization.

Roles of Your Board Members and Officers

One of the most frequent issues in Boards is that members do not understand their roles. Each of your Board members should have general description of their own role and also the roles of the Board officers and current Board committees, if your Board chooses to have officers and committees. These descriptions should be reviewed during orientation for new Board members and provided in the Board Manual given to each Board member.

See "Typical Contents of Board Manual" on page 245.

See "Sample Board Job Descriptions" on page 250 for descriptions of Board member, Board Chair, Vice Chair, Committee Chair, Treasurer and Secretary.

Leadership Role of Your Board Chair

The role of Board Chair is critical to the effectiveness of a nonprofit Board of Directors. Leadership on the Board starts with the role of Board Chair. (The other important aspect of Board leadership is the Executive Committee.) Therefore, it is important to understand the role and how it is carried out. Here are some observations about what makes for a highly effective Board Chair.

General Guidelines for Board Chair Effectiveness

In addition to the specific activities listed in the Board Chair job description referenced above, the Board Chair should:

1. Clearly understand the roles and responsibilities of the nonprofit Board of Directors. (The Board Chair should have this guide!)

2. Clearly understand the roles and responsibilities of the Board Chair position.

3. Maintain clear focus on the organization's plans, particularly its mission, when guiding Board operations. The Chair should be very familiar with the strategic plan.

4. Focus as much as possible on Board processes and not personalities.

5. Model the strong participation and team building required for a highly effective Board.

6. Highly value a strong, working relationship with the Chief Executive. Guidelines for maintaining a strong relationship between the Chair and the Chief Executive are in the section, "Board Coordination with Chief Executive and Staff."

7. Highly value the participation and opinions of Board members.

8. Possess good decision making and problem solving skills. Have strong facilitation skills during Board meetings, particularly regarding reaching consensus and time management.

For basic guidelines for decision making and problem solving, go to http://www.managementhelp.org/misc/mtgmgmnt.htm .

9. Play a leading role in fundraising activities, including visiting funders with the Chief Executive, co-authoring solicitations to funders, etc.

10. Be willing to ask for help.

11. Understand the basic principles of effective delegation.

For basic guidelines about delegation, go to http://www.managementhelp.org/guiding/delegate/basics.htm .

12. Have basic understanding of parliamentary procedure.

For basic guidelines about Robert's Rules, go to http://www.managementhelp.org/boards/boards.htm#anchor1463640 .

Leadership Role of Your Executive Committee

The Executive Committee, if a Board chooses to have such a committee, is often appointed by the full Board to act on the Board's behalf if a matter must be addressed before a full Board meeting can be convened. The Executive Committee is sometimes referred to as the Executive Board or Leadership Team.

The Executive Committee can be comprised of officers of the Board (for example, Board Chair, Vice Chair, Secretary and Treasurer) and/or Chairs of various committees. The Chief Executive Officer might serve as a non-voting member of the Board. (Many experts assert that the Chief Executive should not be a member of the Board itself. However, particularly during the first few years of the life of a nonprofit, the Chief Executive is frequently a member of the Board.)

The Board should specify in the By Laws that the Executive Committee must make recommendations to the full Board for full Board approval before such recommendations can be implemented. An option is to carefully specify what decisions can be made by the Executive Committee. Note that this specification cannot conflict with other terms of decisions as specified in the By Laws.

This committee might address time-sensitive and proprietary matters such as performance and compensation of the Executive Director, development and monitoring implementation of the strategic plan, review of the annual budget, etc.

Some Boards might be designed such that the Chief Executive reports to the Executive Committee, rather than to the entire Board. Such an arrangement should be done carefully because all Board members are legally responsible for the governance of the nonprofit corporation. Thus, the Executive Committee that "supervises" the Chief Executive must be careful to ensure that the entire Board is continually aware of the status of the performance of the Chief Executive.

The Board must be careful that the Executive Committee does not acquire the same roles and responsibilities as the entire Board. Note that all Board members are responsible for the entire Board matters and governance of the nonprofit, despite the power granted to the Executive Committee.

Some experts on nonprofit Boards recommend that a Board not have an Executive Committee because of the confusion and conflicted roles that might occur between the charters, or assigned responsibilities, of the entire Board "versus" the Executive Committee.

Board and Staff – How Do Their Roles Compare?

Board/Staff Responsibilities Are Fuzzy Early On

Early on in the life of a nonprofit, the Board might do much of the work that staff would be doing in a more mature organization such as installing faxes, doing mailings, serving clients, managing facilities. This type of Board is often referred to as a "working" Board. Hopefully, as the organization continues to effectively serve its clients, the organization grows to have more resources to serve more clients and serve them more efficiently. That growth often includes adding staff. The addition of staff would permit Board members to back off from the day-to-day activities to attend more to matters of policy, if Board members prefer. Essentially, the Board becomes more of a policy governing Board. This all depends on the type of Board model that the nonprofit prefers.

During that time of growth, it can be particularly confusing as to what Board members should be doing and what staff members should be doing. Therefore, it is important to establish policies that clearly communicate what the nonprofit expects the Board to be doing and the staff to be doing.

To further understand suggested roles for Board in comparison to staff, see the policy "Sample Comparison of Board and Staff Roles" on page 258.

General Areas of Board-Staff Overlap

The extent of overlap depends very much on the particular Board structure chosen by members, for example, a working Board, policy Board, collective Board, etc. Here are some areas where Board and staff activities can overlap:

1.   Mutual membership in Board committees.

2.   Staff attendance at Board meetings to make presentations.

3.   Staff participation in strategic planning, particularly during action planning.

Table II:5 in the next section depicts a common type of relationship between the Board, Board committees, Board Chair, Chief Executive and other staff.

To further understand suggested roles for Board in comparison to staff, see the policy "Sample Comparison of Board and Staff Roles" on page 258.

For more information about the level of involvement of Board members in managerial activities with staff, see "Variety of Board Models for You" on page 27.

Organization Chart of Board/Staff Relationships

This drawing depicts the typical arrangement in a policy (traditional) Board structure. The solid lines indicate formal lines of authority – authority that is official to the position. For example, corporate law asserts that the Board of Directors is legally responsible for the nonprofit corporation. Therefore, the Executive Director formally reports to the Board of Directors. The official authority of the Executive Director position is derived from the Board's specification for the position, for example, in the By Laws and/or Board-approved job description of the Executive Director.

The power of the Board is vested in the Board as an entirety of all of its members – no one member has the full authority of the Board. Therefore, the Board Chair (a single Board member) formally reports to the full Board. Committees formally report to the Board Chair or the full Board, depending on the official specification in the By Laws. Staff members, other than the Executive Director, typically report to the Executive Director, as specified in the By Laws and/or Board-approved job description of the Executive Director.

(Used and adapted with permission of Greater Twin Cities United Way)

Table II:5 – Board / Staff Relationships

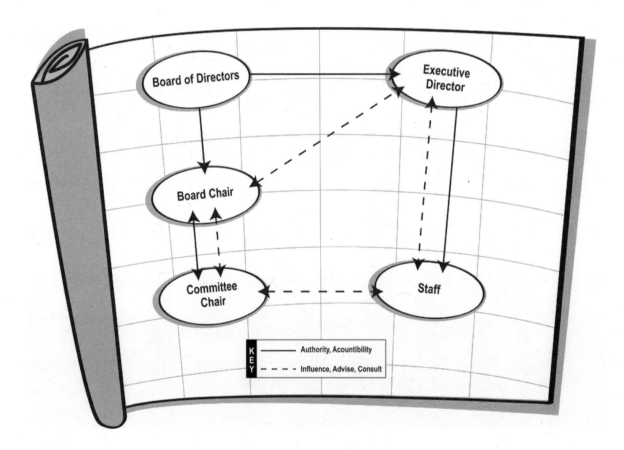

PART III:

HOW BOARDS

DO THEIR WORK

Your Board Calendar
(Your Board's Annual Important Tasks)

When we talk about how Board members do their work, we naturally describe many of the most important activities conducted by a Board of Directors. Board members conduct those activities at certain times of the year. Often, the By Laws and/or Board policies specify when certain activities will be conducted and when. Activities include: conducting regular Board meetings (every month, two months, etc.), conducting the Board self-evaluation, evaluating the Chief Executive, reviewing and updating Board and personnel policies, conducting strategic planning, recruiting new members, holding an annual meeting, reviewing and authorizing the yearly budget, conducting fundraising, etc.

One of the ways that Board members remember to do those activities is by continually referencing a Board Calendar. Therefore, one of the most important Board policies is the calendar of activities. If Board members used only one policy, this is the policy that might produce the most benefit because the calendar would continually remind members to do all of the important activities required in strong governance. Therefore, in addition to the By Laws, one of the first policies that Board members should develop and adopt is the Board Calendar.

See the "Sample Annual Calendar of Board Activities" on page 257.

Strategic Planning: Direction for Nonprofit and Your Board

The primary purpose and direction of a nonprofit and its programs should be established during the strategic planning process. Along with ensuring that the nonprofit is indeed meeting a strong public need, the Board is responsible to ensure that the purpose of the nonprofit is clear to all. Therefore, no guide intended to help a nonprofit to develop its Boards of Directors would be complete without including at least basic guidelines to develop a short-term strategic plan. This section provides guidelines sufficient for you to develop a short-term, strategic plan that is more complete than the simple plan that you drafted in the earlier section, "Conduct Basic Strategic Planning for Now."

It will be helpful to recruit the involvement of a Board Planning Committee. This committee might be comprised of Chairs of the other Board committees or of officers on the Board.

 It is not within the scope of this guide to provide comprehensive guidelines and procedures to carry out a complete, in-depth strategic planning process. You can get step-by-step guidelines for developing an in-depth strategic plan from the guidebook, *Field Guide to Nonprofit Strategic Planning and Facilitation,* from Authenticity Consulting, LLC. Additional resources are suggested at the end of this topic.

All Else Flows From Your Strategic Planning

Strategic planning influences numerous aspects of the organization including:

1.   Identification of existing needs among the nonprofit's stakeholders. This information is critical to the job of nonprofit Board member.

2.   Programs and services to be provided by the nonprofit in order to meet certain needs among stakeholders, and how those programs and services will be designed. This information also is critical to the job of Board member.

3.   Organizational and program design and roles needed by the organization.

4.   Board committees to be developed.

5.   Performance goals established for positions throughout the nonprofit.

6.   Resources needed to reach those goals and consequently, how much money is needed to procure those resources – ultimately, the goals determine the content of various budgets.

7.   Amounts of money needed for inclusion in fundraising plans.

The most important part of strategic planning is not the plan document itself, but rather the planning process, which, in reality, is always an ongoing process. Good governance and management are essentially an ongoing process of good strategic planning and implementation. Many organizations carry out some form of a strategic planning process. They just do their planning in an implicit manner, that is, they do not do it in a systematic and documented approach. Consequently, the quality of their planning often suffers.

Particularly for small nonprofits, the process of strategic planning should be carried out in a highly practical fashion. It is important during planning to do the 20% of effort that generates 80% of a good plan. The remaining 20% of a good plan often comes from actually implementing the plan itself. While matters about the mission, vision and values are certainly very important, do not get distracted into spending most of your planning time and energy on those matters. Strategic planning should always include solid action planning, specifying who will do what and by when in order to achieve goals. However, be careful not to engage in so much analysis and detail that planning members become fatigued, lose perspective and eventually lose interest in the planning process.

Strategic Planning – What, Who and When

What is Strategic Planning?

Simply put, strategic planning is determining:

1.   Why the nonprofit exists (its purpose, or mission).

2.   Where the nonprofit wants to be (vision and goals), usually in the next one to three years.

3.   How it is going to get there (via values, strategies and action plans).

4.   What is needed (money, people, equipment, etc.) in order to get there.

5.   How to make sure that the nonprofit is on track to get there.

There are many perspectives on the strategic planning process, including on the various terms and steps in the process. Some experts assert that organizations should start by examining their mission, vision and values statements. Others assert that organizations should start by analyzing what is going on in their external and internal environments, and then using the results of that analysis to update the mission, vision and values statements. Most experts assert that planners should identify major goals, set strategies to achieve the goals, and perform action planning that identifies who will be doing what and by when in order to achieve the goals. Action planning is followed by identifying what resources are needed to implement the strategies and specifying those resources, for example, in an annual operating budget.

Who Should Develop the Plan?

Board members must be highly involved in clarifying the mission statement. They also should be involved in writing the vision and values statements, if the organization decides to develop vision and values statements. They also should be highly involved in identifying strategic goals.

Staff members are often involved with the Board in identifying strategic goals and strategies to achieve the goals. Staff are also highly involved in action planning.

If you have not done strategic planning before, consider recruiting an experienced facilitator. A nonprofit should obtain an outside facilitator (that is, someone to facilitate who is not a member of the nonprofit) if any of the following are true:

- ▪   The nonprofit has not conducted strategic planning before.

- For a variety of reasons, previous strategic planning was not deemed to be successful.

- There appears to be a wide range of ideas and/or concerns among organization members about strategic planning and current organizational issues to be addressed in the plan.

- There is no one in the nonprofit who feels that he/she has sufficient facilitation skills.

- No one in the nonprofit feels committed to facilitating strategic planning for the nonprofit.

- Leaders believe that an inside facilitator will either inhibit participation from others or will not have the opportunity to fully participate in planning themselves.

- Leaders want an objective voice, that is, someone who is not likely to have strong predispositions about the nonprofit's strategic issues and ideas.

When Should Strategic Planning Be Done?

- Strategic planning should be done when an organization is just getting started.

- Strategic planning should also be done in preparation for a new major venture, for example, developing a new program.

- Strategic planning should also be conducted at least once a year in order to be ready for the coming fiscal year.

Sample Planning Process for Short-Term Strategic Plan

The length of time for strategic planning depends on whether the organization has done planning before, how many strategic issues and goals the organization faces, whether the culture of the organization prefers short or long meetings, and how much time the organization is willing to commit to strategic planning. However, for small nonprofits in particular, the planning process might be too long if it drags out over several months. Therefore, it is often much better for small nonprofits to spend several weeks in order to do a top-level, yet short-term strategic plan than to spend several months or longer doing a more detailed, long-term strategic plan.

Here is an example of a very basic strategic planning format, which results in a short-term, strategic plan that can be embellished later by staff adding more detailed action plans, if necessary. The plan is focused on the coming six-month period. Some strategic planning experts might complain that the following procedure does not produce a highly "strategic" plan, that is, the procedure does not include getting input from all major stakeholders, analysis of external factors, etc. However, the following recommended procedure is likely to "jump start" a highly practical plan from which you can gain guidance to continue directing and refining development of a nonprofit program.

1. **Have a meeting to announce planning process to Board members and key staff.**
   a. The Board Chair and Chief Executive announce to Board and staff that a strategic planning process will soon be underway. The announcement includes explanation of the purpose and benefits of strategic planning, and the role of Board and staff in the process. The Chair and/or Chief Executive explains who will be involved in the planning process. Time is allowed for Board and staff to ask questions in their respective meetings.

b. All Board members and certain staff are asked to think about current challenges that the organization faces and/or goals that they recommend for the organization to achieve over the coming six months. Staff are encouraged to talk to other staff to get ideas, as well.

c. The next upcoming planning sessions are scheduled.

2. **In a half-day Board retreat, identify major challenges over next six months.**
Include Board members and key staff. Activities include:

a. Introductions by the Board Chair and/or Chief Executive along with their explanations of the organization's benefits from strategic planning and the organization's commitment to the planning process. Explanations should indicate that the planning process will focus particularly on the next six months.

b. The facilitator provides an overview of the process. The facilitator might be an external facilitator, that is, someone from outside the organization, or an internal facilitator who has previous experience in strategic planning.

c. Brief review of the mission (and the vision and values, if applicable) with the bulk of time spent on identifying current, major challenges to address over the next six months. Challenges are clarified and prioritized. Participants may suggest strategies to meet the challenges, as well.

d. Finalize which challenges will be targeted over the next six months.

e. Finalize which strategies will be used to address the challenges.

f. Before the next meeting, a subcommittee is asked to draft the plan document that describes the major challenges and the strategies to address each challenge.

3. **Finalize action plans for each strategy and draft plan document.**
The next planning meeting is attended primarily by staff. All or certain Board members can attend, as well, especially Board leadership and any Board members assigned to Board committees whose activities are affected by strategies.

a. An action plan is developed for each strategy, including who will be doing what and by when in order to implement the strategy.

b. A subcommittee is asked to update the drafted plan to include the action plans, and provide the plan to Board members before the next Board meeting.

4. **In the next Board meeting, members authorize the strategic plan document.**
Board members:

a. Discuss the drafted plan document.

b. Suggest any changes. If changes are in order, they should be coordinated promptly with staff.

c. Approve the final draft of the document by signing the document.

Note that in the above example, various subcommittees might be charged to gather additional information and distribute it between meetings.

No matter how serious organizations are about strategic planning, they usually have strong concerns about being able to find time to attend frequent meetings. This concern can be addressed by ensuring meetings are well managed, having short meetings as needed rather than having fewer but longer meetings, and having realistic expectations from the planning project.

Developing Your Initial Strategic Plan for Now

The following guidelines and examples will help you to get started on a short-term, strategic plan. You may already have a pretty good sense about your organization's mission, groups of clients that your organization will serve, and major methods that the organization will use to meet those client's needs. Thus, you have probably already done some strategic planning. You have just been implicit about your planning. Make your planning explicit now so that it can be reviewed and communicated to others, including Board members and program staff.

For a complete set of worksheets that you can use to fill in the draft of your strategic plan, go to
http://www.managementhelp.org/np_progs/sp_mod/sp_frame.htm .

Draft Your Initial Mission Statement

Your description of your mission statement should briefly describe the purpose of your organization, whom it serves and how it serves them. The mission is the compass for Board decisions. Your mission statement is particularly important to program planning because it guides the overall relationship between the activities of your overall organization and your program. There should be strong alignment between the mission of your organization and the goals of your program. Therefore, you should give careful thought to the development of your mission statement.

Example:

> "To support individual and community development in Minneapolis by ensuring all adults between the ages of 18 and 65 achieve gainful employment in the community."

Draft Your Initial Vision Statement

Your description should depict the overall benefits that your community and clients will achieve from participating in your program. It should help guide Board members' decisions.

Example:

> "Every adult in Minneapolis is fulfilled by employment that contributes to his or her individual development as well as community development."

Draft Your Initial Values Statement

The values statement should describe the overall priorities, or principles, that guide how you want the nonprofit or program to operate.

Example:

> "We believe that:
>
> - Employment provides opportunity for adults to develop community and themselves;
>
> - Every person deserves opportunity for gainful employment;
>
> - Gainful employment of all citizens is a responsibility of all citizens."

Analyze Outside of Nonprofit Now

Take a wide look around at the world and how it might affect the nonprofit and its clients. This external analysis looks at societal, technological, political and economic trends affecting the organization. This may include trends in donations, recent or pending legislation, federal funds, demographic trends, or degree of access to trained labor and competition. Here is where a well-developed Board can be especially useful, if its members have strong understanding of the needs and resources in the community. (If you are starting the nonprofit now, your Board might not be that well-developed, but it should be within the next year or so, including by using this guide to staff your Board.) In your external analysis, do not forget to look at stakeholders' impressions of the organization including funders', clients', community leaders and collaborators.

 For another comprehensive list of considerations about the external environment, go to http://www.managementhelp.org/plan_dec/str_plan/drvnforc.htm .

From your external analysis, identify any perceived major threats to the nonprofit, for example, shortage of labor or decreased number of funders. Also, identify any major opportunities, for example, increased interest from the public in your programs or new nonprofits with which you might collaborate. Planners refer to this step as part of the SWOT analysis. SWOT is an acronym for strengths, weaknesses, opportunities and threats. You will identify the strengths and weaknesses in the next section.

 The following sites might have examples of SWOT analyses:
1. http://www.lakeheadu.ca/~eventswww/strategy/swot.html .
2. http://www.historyoftheuniverse.com/human.html#swot .
3. http://www.uk.amsat.org/swot.htm .
4. http://www.consultancymarketing.co.uk/swot.htm .
5. http://erc.msh.org/quality/example/swot.cfm.

Analyze Inside of Nonprofit Now

One of the best ways to measure the internal health of the organization is by using an organizational assessment. (See the reference immediately below.) Consider the strengths and weaknesses of the operations of the Board, staffing, programs, marketing, finances, fundraising, facilities and evaluations. Strengths might be clients' positive feedback about programs, strong reputation of the organization and expertise of staff, suitable and stable facilities, strength of finances, and evidence of solid administrative offices and operations. Weaknesses could be a deficiency in any of these areas.

 See "Tools to Measure Health of Nonprofits" on page 227 for a list of organizational assessment tools that could be used examine the operations inside the nonprofit.

Identify Your Most Important 5-7 Challenges to Address For Now

Think about the threats and weaknesses facing your organization. As a result, what challenges might arise for the nonprofit over the next six months? (A new nonprofit is often better off to focus on the major obstacles or issues that it will face over the next six months. After this initial period, the organization can identify the more forward-looking, developmental goals to accomplish over the next 12 months or so. For example, challenges over the next six months might be that the Chief Executive is not being paid, the Board is not achieving a quorum in Board meetings, there is no money at all, etc.) To identify the key challenges identified from your strategic analyses, consider the following guidelines:

1.   From considering the effects of threats and weaknesses you identified, what are the major challenges that you see? List as many as you can. Many organizations have stumbled badly because they ended up "falling over their feet" while being focused much too far down the road.

2.   Consider each of the challenges. Ask whether it is important or urgent. Often, challenges seem very important when they are only urgent. For example, changing a flat tire is an urgent issue – but you would never put "changing a tire" in your strategic plan. Attend only to the important challenges and not the urgent issues.

3.   Deal with challenges that you can do something about. Challenges that are too narrow do not warrant planning and challenges that are too broad will bog you down.

4.   Challenges should be clearly articulated so that someone from outside of the organization can read the description and understand the nature of the challenges.

Identify Your Goals (and Optionally, Strategies) for Now

Think about goals needed to address each of the major challenges. When thinking about goals, think about the opportunities and the strengths you identified. Use your strengths and opportunities to shore up weaknesses and to take advantage of opportunities to ward off threats. Goals should be written to be as specific as possible. Think about the strategies, or methods, to achieve each goal.

Example:

> Challenge #1: Establish full-time CEO position.
>
> 1) Strategy 1.1: Obtain funds to pay CEO for at least one year.
>
> 2) Strategy 1.2: Establish and operate Board Search Committee.
>
> 3) Strategy 1.3: Search Committee recommends CEO candidate.
>
> 4) Strategy 1.4: Board selects new CEO.

Develop Action Plans (Short-Term?) for Each Goal

For example, for Strategy 1.1 above:

Actions for Strategy 1.1	Date of Completion	Responsibility	Status and Date
1.1.1. Recruit fundraiser/trainer.	1/1/09	Program Director	
1.1.2. Schedule Board and CEO training about fundraising.	1/1/09	Program Director	
1.1.3. Conduct training.	1/21/09	Program Director	
1.1.4. Draft short-term fundraising plan.	2/1/09	Program Director	
1.1.5. Board approve plan.	2/8/09	Program Director	
1.1.6. Implement plan.	2/8/09	Program Director	
1.1.7. Pay CEO salary.	6/1/09	Program Director	

How Do You Ensure Implementation of Your Plan?

The following guidelines will help ensure that the plan is implemented.

1. **Involve the people who will be responsible for implementing the plan.**
   Use a cross-functional team (representatives from each of the organization's major products or services) to ensure the plan is realistic and collaborative.

2. **Ensure the plan is realistic.**
   Continue asking planning participants "Is this realistic? Can we really do this?" Adjust deadlines as needed in order to keep the plan relevant.

3. **Board Chair and Chief Executive should show visible support.**
   For example, they might explain the purpose of the plan to staff in a meeting.

4. **Organize the overall strategic plan into smaller action plans.**
   Include an action plan (or work plan) for each committee on the Board.

5. **In the overall planning document, specify who is doing what and by when.**
   Action plans are often referenced in the implementation section of the overall strategic plan.

Some organizations may elect to include the action plans in a separate document from the strategic plan (so that the strategic plan would include only the mission, vision, values, challenges and strategies). This approach carries some risk that the Board will forget to monitor implementation of the action plans.

6. **Build in regular reviews of status of the implementation of the plan.**
    Board and staff meetings are very good opportunities to quickly review status.

7. **Translate plan's actions into job descriptions and personnel performance reviews.**
    Unless the plan is integrated into the day-to-day activities in the nonprofit, the plan document is likely to sit on a shelf collecting dust.

8. **Document and distribute the plan, including inviting review input from all.**
    Invite input from leaders in the community. Ideally they should have been involved even earlier when deciding the mission and goals to include in the plan as well.

9. **Be sure one internal person has ultimate responsibility to ensure implementation.**
    Even though one person is responsible to coordinate the plan's activities (often the Chief Executive Officer), Board members are still responsible to monitor the implementation of the plan.

10. **Ensure Board members regularly review status reports on the plan's implementation.**
    This is one of the members' most important jobs – to be sure that the nonprofit is meeting the needs of the community by implementing a community-driven strategic plan.

11. **Have designated rotating "checkers."**
    They verify, for example, every quarter or three months, if each implementer completed his/her assigned tasks.

12. **Have pairs of people be responsible for tasks.**
    Have each partner commit to helping the other finish tasks on time.

13. **Communicate the method of follow-ups to the plan.**
    If people know the action plans will be regularly reviewed, implementers tend to do their jobs before they are checked on.

For more information on strategic planning, go to http://www.managementhelp.org/strt_org/strt_np/strt_np.htm .

Consider the *Field Guide to Nonprofit Strategic Planning and Facilitation* from Authenticity Consulting, LLC, available by clicking on the link "Publications" at http://www.authenticityconsulting.com/ .

How to Staff and Fully Equip Your Board

Different Approaches You Can Use to Staff Your Board

One of the most important aspects of Board operations is Board staffing. Just like the careful staffing that is usually done with employees, Board members should be carefully selected, trained and evaluated, as well. Board members and other leaders must appreciate the strong value that Board members can bring, rather than tolerating Boards as if they are some necessary evil to be avoided at all costs. Leaders should not approach recruitment and selection as if they are somehow lucky just to get Board members who will show up at Board meetings. Leaders must act as if they deserve a very dedicated and participative Board – that attitude alone can make a huge difference in achieving highly effective Boards.

The philosophy for staffing the Board depends on the Board model that the nonprofit prefers. For example, a policy governing Board might prefer members who have strong Board experience. In a collective, the nonprofit also would prefer members who were comfortable working as equals with members of the staff. Nonprofits often use a mix of the following approaches.

- **Functional approach**
  Boards staffed primarily with members who have the skills and knowledge to address current strategic priorities, for example, Boards, planning, programs, staffing, finances and fundraising. This approach is useful when starting a nonprofit because Board members can help build the various management functions. It also is useful to ensure strong governance of the various management functions on an ongoing basis. The number of Board members that you might have depends on the types of skills that you need on your Board, which, in turn, depends on the range and complexity of issues or goals to be faced by the nonprofit.

- **Diversification approach**
  Boards staffed primarily with members that represent a variety of different cultures, values, opinions and perspectives. This approach is useful to ensure that Board planning, deliberations, decisions and policies truly consider many different perspectives and that they do not forget about, or discriminate against, certain groups of people. The number of Board members to have on your Board depends on the range of diversity that you want to involve.

- **Representative approach**
  Boards staffed primarily with members who represent the major constituents of the organization, for example, members from different regions or groups of clients. This approach is useful to ensure that specific constituents, for example, subchapters of a national organization, always have strong input to the Board's planning, deliberations, decisions and policies. The number of Board members to have on your Board depends on the number of different constituents that you want represented.

- **Passion approach**
  Boards staffed primarily with people who have a strong passion for the mission of the organization. Too often, that approach only makes for passionate meetings, not for passionate results. Passion alone is not enough – Board members also must have the time and energy to actively participate in the Board.

Often, nonprofits use a mix of these approaches, for example, the functional approach to ensure that governance has strong oversight of management activities, and diversification and representative approaches to ensure that all important perspectives and constituents are represented on the Board.

If you are using this guide to start a nonprofit (rather than to further develop or to repair your Board), then at this point in your use of this guide, you have probably already got at least three or four Board members who are helping you to start the organization. After conducting your basic strategic planning, you have got a better sense of what goals you need to achieve over the coming years and what resources and skills you need to achieve those goals. You very likely need more Board members to provide those resources and skills. For example, if you are struggling with finances, then seek a new Board member with strong financial skills.

Depending on the particular Board structure that members prefer (working, policy, collective, etc.), a Board Nominating Committee, Board Development Committee or Executive Committee might carry out the activities listed in this section of the guide.

Adopt Comprehensive, Yet Practical, Board Staffing Policy

Board members should formally adopt a Board staffing policy, by voting to accept the policy and documenting the vote in the Board meeting minutes. It should provide guidelines about how Board members:

- Identify what expertise is needed on the Board.

- Identify and keep an up-to-date list of potential new Board members.

- Invite new members to the Board (or nominate themselves).

- Finalize a "slate" or list of potential new members for a currently open position on the Board.

- Select or elect the new Board members.

    Note that the election procedure to add new Board members is often included in the By Laws as well. A common practice is that new Board members are elected during the nonprofit corporation's annual meeting (in many places, corporations are required to hold an annual meeting). If the nonprofit is a membership-based organization (not referring to Board members here) such as an association, then usually the By Laws specify that those members elect new Board members.

See the "Sample Board Staffing Checklist" on page 260.

How to Identify the Best Potential Board Members

1. **First, check your attitude – realize that you deserve an active Board!**
    Do not approach Board recruitment as if your Board is lucky to get a "warm body" – otherwise, that is what you will get: a warm body! The public has entrusted the nonprofit Board (and probably given certain tax privileges to the nonprofit, as a result) to ensure that

the nonprofit is governed effectively, to represent and meet the community's needs. You are "cheating" the public if you do not treat Board recruitment as if the Board deserves the best members that it can get. Consider it a privilege for people to join your Board! If you are cynical about that statement, then you really need to check your own attitude.

2.   **Next check your By Laws.**
      If your By Laws specify that your Board members must come from among your membership (if the nonprofit is a membership organization), then you will first need to look to your membership for new Board members, but follow the next guideline, too!

3.   **Be sure to avoid anyone who has a clear conflict of interest.**
      One of the fiduciary responsibilities of a Board member is the duty of loyalty to the nonprofit organization that they serve. That duty suggests Board members' careful deliberation and disclosure about potential, or actual, conflict-of-interest situations. These are situations which may compromise, or have the appearance of compromising, a Board member's judgment and priorities in carrying out the roles and responsibilities of Board members. Specifically, conflict-of-interest situations might enable a Board member to influence the nonprofit's activities with an outside person or other organization in way(s) leading to the personal gain or improper advantage for the Board member or other person.

4.   **Identify which basis to use when staffing the Board.**
      Functional staffing is recruiting based primarily on the person's knowledge and skills, diversification is recruiting based on unique cultures or values, and representative is recruiting based on ensuring that major constituents are represented on the Board.

5.   **Look for new Board members who can commit the time.**
      The "rule of thumb" is that Board members should plan to spend 4-8 hours a month working as a Board member. Of course, this amount of time depends very much on the amount of work to be done by the Board in the first place.

6.   **Do not recruit Board members just because they are "big names" or are wealthy.**
      You want Board members who can help you achieve the goals of the organization by bringing the necessary skills and promising strong participation in Board activities. "Big names" often got that way by being very busy – they may not have to time to be effective on your Board. Besides, funders are not giving money lately because of "big names" on the Board; rather, funders are giving money because of seeing results. Get Board members who can help the nonprofit to achieve results.

7.   **Look for new Board members who also understand your clients and their needs.**
      This understanding can be very precious to the overall skill-set of the Board!

8.   **Look for members who suit the culture of your organization.**
      For example, if the members of the organization highly value egalitarian and participatory values, then autocratic Board members who highly value hierarchy and authority would probably clash with the style of other Board and staff members.

9.   **Look for independent Board members.**
      These are people who are not on the staff, have no business affiliation with the nonprofit, and are not close, personal friends of the CEO. Independent Board members are much more likely to be objective, and to be able to challenge the opinions and decisions of other Board members and the CEO.

10. **Maintain an up-to-date list of potential Board candidates.**
Consider the particular skills they can bring to the organization in order to address current strategic priorities, and whether they represent certain constituencies that should be represented on the Board.

Skills Typically Needed By New Nonprofits

When starting a nonprofit, certain types of skills are commonly needed among Board members. Of course, the nonprofit may need different skills. That depends on the results of your preliminary strategic planning. Typically needed skills are listed below in the form of suggested committees. If your Board prefers to work without committees, you might consider a short-term task force.

1. **Finance Committee (or task force)**
You will probably need someone to help you construct your first budget and track your expenses over the first year. They might form a Finance Committee.

2. **Fundraising Committee (or task force)**
Ideally, you can find someone who has a basic sense about what it takes to raise funds. Boards are responsible to play a major role in fundraising (although many Board members hate the thought), and it helps to focus the Board's involvement via a Fundraising Committee. Fundraising is more than just doing annual events and writing grants. It should include prospect research – identifying all of the possible sources of funding among individuals, foundations, corporations and government.

3. **Marketing Committee (or task force)**
It is very useful to have someone who has a basic sense about marketing, including to identify each of the different stakeholder groups, how each group prefers to get information, and how to advertise and promote the organization and its programs to each group. Sometimes new nonprofits combine the Marketing Committee with the Fundraising Committee. However, fundraising is much more than doing promotions, and effective marketing requires much more than working to get donations and funding and more than just promotions.

4. **Programs Committee (or task force)**
A good Programs Committee can be very helpful to ensure that each program is carefully designed to effectively and efficiently meet needs in the community. This committee also can be helpful to ensure that the program is being evaluated, so that it can prove that the program is meeting those community needs.

5. **Personnel Committee (or task force)**
You might not need this committee if you are not planning to hire staff or recruit many volunteers (yes, a Personnel Committee should guide and support management of volunteers, in addition to staff). However, a Personnel Committee can be extremely useful in guiding Board members and/or the CEO to effectively hire, train, supervise, deal with performance issues and fire personnel. (Keep in mind that the Board supervises the CEO, who also is a staff member.)

See "What Each Committee Typically Does" on page 85 for a listing of goals that might be associated with standard committees.

Common Sources of Board Members

When you are staffing your Board, it might be helpful to decide what skills you need by using the "Sample Board Member Recruitment Grid" on page 261. It also might be useful to use the "Sample Board Staffing Checklist" on page 260 to be sure that you effectively recruit, orient and train your new members.

The following list includes the most common places to look in order to find Board members. Your choices for Board members will depend on your approach to staffing, for example, functional, diversification, representative, etc.

1. **By Laws might specify where Board members are to come from.**
   First consult your By Laws about where new Board members should come from. For example, if yours is a membership organization, then Board members might have to come from the general membership of your organization.

2. **Consider members of nonprofits that provide services similar to yours.**
   If your services are similar to, but different enough from, other nonprofits that provide your types of services, then they might provide Board members. For example, if you plan to provide day-care as a social service, then people who work in nonprofits that provide family and child development as a social service may be interested in joining your Board.

3. **Consider past clients of nonprofits that provide services similar to yours.**
   These people often make ideal Board members because they truly understand the needs of your clients and how those needs can be met. Include past clients of your nonprofit's programs.

4. **Consider members of large corporations in your community.**
   Frequently, large corporations want to provide community services, in part, by supporting their employees to volunteer to nonprofits. These employees bring a wide range of valuable expertise such as financial management, general management, planning, computers, etc.

5. **Talk to nonprofit service organizations and associations.**
   Many cities have service organizations that are focused on serving other local nonprofits. Some examples are: National Council of Nonprofit Associations, Alliance for Nonprofit Management, Executive Service Corps, SCORE, etc.

6. **Consider members of local professional organizations.**
   Many professionals join these organizations to find opportunities to apply their skills, for example, facilitator's network, an organization development network, or a training and development network.

7. **Consult volunteer service organizations.**
   Look in the phone book under "Volunteers" and you are likely to find a range of organizations that provide volunteers for activities, such as yard cleanup, mailings, technical expertise, etc.

8. **Talk to local universities or colleges.**
   Educators can bring a wide range of expertise. Management, financial, legal, and planning

abilities are a few examples. Call the Human Resources Department, Training and Development or Business Administration.

9. **How about friends and colleagues?**
    Often, when starting an organization, it is critical to have Board members who can even just provide the time to attend meetings! (You will want to grow to include more expertise, certainly!) Therefore, you might solicit friends and colleagues who can provide the time and energy to support the organization as it gets off the ground.

10. **Are there "Board Banks" in your area?**
    These are organizations that recruit and often train people to be members of nonprofit Boards. Ensure that the members that they suggest provide skills that will be useful to achieve the goals identified during strategic planning.

11. **Consider current or recent volunteers to your organization**.
    Volunteers (who are not yet Board members) on Board committees might be prospects – they are already familiar with some of the work of the Board and organization. Also consider volunteers to your fundraising events and programs.

How Potential Members Apply to Your Board

Do not forget that, ultimately, you will have to follow any process specified in your By Laws. For example, at this point in your recruitment process (if yours is a membership-based organization) you might have to pose the "slate" of eligible Board candidates to the general membership for an upcoming vote – and the rest of these guidelines might not be applicable to your organization.

It might be helpful for you to reference the "Sample Board Member Application Form" on page 262.

Your first Nominating Committee or Board Development Committee might carry out the following tasks.

1. **Develop a basic application form for prospective new Board members.**
    The form should solicit information about the potential new members including: biographical information, why they want to join this Board, what they hope to bring to the Board, what they would like to get from their Board membership and any questions they might have.

2. **Narrow down to a list of highly preferred, potential new Board members to recruit.**
    Suggest the list to the Board for discussion and final selection to contact for recruitment for Board membership. Again, be sure that the potential Board member has the skills that your Board requires to achieve the current strategic goals.

3. **Have the Board Chair call each potential Board member.**
    Have the Chair introduce him/herself and explain why he/she is calling. Ask if the person would consider joining the Board. Ask if the person might have conflicts of interest as a Board member. (For example, is the person closely affiliated with a "competitor," doing work for the nonprofit, etc.?) Ask if the person would mind receiving some information.

4. **If they do not mind having information sent, then send a solicitation kit, including:**
    a. A cover letter that:

        1) Briefly explains why you are sending the kit to that person.

        2) Asks them to consider membership on your Board of Directors.

        3) Lists the benefits of their joining your Board.

        4) Explains why you chose to send the kit to them, including mention of the particular skills that they possess and why you need them now.

        5) Specifies the commitment that you are asking for, in terms of hours per month.

        6) Suggests next steps for them if they are interested (calling the Board Chair).

    b. Information about your organization, including its mission, programs, list of current Board members, etc.

    c. A Board Job Description.

    d. A Board Member Application form.

5. **Review the candidates' completed application forms.**
    Carefully review and compare the forms. Were they complete? Have they got strong volunteer experience? Why do they want to join your Board? Does it seem like they will even have the time? Do they have references? If so, always check them.

6. **Invite the prospective new members to a Board meeting.**
    Notify current Board members that a potential new member will be attending. Consider nametags to help the potential new member be acquainted with Board members. Introduce the member when the meeting begins and again at the end. Ask the potential new member if they have any questions. Thank them for coming.

7. **Shortly after the meeting, call prospective new members to hear if they want to apply.**
    If so, submit their names to the entire Board as interested candidates for the Board openings.

8. **Hold elections to fill the open or new Board positions.**
    Elections will be among fellow Board members and/or members of your general membership, depending on the terms of your By Laws.

9. **Notify elected new members and invite them the Board orientation.**
    Follow the guidelines in the following section, "Guidelines to Orient New Board Members."

10. **Do not forget to formally document the new member(s) of the Board!**
    Board decisions and quorums are not official unless all of the Board members are somehow formally designated as Board members. It is not uncommon that someone gets elected to the Board, but the formal list of Board members is not updated, the Board organization chart is not updated, and the Board meeting minutes do not list the new person as a Board member. Be sure to formally document that the newly elected members are officially Board members.

"Contract" for Board Members

Sometimes it is quite helpful to Board members to sign a document that specifies what services they will provide to the organization so that there is no misunderstanding. Do not be reluctant to ask members to sign a contract. The contract often benefits the member as well as you because it conveys the specific expectations that the Board has of each of its members.

It might be helpful for you to reference the "Sample Board Member Contract" on page 266.

How to Orient New Members About the Nonprofit

Board orientation and Board training are intended to equip new Board members with the knowledge and materials necessary to be an effective Board member for the nonprofit. Board orientation is about the unique aspects of the nonprofit. In contrast, Board training is training members about the roles and responsibilities of members of any governing Board.

See "How to Train Members About Their Roles" on page 73.

Guidelines to Orient New Board Members

The following guidelines and sample Board orientation agenda might be useful to you when designing orientation plan and agenda.

1. **Conduct Board orientation shortly after new members are elected to the Board.**
   This scheduling helps new members to quickly gain understanding of their roles and potential contributions to the organization. This understanding often increases their participation and fulfillment regarding their roles as Board members.

2. **Board orientation should be done by the Board Chair, and perhaps with CEO.**
   Ideally, the organization also has a Board Development Committee whose Chair can provide strong participation in the meeting. If timing permits, discuss ideas with all Board members to collect their feedback and review before the orientation session is conducted.

3. **Provide the orientation agenda and materials to members before the meeting.**
   Ask them to review the materials before the meeting.

4. **The Board Chair and the Chief Executive typically facilitate the orientation session.**

5. **Ensure introductions and consider using nametags.**

6. **Ensure adequate time for questions and answers.**

7. **Consider assigning a "buddy," or current Board member to each new member.**

8. **As soon as possible, involve new members in relevant Board committees.**

9. **In the orientation, consider reviewing the following items:**

a. Introduction to all Board members and key staff.

b. Listing of current Board officers, committees and committee Chairs.

c. Overview of the organization, including history, mission, vision and values of the organization, along with any major accomplishments.

d. Board policies, especially By Laws, Board calendar, comparison of Board and staff roles, Board attendance, conflict-of-interest, Board self-evaluation, CEO's job description, committees and ethics policy.

e. Overview of organization's Board roles, role of Chief Executive, and clarification of organization's "boundaries" between Board and staff.

f. How Board decisions are made.

g. Board annual calendar.

h. Committee work plans.

i. Strategic plan, including review of strategic goals and strategies.

 Much of the information provided for Board orientation is included in a Board Manual. See "Typical Contents of Board Manual" on page 245.

The agenda in Table III:1 can be modified by the organization to meet its own nature and needs.

How to Train Board Members About Their Roles

Board training is used to teach people about the fiduciary, or legal, roles and responsibilities of a governing Boards of Directors and how to fulfill those duties. This is in contrast to a Board orientation session, which is a customized session held usually for new Board members to learn about a specific Board and organization (see the preceding section, "How to Orient New Members About the Nonprofit").

It is amazing how many experienced Board members admit that they really do not know the roles and responsibilities of a member of a Board of Directors! One of the best ways to ensure a high-quality Board is to conduct an annual Board training for members. Even a fast-paced, highly condensed, one-hour training can be very useful. For even the most experienced Board members, training tends to ground and integrate their current knowledge, making them more effective Board members. For new members, they can learn the 20% of information needed to do the 80% of tasks that are critical to being an effective Board member. The training ensures that all Board members are working from "the same script." It reminds them that they are Board members and have a certain job to do, especially to verify that the nonprofit is indeed meeting the needs of the community.

Table III:1 – Sample Agenda for Board Orientation Session

Topics marked with an "*" should include a brief presentation about the topic and then time for open discussion and questions from participants.

Topic	Who Should Lead This Portion of the Training
Welcome	Board Chair
Review of agenda*	Board Chair
Introduction of participants	Each person introduces him/herself.
Overview of organization*	Chief Executive reviews mission, history, and programs and introduces key staff.
Orientation to Board manual*	Board Chair
Roles and responsibilities of governing Board*	Board Chair reviews overview of roles, role of Chief Executive, and comparison of roles of Board and staff.
Overview of Board structure	Review listing of current officers, committees, and committee Chairs.
Overview of Board operations*	Board Chair reviews key points from By Laws and Board policies, Board operations calendar, sample committee work plans, and sample meeting agenda and minutes.
Review of strategic plan*	Board Chair reviews format of plan, highlights from plan, key points about status of implementation of plan.
Administrative activities	May include: setting the schedule for next year's Board meetings, refining the Board operations calendar, updating the list of Board members, etc.
Next steps	Board Chair poses reminders of upcoming activities and events.
Meeting evaluation	Board Chair

Topics to Cover in Board Training

A Board training session should quickly cover the most important information and practices to be an effective Board member. A fast-paced, highly-condensed, Board training session might cover:

1. Fiduciary duties and associated roles and responsibilities of Board members.

2. Job descriptions of Board members.

3. Typical types of decisions made by Board members.

4. "Best practices" in Board operations.

5. Types of problems that can occur in Boards and how to overcome them.

6. The Board's self-evaluation tool, including which Board practices are evaluated.

How to Keep Your Board Members Fully Informed

Board members are legally responsible for the governance and operations of a nonprofit. Therefore, it is critical that all members have access to the necessary information to carry out their roles as Board members. Each Board member has the right to see anything they want to see regarding the nonprofit. At a minimum, the following communications should occur:

1. **Each new member should have Board orientation and Board training.**
    See guidelines in the preceding sections on Board orientation and training.

2. **Each member should have a Board Manual, which includes a great deal of information.**
    The manual includes key information, for example, legal/charter information, strategic plan, Board policies, fiscal policies, personnel policies, most recent annual audit, etc. The material should be reviewed during Board orientation.

     See "Typical Contents of Board Manual" on page 245.

3. **Financial information should be reviewed on a monthly basis for new nonprofits.**
    This includes especially the cash flow, budget-versus-actual report, and Statement of Financial Activities (income statement). The Statement of Financial Position (balance sheet) is also reviewed at least on a quarterly basis.

4. **Chief Executive's report should be provided on a regular basis.**
    It should describe the highlights, trends and issues regarding all important management functions, including planning, programs, staffing, marketing, finances, fundraising, facilities and evaluations. Information should be provided about any new developments and priorities among stakeholders, including clients, funders, collaborators, community leaders and governmental agencies.

5. **Provide meeting materials at least a week before the Board meeting.**
    This should include at least the agenda for the Board meeting, any financials, and the CEO's report to the Board.

How to Thank and Reward Your Board Members

Board members bring strong expertise to the nonprofit. If that expertise were purchased from other experts it would cost the nonprofit a great deal of money. Board members often contribute at least 4-8 hours a month in their service as Board members to a nonprofit. In addition, Board members assume a major responsibility to oversee the direction and development of the nonprofit. They do not have to assume that responsibility – they do it on a volunteer basis to serve their communities. Their service should be recognized accordingly. Here are some ideas to show recognition and gratitude to Board members who have done a good job in their roles as Board members.

1.   **Include mention of the people joining your Board.**
      It is common in business sections of newspapers to mention who is joining which Boards.

2.   **Mention members' accomplishments during Board meetings.**
      Celebrate the accomplishments of committees, including the individuals on those committees.

3.   **Include mention of the members' accomplishments in the meeting minutes.**
      The minutes reflect what "officially" happened during the meeting, making the members' accomplishment that much more legitimate and recognized.

4.   **Include mention of the member s' accomplishment in the nonprofit's newsletter.**
      This form of recognition ensures that clients and other nonprofits in similar services get to recognize the accomplishment of the Board member.

5.   **Present a certificate of gratitude.**
      Make this presentation during a Board meeting, or ideally, during the annual meeting.

6.   **Offer to write references for their jobs searches and personnel files.**
      Their places of employment usually keep files on their employees, including their community service. A letter from the nonprofit would be a welcome addition to the Board members' employer personnel file.

7.   **Include their names on your Website and stationery.**
      The names of Board members are often included on the nonprofit's stationery, for example, along the left side of the paper. Nonprofits can also list their Board members on their Websites.

8.   **Let them see the results of programs on clients.**
      Probably the most powerful form of recognition and fulfillment for a Board member is to hear from a client that has benefited from the nonprofit's programs. Have a client come to a Board meeting to provide testimonials about the success of the program.

9.   **Probably the most fulfilling for Board members is to do useful work.**
      Ensure that the Board member is doing what they want to be doing. Ask them what they want to do and help them to get that kind of work on the Board.

How to Retire Board Members

When a Board member decides to leave the Board, or his or her term has expired without a run for re-election, then the retirement must be done very carefully. Here are some basic guidelines to help ensure that the transition is carried out effectively.

1. **If the staffing policy was well planned, there are no surprises.**
    All Board members will have known about the Board member's upcoming departure for at least a few months and will be quite prepared for it.

2. **Ensure succession planning for the departing Board member.**
    Before the member leaves, be sure that another Board member has been assigned to adopt that departing member's role. The new member should gain information and materials to carry out his/her role, and feel secure that he/she can operate effectively as a Board member.

3. **After announcement of departure, have the departing member attend a meeting.**
    It can be quite confusing and unsettling to suddenly have a long-term Board member leave the team. Provide a chance in a Board meeting for people to ensure that the departing Board member is fine and leaving for good reasons.

4. **Have a specific celebration for the departing Board member.**
    Some people may feel that parties are frivolous. Often, they underestimate the affect that it has on a team when a long-term member leaves. For thousands of years, societies have recognized the wisdom in rituals – they do not just do them for the sake of doing them. Hold a special event for the departing Board member. List the accomplishments of the organization during the member's tenure. Award the member a plaque or something that will be meaningful to him or her. (For more ideas, see the above section, "How to Thank and Reward Board Members.")

5. **Consider having the departing Board member on an Advisory Board.**
    Or you might place the member on some other similar type function, so that the departing member's expertise and history is not lost to the organization.

6. **Ensure that the person does not act as an "unofficial Board member."**
    Sometimes, long-standing Board members struggle to no longer be Board members, for example, they continue to refer to themselves as Board members and they attend meetings. That can be very confusing to other Board members, senior staff and particularly to new Board members. It also diffuses the sense of responsibility for Board members when they notice an "unofficial" Board member taking part in Board deliberations.

How to Remove a Board Member

Procedures for Removing Members Should Be In By Laws

The process for terminating a Board member should be specified in the By Laws. If there is no such wording in the By Laws, then the Board should establish such wording as soon as possible. In many cases, Boards arrange to be able to remove a Board member by accomplishing a two-thirds vote among all of the Board members, or even a quorum of the members (a quorum is the minimum number of Board members that must be present in order for a Board meeting to be considered an "official" meeting).

Typical reasons for removal include:

- Continued absence involving more than a minimum number of meetings in a calendar or fiscal year.

- Breach of Board ethics such as confidentiality or conflict-of-interest issues, or violation of some other major Board policy.

Some Boards do not specify reasons for removal. Instead they leave wording in the By Laws to enable a Board member to be removed by a strong majority vote or a quorum vote of members. These situations are often reserved for Board members that are perceived by the majority of other members as continuing to act in a manner that is destructive to the effectiveness of the Board, for example, showing continued hostility, major interruptions during meetings or continued refusal to do any work outside of Board meetings.

Before starting the removal process, be sure you have contacted the Board member to discuss the issue. The cause of the member's issue might be from a larger problem in Board operations, for example, mismatch between the member's skills and assignments, meetings focused on too trivial of information and unfocused facilitation during meetings. Be sure the member had been given clear and specific means to provide value, for example, an assignment to a committee that had specific work plans. The least productive Board members can become the most productive when given straightforward means by which to provide value.

Guidelines for Removing Board Members

Removal of a Board member must be done carefully. If the member was elected by the general membership of the organization, that member may have a legal right to that Board seat. Just like the termination of an employee, the termination of a Board member should be done according to official policies reflected in the By Laws, or at least in the approved Board policies.

1. **If possible, the Chair should first warn the member about his/her offending behavior.**
    On occasion, a member's behavior might turnaround with even a short amount of attention to his or her problem. This guideline might apply, for example, when a member continues to disrupt meetings by interrupting other members or resorting to hostility during deliberations. Of course, there are occasions where the member's behavior is of such a magnitude (for example, committing theft or fraud) that the act must be dealt with promptly, including notifying the appropriate legal authorities and terminating the member from the Board.

2.   **No one Board member should make the decision to terminate a Board member.**
Termination is a matter for the entire Board to address according to its By Laws and approved Board policies.

3.   **Bring the behavior of the member to the attention of the entire Board.**
Notify the member of the issue pending against him or her as well as when and where the issue will be brought before the entire Board. This gives the member a fair opportunity to explain him/herself. Schedule an Executive Session (Board meeting in which only Board members attend – sometimes called "in camera") to discuss the issue and arrive at a suitable action to address the matter, preferably by vote of Board members. Be sure that the issue was not inadvertently caused by the structure or operations of the Board itself, rather than by the behaviors of one Board member. For example, if Board meetings are not facilitated according to an agenda, it is no surprise that a member might become very irritated and interrupt others at will.

4.   **After the matter has been reviewed, establish a new Board policy?**
The new policy would be aimed to addressing the kind of behavior(s) exhibited by the Board member.

 The "Sample Board Attendance Policy" on page 275 and "Sample Board Conflict-of-Interest Policy" on page 264 might be relevant to your situation now.

5.   **After the member has left, update Board correspondence to not include that member.**
Remove his or her name from Board lists, etc. Attempt to recover any materials held by the departing Board member (Board manuals, etc).

Some Frequently Asked Questions About Board Staffing

How Large Should Board Be? Depends On Staffing Approach

The size of your Board is determined by the philosophy or approach that you use to staff your Board.

 See "How to Staff and Fully Equip Your Board" on page 65.

Most new nonprofits start with a fairly small Board (5-7 members) with members who do a lot of "hands on" tasks, like fixing faxes, doing mailings, etc (this is a working Board). As the nonprofit grows, it needs more Board resources and those resources will probably be more strategic in focus (evolving to a policy Board). At the time of this writing, the trend seems to be toward smaller Boards, however. Some nonprofits prefer a collective Board model, where the number of Board members is influenced by the number of staff members because Board and staff members work together as a team of equals.

If you follow a functional approach to staffing, then conduct strategic planning to determine what the nonprofit needs to achieve, especially over the coming year. Identify what resources, including skills, are needed to achieve those goals. Organize those skills into Board committees. Ensure that each committee has at least three people. Two of those people should be Board members. This process suggests how many Board members to have.

Note that it is possible to include more people and skills by putting them on an Advisory Board or by having them volunteer as non-Board members of committees or task forces.

See "Guidelines to Form Your Advisory Board" on page 217.

States usually have a minimum size for a Board, often three members. Specify the size of your Board in your By Laws by specifying a range, for example, "at least seven and not more than nine members."

Should You Have Term Limits? What Should the Terms Be?

A term limit is the specified length of time that a person can serve as a Board member. The term is specified in the By Laws. Term limits are a good means to ensure that the Board always has fresh perspectives and energy and that no one person comes to dominate the Board for the long term. However, in small communities, it often is quite difficult to regularly find new members. Unless you live in a small community, you should be very sure of any reasons not to institute term limits.

The most common arrangement seems to be three-year term limits with staggered terms, where one third of the Board rotates off and one third comes on new each year. That approach ensures that there is "new blood" on the Board every year and that other members retain their three-year terms. That three-year term can be re-elected for one more consecutive term, resulting in six consecutive years on the Board for the member. Some organizations start with a one-year term, believing that is an appropriate probationary period in which the member can get to know their role and the nonprofit. After the first year, if there is not a good fit, then the Board member leaves the Board. However, it often takes at least a year for a Board member to really learn about the role of Board member. Officers often serve a one-year term.

Should Your Chief Executive Be On the Board?

There is not a clear consensus on this question. It is this author's belief that it is probably fine to have the Chief Executive on the Board for the first year or two, while the Board is developing itself and getting to know the new organization. However, after that first year or two, it is best if the Chief Executive leaves the Board as an official Board member. With that arrangement, Board members might provide more objective assessment and supervision of the Chief Executive. Additionally, Board members might develop more of their own "strategic identity" without the Chief Executive on their team. That is, Board members begin to see themselves as the primary strategic role in the organization, regardless of the input from the Chief Executive. That strategic role, after all, is the Board's job.

The Chief Executive can still attend Board regular meetings, of course (unless the Board is in Executive, or in camera, Session). The Chief Executive, when not attending as an official Board member, cannot vote in Board decisions.

Should Your Staff Members Be On the Board?

This guide explains that there are several different types of Board models, for example, a working Board, policy Board, collective Board, etc. It is probably more common to have staff members on a working or collective Board than on a policy Board.

Many experts assert that staff should not be on the Board because it is an inherent conflict of interest. Board members who are also staff might struggle when trying to govern for the best interests of the organization as a whole. This happens when they encounter the opportunity to make decisions that might benefit themselves personally, such as deliberation over staff salaries. Also, it might be a major challenge for Board members to remain strategic when attending to their staff roles.

As with membership of the Chief Executive to the Board (mentioned above), it is probably best if staff members are not Board members. This is for some of the same reasons that the Chief Executive eventually should not be a member of the Board. Staff can attend Board meetings (unless the Board is in Executive Session) to make presentations, be acquainted with Board members, etc. Staff, when not attending as official Board members, cannot vote in Board decisions.

Should Your Staff Members Attend Board Meetings?

It is often a major benefit to have staff attending at least portions of a Board meeting. Remember that the CEO is a staff member, as well, and his or her presence in Board meetings is often critical to the success of the Board and the CEO role. Attendance of other staff members can be a major benefit as well. For example, presentations by staff members to the Board are often very enlightening for Board members. They learn more about staff roles and the benefits staff provide for clients. Staff attendance to Board meetings should not be discouraged, just coordinated carefully.

There are times (for example, in Executive or in camera Sessions) when Board members should hold meetings that are private amongst themselves. This may be to consider the CEO's performance or deliberate about how to handle a pending lawsuit.

How to Organize Committees (If You Use Them)

The Board's use of committees depends on the Board model used by members. The policy governing Board (traditional Board) structure often uses Board committees, perhaps with some staff members on committees. A working governing Board often uses committees with staff members on many committees. Ideally, committees are organized primarily in order to focus Board expertise on certain strategic priorities, and when those priorities are addressed, the committees are terminated. Committees do not replace the authority of the Board; rather committees make recommendations to the full Board for all members review and decisions. Each committee should have a charter, as explained later on in this section. The charter describes the purpose of the committee, its membership and how it makes decisions. Committees are often most useful if each has a work plan that specifies the goals to be achieved by the committee and by when.

Advantages and Potential Disadvantages of Committees

Over the past few decades, opinions on the use of committees have changed back and forth from favoring them to suggesting they not be used at all. One Board model, Policy Governance®, asserts that no, or very few, committees be used. In contrast, the major feature of the policy governing ("traditional") model of governance is regular use of committees. Another consideration is what committees to use, if they are used. Yet another consideration is how long a committee would exist, for example, permanent or temporary use.

Advantages of Committees

Advantages of the use of committees, when each is designed and used well, can include that:

1.   They efficiently match the most appropriate Board resources to each of the most important priorities of the nonprofit (for example, match members with financial skills to financial priorities and fundraising skills to fundraising), rather than inefficiently matching all Board resources on all priorities at the same time.

2.   Collectively, committees can more fully engage all of the Board members when each member feels challenged and fully utilized on an appropriate committee. This is compared to trying to engage all Board members on the nature of the current topic on the agenda in a Board meeting.

3.   Similar to the above point, if all Board members are engaged in focused committees, then the entire Board usually has strong understanding of the status of the most important management functions (for example, programs, marketing and facilities), which can be an advantage if the Chief Executive or another key staff member suddenly leaves and the functions need quick attention.

4.   Committees can increase the likelihood of Board members' understanding of the nonprofit's various management functions, thereby increasing the Board's effectiveness in governing these functions.

5.   Board meetings can be held less frequently if committees are productive between Board meetings. For example, Board meetings could be held every other month with committee meetings in between those months.

82

6.   Committees can lower the likelihood of burnout among staff if the committees result in Board members assisting with activities that staff otherwise would undertake.

7.   For nonprofits that value Board and staff members working together, committees can be an efficient means to organize members to work together in a focused and productive manner.

Disadvantages of Committees

Many disadvantages of committees can occur if the committees are not designed and used well:

1.   Board resources are very poorly used when committees are established merely for the sake of having committees. For example, new nonprofit leaders might hear that nonprofits usually have a Personnel Committee, so they might establish that committee and hope that its members somehow find something useful to do. That approach is rarely successful.

2.   A similar situation exists if the original priority that the committee was meant to address is no longer a priority. Instead of terminating the committee, it struggles on, trying somehow to be useful.

3.   Burnout can occur among committee members if too much is assigned to the committee. This can occur, especially during the early years of nonprofit when it has no, or few, staff members so that much of the nonprofit's work is assumed by Board members.

4.   If committees are not carefully chartered (with relevant, specific goals and timelines), then members of the committee can become frustrated and conflicted, wondering what their role is and not feeling useful on the Board.

5.   Effectiveness of the Board can be damaged when there are too many committees, many of which are ineffective. That results in a large amount of wasted resources, including time in committees that do not seem to have any purpose.

6.   Committees require additional workload on the Board to coordinate the work of all of the committees. This is often an additional responsibility of the Executive Committee.

7.   A Board can become splintered if its various committees end up working apart from each other, without some Board function (for example, an Executive Committee) that monitors and integrates the work of the various committees.

Some problems occur because of members' arbitrary philosophies about their Board. For example, some Board members adopt a philosophy "to keep the Board small" or "to have few committees." This is like adopting a philosophy to always keep one's toolbox small – even though some very important tools might not be available because they do not fit in the chosen size of the toolbox. Those philosophies can become a major, unnecessary obstacle to the members doing their job on the Board.

In summary, committees (or temporary task forces) can be tremendous assets to a Board if each is carefully chartered with specific goals aligned with important and current priorities, and has regular assessment of effectiveness to validate whether the committee should continue to operate. Otherwise, committees can be a major hindrance to the effectiveness of the Board. (More information about chartering committees, and typical "best practice" goals of each, are included later on in this section.)

How to Organize Your Committees (or Your Task Forces)

1. **Ensure the committee has a specific charter and work plan (set of tasks to address).**
   (More on charters and work plans later on below.)

2. **Have at least one Board member on each committee (especially Finance).**
   Many Boards tend to defer finances to one person, the Treasurer. The rest of the Board members tend to rely completely on the Treasurer, which is very high-risk.

3. **Try not to have a member on more than two committees.**
   Membership on more than two committees often leads to burnout.

4. **In each Board meeting, have each committee Chair report on the committee's work.**
   Board reports are usually a standard part of a Board agenda.

5. **Consider having non-Board volunteers as members of the committee.**
   This is useful especially on committees, including Fundraising, Marketing and Programs.

6. **Consider having a relevant staff member as a member of the committee as well.**
   Depending on the Board model, Board members and staff can work together, for example in policy governing and working governing Boards.

7. **Consider having Board and committee meetings on alternating months.**
   That is, Board meetings might be held every other month with committee meetings during the months between the Board meetings. That arrangement works well if committees are active between Board meetings.

8. **The Board Chair and/or CEO could service ex officio on any relevant committees.**
   Some organizations might consider placing the CEO as a member of the Board – this decision should be made very carefully, as discussed earlier. ("Ex officio" means membership by virtue of the position. Whether the person in the role has all of the rights of membership is up to the nonprofit.)

The diagram in Table III:2 is not meant to suggest what committees you should have, rather to depict the typical members on various types of committees. It also shows that the Executive Committee might be made up of the chairs of the committees, though it might also be made up of Board officers. Note that the some committees are unlikely to have community volunteer members and some, such as Board Development or Personnel might not even have staff members.

How Many Committees Should the Nonprofit Have?

When answering this question, it is useful first to review how to decide if a committee is even needed. (As a reminder, not all nonprofits choose to have committees – some might use task forces, or even less organized and temporary forms.) It is best to form committees to address each of the types of current strategic priorities, rather than to have committees just for the sake of having them. Thus, if the nonprofit is building a facility, then a temporary (ad hoc) Facilities Committee might be appropriate. When the building is completed, then dissolve the committee. Similarly, if a nonprofit plans to have a substantial portion of its budget to include revenue from fundraising, then perhaps a Fundraising Committee is appropriate.

Table III:2 – Staffing of Board Committees

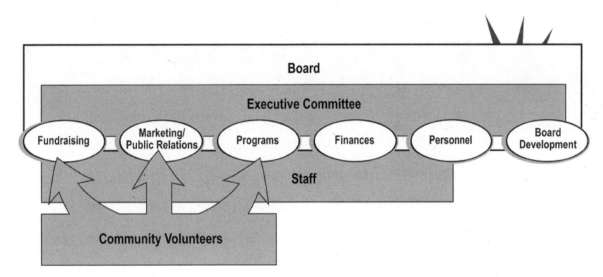

So the number of committees you might have should be determined primarily from the number, or different types, of current strategic issues facing the nonprofit. For example, if it has a large number of issues across a wide range of internal functions, or if its strategic plan calls for developing new programs, or if there are many changes expected in the nonprofit, then a nonprofit might have numerous committees, including, for example: Board Development, Programs, Personnel, Finance, Marketing and Fundraising. In contrast, if the nonprofit has very stable programs, its internal workings are fairly stable, and the needs of its clients are not likely to change much, then the nonprofit might have just a few committees – such is the case with many long-established associations, churches and museums.

What Each Committee Typically Does

If committees are formed, they should correspond to current strategic priorities. For example, if the nonprofit wants to expand the number of clients that it serves, then it might start a Marketing Committee to spread awareness of the nonprofit's programs. Each committee should have a work plan that specifies the goals and associated objectives, deadlines and responsibilities to achieve each objective. The following is a list of standard committees and the typical goals of each committee. Committees include: Board Development, Finance, Fundraising, Facilities, Programs, Personnel and Marketing/Communications.

Board Development Committee

1.   Ensure new Board systems (new members, committees, work plans, etc.) are successfully incorporated into Board operations.

2.   Ensure Board is fully resourced to govern the organization.

3.   Ensure full participation and dedication of all Board members to the organization.

4.   Ensure all Board meetings are highly-focused and strategic.

5.   Ensure the Board leadership rigorously monitors implementation of work plans.

6.   Ensure continuous improvement of the Board.

See "Goals and Objectives for Board Development Committee" on page 243.

Finance Committee

1.   Ensure the update of fiscal policies and procedures and also ensure the Board approves the policies on an annual basis.

2.   Guide development of the annual budget. Consider developing a program-based budget that organizes overall expenses and revenues to be per program. Also specify the overall fundraising target for the year, working with the Fundraising Committee if there is one.

3.   Ensure an annual audit, if the organization's budget is of sufficient size to warrant an audit, and ensure Board's approval of the audit and associated recommendations.

4.   Establish financial sustainability policies, as needed, for example, to develop financial reserves, contingency planning, etc.

5.   Train Board members to understand financial information sufficient to make decisions regarding financial resources.

Fundraising Committee

1.   Identify fundraising target (amounts to be raised) in conjunction with the Finance Committee.

2.   Ensure effective prospect research to identify percentage desired mix of donors, among individuals, corporations, foundations and government, as based on the nature of each program in the organization.

3.   Identify specific potential donors for each mix and how to approach each.

4.   Develop action plans, including who will approach each donor and by when, not only to solicit funds, but to develop relationships with funders.

5.   Ensure the organization has the administrative and database resources to manage donations.

6.   Establish and implement a Fundraising Plan that contains the information from goals 1-5.

Facilities Committee

1.   Oversee development of a Facilities Plan, including specification of the nonprofit's requirements for facilities (buildings, information technology, equipment, etc.), how those facilities should be obtained (lease, buy or rent) and maintained.

2.   Guide development of Facilities Development Plan, including costs to develop all facilities.

3. Guide development of Facilities Operating Budget, including costs for expertise and materials to operate and maintain facilities.

4. Provide input to the Finance Committee to develop budgets for capital and operating needs.

5. Oversee and guide activities to ensure sound maintenance of all facilities.

Personnel Committee

1. Ensure the organization's personnel policies are updated to guide all staffing activities in the organization, including for paid and volunteer staff.

2. Ensure a comprehensive, fair and equitable employee performance management system.

3. Ensure a comprehensive, fair and equitable compensation system.

4. Guide a staffing analysis to identify the necessary expertise, roles and organization of roles to achieve the new strategic goals and programs.

5. Ensure sufficient succession planning of key staff positions.

6. Coach (support and guide) the CEO, especially regarding top-level work priorities and any stress management needed during major changes.

Programs Committee

1. Ensure each program has goals and services that are designed to meet verified needs in the community, achieve desired outcomes among specific groups of clients, and be in accordance with the mission. This could include identifying collaborators, competitors, pricing, etc., for each program.

2. Ensure programs are fully resourced to deliver desired services.

3. Ensure services in each program are evaluated to verify that desired outcomes are achieved.

4. Ensure continuous improvement of programs.

5. Ensure program operations remain effective and efficient.

Marketing / Communications Committee

Note that the Programs Committee does some "inbound" marketing, including clarifying needs of clients, which groups of clients to serve, collaborators, competitors, pricing, etc.

1. Define overall public image and identity (branding) desired by organization.

2. Develop and implement a Communications Plan that identifies:

    a. Each of the different groups of stakeholders.

    b. What the organization wants each group to know about the organization.

    c.   What messages to convey to each stakeholder group.

    d.   How to convey the message.

    e.   Who will convey the message.

    f.   When they will convey the message.

3.   Ensure major communications tools (Website, newsletters, etc.) effectively represent the branding and also effectively communicate according to the Communications Plan.

How to Successfully Start Each Committee (or Task Force)

First, we should review what successful delegation is. Delegation is the skill of assigning someone or a group to achieve a certain result by a certain date, but leaving it up to them to decide how to achieve the result. Delegation is a critical skill for leaders and supervisors to acquire. It can be quite a challenge for some Board members to delegate to a committee or even to the CEO. Consequently, Board members should give attention to this potential issue before it becomes one. One of the best ways to effectively delegate to a committee is to effectively charter it in the first place. Consider the following guidelines.

1.   **Board meeting minutes should reflect the Board's decision to charter the committee.**
The committee becomes official once its inception is listed in Board minutes or By Laws.

2.   **Draft a charter document for committee members.**
The document should include information mentioned in the guidelines below.

3.   **Describe the strategic intent of the committee.**
Include the strategic goal(s) that are to be addressed by the committee, the relationship between the committee's activities and the mission of the organization, etc.

4.   **Explain brief history or background regarding Board's decision to form the committee.**
This information helps others to understand why the new committee was formed and what might be expected from its members.

5.   **Specify if the committee is "standing" (permanent) or ad hoc (temporary) committee.**
If the committee is a standing committee, then probably the By Laws should be modified to reflect addition of the new permanent committee.

6.   **List the desired outcomes, or results, Board members want and by when.**
This information is extremely important when evaluating the success of the committee.

7.   **Specify availability of any resources for use by the committee.**
For example, consider certain amounts of funding, personnel, materials, etc., for committee use.

8.   **Suggest, or require, any boundaries within which the committee should work.**
For example, the full Board might prefer that the committee not make formal contact to recruit members from, or collaborate with, other organizations.

9.   **Specify how the committee is to coordinate with the Board.**
     For example, the Board might prefer regular written reports about certain topics and at certain times.

10. **Specify terms of leadership for the committee.**
     For example, the Board might prefer that a fellow Board member be Chair of the committee to ensure adequate representation between the Board and committee.

11. **Specify indicators of success.**
     Indicators should specify what the Board would consider to be successful results from the committee. Some examples are: level of engagement among general membership, number of events held and participation to them, etc.

12. **Staff the committee if it is not already staffed.**
     Staffing could be carried out in the same fashion as the guidelines in the section for staffing the Board.

 See "Sample Board Committee Charter" on page 259.

Work Plan – Each Committee's "To do" List

One of the best ways to ensure effective Board committees and accomplishment of strategic goals is through use of a committee work plan. The plan specifies goals for the committee, strategies to meet the goals and timelines for completion of the goals. The goals of the committee should be closely aligned with achieving the strategic goals determined during strategic planning. Essentially, the work plans specify the operational goals of the committee for the year.

A work plan is the plan that each Board committee and relevant staff members reference to guide completion of their portion of the organization's strategic plan. For example, the Finance Committee works from Finance work plan, Marketing Committee from Marketing work plan, etc. Each work plan might reference the related goal(s) from the strategic plan. Work plans include objectives that, in total, implement the respective strategy.

For example, the following work plan describes one strategy which, together with other strategies, meets Goal 3 from the strategic plan. This strategy has five objectives including x.x.1 to x.x.5. This sample represents one example of the format and content of a work plan. This sample should be customized to the particular culture and purpose of the organization.

Year 2009 Actions	Jan	Feb	Mar	Apr	May	Jun
Strategy 3.1: Develop Strategic Plan						
3.1.1. Recruit consultant help	---					
3.1.2 Planning with Chief Executive		---	---	---		
3.1.3 Draft first version of strategic plan					---	
3.1.4 Board review of plan					---	
3.1.5 Obtain Board approval of plan						---

Another example of a work plan is "Goals and Objectives for Board Development Committee" on page 243.

Board Decision Making

The major responsibility of a nonprofit Board of Directors is to provide ongoing direction and oversight of the nonprofit organization ("oversight" as in monitoring, not "oversight" as in inadvertently missing a point or task). At the heart of this responsibility is making decisions regarding strategic direction and policy. Making decisions can be a major challenge, particularly for new Boards. Guidelines in this section help Board members to focus on issues and make decisions in an effective and timely fashion.

Typical Types of Decisions Your Board Should Make

The specific types of decisions made by Board members depend on the level of involvement of Board members in the management of the nonprofit. Members of working Boards and collective Boards (both are types of governing Boards) might be very involved in day-to-day affairs. In contrast, members of Policy Governance® and policy Boards are not very likely to be involved in those affairs.

However, there are some decisions that major stakeholders, such as funders, expect Board members to make – and to formally approve, regardless of the form of Board structure or involvement used by the Board.

1.   Add or remove Board member(s).

2.   Hire and terminate the Chief Executive Officer.

3.   Approve the strategic plan.

4.   Approve major organizational changes, for example, new program or a merger.

5.   Approve the annual budget.

6.   Approve personnel policies.

7.   Approve expenditures above a certain limit (the limit is often specified in the By Laws).

8.   Approve contracts with expenditures over a certain limit.

Certainly, there are other decisions that a nonprofit might wish that Board members attend to (again, depending on the structure used by the Board), such as modifying compensation and benefits to the Chief Executive, selecting major vendors for certain services and when to conduct major fundraising activities.

How to Ensure Your Board Makes Useful Decisions

1.   **Be sure to conduct strategic planning in some form – and clarify community needs.**
      That includes specifying and communicating the purpose of the organization (its mission), goals to work toward that mission, and action planning (who will do what and by when). The plan should provide ongoing direction and priorities when making decisions.

2.   **Have a Board policy regarding how certain types of decisions will be made.**
The policy might specify that decisions are made about topics, first by getting the topic on the agenda, specifying a time on the agenda to make the decision, attempting to achieve consensus, then resorting to a majority vote.

See the "Sample Board Decision-Making Policy" on page 268.

3.   **Consider whether the decision is clearly in regard to a strategic matter.**
For example, is it in regard to a current strategic goal in the strategic plan, or is it a new and major goal or issue? Or, is it an operational matter that is best left for the CEO to address (for example, implementation of a strategic plan or policy)? If the matter is best left for the CEO to attend to, then delegate the matter to him/her if your Board follows a policy governing model. In a collective Board model, have a team of Board and staff members attend to the matter.

4.   **Be sure that the CEO and Board Chair work together to design Board meetings.**
Give Board and staff members an opportunity to contribute topics to the agenda.

   a.   Specify what type of outcome is needed by the Board regarding each topic on the agenda, such as, approval of a plan.

   b.   Ensure sufficient time for debate of each topic.

   c.   Include topics near the beginning of the agenda that might require the most attention and deliberation, in order to take advantage of members' fresh energy at the start of the meeting.

   d.   Ensure the agenda is sent out at least one week before the Board meeting.

   e.   The Board Chair *has* to closely manage time during discussion and any debate.

   f.   Ask for a decision near the end of the time allotted to the topic. Members might prefer a variety of methods to making decisions, for example, voting or consensus. Consensus decision making seems increasingly popular because it helps to ensure that many perspectives are heard and members can compromise to reach a team-based decision.

5.   **Record all decisions made by members in the Board meeting minutes.**

6.   **Ensure that all decisions are in accordance with:**
   a.   Federal, state/provincial and local laws and regulations.

   b.   Plans and policies.

How Your Board Members Can Come to Consensus

First, let us understand what consensus means because there often is some confusion around that term. Consensus means that every Board member can at least live with the Board's final decision, for example, a decision reached by at least a quorum of Board members. It does not mean that everyone completely agrees with the decision. Consensus is often the means by which highly participative Board members reach their decisions.

Before Board Meeting

Members receive information that:

1.   Clarifies the decision to be made.
        It is often best if the decision is written in the form of a "yes/no" question or a choice from among alternatives, for example, "Should we approve ___?" or "Should we hire ____?", etc.

2.   Is sufficient for each member to come to some conclusion on his/her own.

Ground Rules During Consensus Activities

The Board Chair explains the following ground rules to other Board members.

1.   Members do not interrupt each other.

2.   Members can disagree with each other.

3.   Members do not engage in side discussions.

4.   Silence is considered agreement with the decision to be made.

5.   If decision is reached by consensus, then all Board members act as united front to support decision.

Consensus Process Among Board Members

The Board Chair facilitates this procedure using the following steps.

1.   The Chair specifies a deadline in the meeting by which to reach consensus in the meeting.

2.   In a roundtable fashion, each member:

        a.   Gets equal time to voice his/her preferences and reasons in regard to the question.

        b.   Focuses perspectives on what is *doable*.

        c.   Does not mention other members' names.

        d.   The Chair voices his or her opinion last.

3.   At the end of each person's time, all members take a quiet minute to:

   a.   Collect their own thoughts in response to the last person's comments or preferences.

   b.   Decide what they would be willing to compromise or have in common with the last speaker.

4.   At the deadline in the meeting:

   a.   The Chair poses what seems to be the most common perspective voiced by members.

   b.   Asks all members if they can support that perspective.

5.   If no consensus is reached, members might choose one of following options:

   a.   Consider further research until specified future time. Decide what additional information is needed and maybe appoint a committee or a temporary task force to do the research. The committee researches and provides recommendations, preferably in writing to each Board member before the next Board meeting. At the next meeting, the Board hears the committee's recommendations and initiates the consensus process again.

   b.   Consider having a vote to decide, for example, by simple majority (at least 51%) or strong majority (two thirds) of the members. (Note that some people would assert that voting is not consensus, but it sure is handy if the consensus process has not reached a conclusion by an absolute deadline.)

Speaking With "One Voice"

Once Board members have made a decision, it is important that all members present a united front when representing the decision to others. It can be toxic to a Board if one or more members later on claim that they did not agree with the Board's decision and, consequently, are not behind it. If someone agrees to be on a Board, then he/she is agreeing to be part of a team effort. If the person absolutely disagrees with a Board decision, then the person can vote "no" and have the Board meeting minutes reflect that vote. Still, the person should not proactively spread the word to outsiders that the Board's decision was a bad one. That kind of behavior not only makes the Board look bad, but makes the Board member look bad, as well.

How to Be Sure Board Members Participate in Decisions

Board members usually make their decisions in Board meetings. Therefore, much of what you do to accomplish participative decisions can be done in the meetings. However, there are some things to do before the meeting, too, as mentioned below.

Before the Meeting

1.   Be sure that all Board members undergo a Board orientation that presents information that is unique to the nonprofit, for example, about fellow Board members, staff members, programs, the nonprofit's history, etc., so that members are comfortable about each other and speaking up about the nonprofit.

2.   Be sure that all members also undergo Board training about the roles and responsibilities of a governing Board so that all members understand their responsibilities to speak up in Board meetings.

3.   As much as possible, ensure that each Board member has a specific assignment and/or role, for example, that he/she is on a Committee with a specific charter or purpose.

4.   When developing the agenda, give all Board and staff members the opportunity to suggest topics.

5.   Include topics near the beginning of the agenda that might require the most attention and deliberation, in order to take advantage of members' fresh energy at the start of the meeting.

6.   Be sure to suggest specific actions and times for each agenda topic, for example, "Fundraising Plan requires approval" and allocate 15 minutes for discussion and a vote.

7.   Be sure the meeting materials are provided in advance of the meeting.

Opening the Meeting

Consider some or all of the following:

1.   Review the agenda to help all members be comfortable with the design of the meeting. Ask if everyone is OK with the agenda, including whether there is a potential or actual conflict of interest for anyone about any of the topics.

2.   At the beginning of each meeting, get them involved early. For example, include introductions or do a brief "check in" from each member, about what they are up to personally or currently doing at work.

3.   If a member is absent from a meeting, the Board Chair or Chief Executive should acknowledge who is missing and find out why.

4.   Review ground rules, including the ground rule that "everyone participates."

5.   If there are several topics in regard to routine matters that will not require much deliberation, for example, approving the minutes, approving promotions recommended by the CEO and approving a Board gesture (for example, sending flowers to someone who is ill), then put those items on a "consent agenda" and have members do one vote for the entire agenda.

During the Meeting

Consider some or all of the following:

1.   If the Board Chair feels the group is in a lull, he or she should say so, and then ask members if they agree and what they can do to get out of the lull.

2.   Build in a 5-minute break so members can get up and walk around.

3.   Bring in some jokes or cartoons and share them at different times.

4. Post the mission, vision and/or values statements on the walls to remind people of why they are there.

5. Do a quick "Round-Robin" about the current topic, asking each member what he or she thinks about the current activity or topic.

6. Specifically address the quiet people, for example, mention, "We haven't heard from you yet." However, do not push hard on people who seem reluctant to speak.

7. Ask questions about the current topic for the members to answer.

8. Use a variety of aids to ensure all learning styles are considered, such as spoken, visual and kinesthetic. This is important to keep members with varying styles equally engaged.

9. Share facilitation roles. Let someone else facilitate as you take the time to record, organize and prepare information. (Be careful that members do not somehow become confused about who is the Board Chair or not.)

Near the End of the Meeting

1. Evaluate the meeting in a process so each member quickly shares his/her opinion of the meeting, including what worked, what did not and what should be done.

2. Quickly acknowledge any members who typically do not speak up, but who did in that meeting.

Shortly After the End of the Meeting

1. Recognize and document results at the end of each meeting. This shows progress, promotes satisfaction and cultivates fulfillment among members of the group.

2. Within a week after the end of the meeting, have the meeting recorder (documenter) issue meeting minutes, including major actions and assignments from the meeting.

How to Govern the Nonprofit

In Any Board Structure, Boards Cannot Forget Strategic Focus

Whatever the Board structure chosen by the Board members (whether members focus only on strategic matters or if members also take part in management matters), if the nonprofit and its community are to thrive well into the future, then Board members (and staff, in the case of a working or collective Board) must concurrently maintain strong strategic focus on all of the important functions of governance and management in the nonprofit organization. They must ensure that, ultimately, those functions continue to be focused on verifying that the nonprofit is indeed meeting the community need that the nonprofit was formed to meet. Functions include:

1. **Collecting and acting on communications from stakeholders (inbound marketing)**
    The nonprofit continually collects input from stakeholders, especially – but not only – during strategic planning, program planning and evaluations, and fundraising activities.

2. **Strategic planning**
    Board and staff members consider stakeholders' input to establish plans that clarify the organization's purpose, overall goals, timelines and resources to serve stakeholders.

3. **Board development**
    Board structure and operations are aligned to effectively achieve the overall goals of the nonprofit, and to ensure fair, equitable and legally compliant operations in the nonprofit.

4. **Programs and services**
    Programs are the primary means to meet the needs of clients in the community, and another means to continually collect input from stakeholders.

5. **Human resources management (paid and volunteer)**
    Staff members are an important asset that must be carefully developed and supervised in a manner that meets the needs of the nonprofit, staff members and volunteers.

6. **Fundraising**
    Once the programs are planned, the nonprofit must ethically solicit, manage and report about resources donated to build and provide programs. Funders are critical stakeholders.

7. **Advertising, promotions and public relations (outbound marketing)**
    Board and staff members inform stakeholders of the benefits to them from participating in programs, and convey a clear and positive image of the nonprofit, overall.

8. **Finances and taxes**
    Meanwhile, all finances and taxes must be under strict control and in conformance with rules and regulations imposed on tax-exempt and charitable nonprofits.

9. **Lobbying**
    Board members and senior staff can work to influence legislation – they just need to do so within the requirements of the law for nonprofits.

10. **Monitoring performance**
    Planning includes specific goals and timelines, such as performance of the organization. Plans can be referenced to monitor Board, Chief Executive, staff and programs.

11.   **Risk management**
        All of the important assets of the nonprofit (its plans, people, policies, facilities, etc.) must
        be protected in order to ensure ongoing reliable provision of services to stakeholders.

12.   **Organizational sustainability**
        Being able to pay the bills requires being realistic in planning, ensuring programs are
        meeting needs of clients, getting the most from staff, and managing finances.

13.   **Regularly measuring the health of the nonprofit**
        The nonprofit cannot be taken apart in pieces and each part managed separately. The
        performance of the entire nonprofit must be evaluated regularly.

14.   **Transparency and accountability**
        The nonprofit is owned by – and responsible to – the public and, therefore, must continually
        disclose to the public, the financial, governance and compliance activities of the nonprofit.

How to Make Sure Stakeholders Are Always Heard

Nonprofits are public trusts. They exist to serve the needs of the community. They are obligated to
the community – a community which often permits nonprofits to be exempt from requirements made
to other forms of business. In return, the public expects to be heard. They count on Boards of
nonprofits to ensure the voice of the community is heard. Therefore, nonprofit Boards must focus
strong attention to listening to their stakeholders. This activity is sometimes called "inbound
marketing." This activity is critical to the primary job of nonprofit Board members to verify that
their nonprofit is indeed effectively and efficiently meeting a specific need in the community.

Far too often organizations focus on aggressive advertising, promotions and media campaigns that
go *at* their stakeholders: funders, clients and other groups in the community. Too many
organizations do not really *listen to* their stakeholders.

Guidelines for Effective Board Oversight of Inbound Marketing

If your Board uses committees, then a Marketing Committee would be helpful in this area, although
a Program Committee could also oversee inbound marketing, which involves market research.

1.   **Understand laws and regulations that apply to the nonprofit.**
        This includes filings with appropriate government agencies, benefits and limitations of
        corporate status, conformance to corporate Articles, By Laws, etc.

2.   **Know who the major groups of stakeholders are for the nonprofit.**
        Consider Board members, staff, clients, funders and community members.

3.   **Establish policies to regularly collect information from stakeholders.**
        Collect information about unmet needs in the community, impressions of the nonprofit, and
        other nonprofits working to meet needs similar to those met by the nonprofit.

4.   **Ensure strategic planning includes feedback from stakeholders.**
        Collect input from Board members, staff, clients, funders, the community, etc. Ask each
        stakeholder especially, "What do you consider to be "success" for the nonprofit?"

5. **Ensure the mission is centered on meeting verified needs in the community.**
    Mission statements should describe at least the community need that is being met among which groups of clients by using which methods. Verify that those needs even exist.

6. **Design and conduct Annual meetings.**
    In the meeting, take time to ask others about what they need from the nonprofit and what would meet that need.

7. **Ensure means to effectively verify results achieved among clients.**
    Conduct practical outcomes-based evaluations that collect information from program clients about whether their desired results are being met or not.

8. **Ensure Board members represent, or understand, your important constituents.**
    Constituents often include clients, funders, collaborators, community leaders, suppliers, government agencies, etc. Also consider diverse groups of clients, regions and values in the community.

How to Ensure Relevant and Realistic Strategic Planning

Strategic planning establishes purpose and overall direction for the nonprofit, including where it should to be at some point in the future and how it is going to get there. In a previous section, this guidebook explained that "all else flows from strategic planning" in a nonprofit. The process has been emphasized so much that a variety of proponents and opponents have voiced their opinions about the process. Some nonprofit leaders recoil at hearing the phrase "strategic planning" because it represents to them a long, tedious process, which, far too often, results in a report that sits collecting dust on the shelf. That need not be the case. Board members can help ensure that the process is carried out in a highly flexible, relevant and realistic fashion.

Whatever process the nonprofit chooses to use when deciding how to go forward, whether it uses a process called "strategic planning" or something else, Board members have the responsibility to ensure that a process is used to establish clear direction and alignment for all of the important parts of the nonprofit. Also, Board members must ensure that, regardless of which planning process is used, the nonprofit is focused on meeting a strong, verified need in the community and is progressing toward meeting that need.

Guidelines for Effective Board Oversight in Strategic Planning

If your Board uses committees, then an ad hoc Strategic Planning Committee would be helpful in this area.

1. **Actively participate in strategic planning, whether formal or informal.**
    A major responsibility of Board members is to ensure that the nonprofit has a clear purpose and direction, and has guidelines to work toward both of these. Developing and implementing a strategic plan usually fills that responsibility.

2. **Ensure strategic planning includes feedback from stakeholders.**
    Far too often, strategic planning tends to include only the opinions of those internal to the organization. Consequently, a "beautiful ladder can be built entirely to the wrong roof" – the plan includes wonderfully worded mission and vision statements, but little else that directly

applies to needs in the community. Therefore, in planning, include the perspectives of Board members, staff, clients, funders and the community.

3. **Craft your mission statement to describe who you serve, for what results and how.**
    The mission statement is the key communication to constituents. Mission statements can be in a wide variety of formats. However, the statements should reflect what you are doing for your constituents, not just for your organization.

4. **During planning, always ask, "Is this realistic?"**
    Many nonprofit plans sit on shelves collecting dust because the vision and goals were completely unrealistic. It is better to have a plan with a few realistic goals than to have a plan with many inspirational goals, most of which are far too ambitious to achieve.

5. **Be sure that the goals from the strategic plan are integrated throughout the nonprofit.**
    The plan specifies the most important priorities for the nonprofit to address. The nonprofit cannot do that if its various functions are not all aligned with addressing those priorities. Functions include Board operations, programs, marketing, staffing, finances and fundraising.

6. **Regularly monitor status reports regarding implementation of the plan.**
    Top-level information about mission, vision and values and lofty goals have no foundation if there is no specification of who needs to do what and by when in order to work towards those top-level priorities.

Consider the free, online self-directed, learning module about strategic planning at
http://www.managementhelp.org/np_progs/sp_mod/str_plan.htm .

See the topic, "Strategic Planning," in the Free Management Library[SM] at
http://www.managementhelp.org/plan_dec/str_plan/str_plan.htm .

Also consider the publication, *Field Guide to Nonprofit Strategic Planning and Facilitation,* from Authenticity Consulting, LLC. Go to the "publications" link at http://www.authenticityconsulting.com .

How to Make Sure Board Operations Are High-Quality

Guidelines for Effective Board Oversight of Board Development

If your Board uses committees, then a Board Development Committee would be helpful in this area.

Like the physician who has an unhealthy lifestyle, but takes very good care of his or her patients, the Board of Directors rarely gives attention as to how it is doing overall. Board development helps ensure that the Board is working smarter rather than harder. All of the guidelines throughout this entire section on strategic oversight apply to Board members as they work to conduct high-quality Board operations. The following guidelines are directly in regard to ensuring that activities within the Board of always of high-quality.

1. **Clarify what skills are needed among Board members to effectively govern.**
   The approach that you use to recruit Board members depends on whether you are staffing according to a functional approach, diversification approach, representation approach or just recruiting based on peoples' passion for the mission. If you see primarily passion, then be sure that the members do more than have passionate meetings.

2. **Orient Board members about the unique aspects of the nonprofit.**
   Ensure members know about the nonprofit's history, programs, successes and other Board members. Be sure to review Board policies, especially By Laws, Board calendar, comparison of Board and staff roles, Board attendance, conflict-of-interest, Board self-evaluation, CEO's job description, list of committees and ethics.

3. **Train members to be effective Board members.**
   Train Board members about the roles and responsibilities of a governing Board of Directors. Review the fiduciary duties and associated responsibilities, job descriptions and the major types of decisions made by Board members.

4. **Effectively organize Board expertise and resources to achieve goals.**
   You might use committees or task forces to organize members around important strategic priorities. The extent of involvement of Board members depends on the particular Board structure that you use.

5. **Use a Board calendar of important events to ensure all those events are conducted.**
   To ensure that all important Board activities are conducted, reference an annual calendar of about when the Board does a self-evaluation, evaluates the CEO, does strategic planning, produces a budget, approves updated policies and procedures, etc.

6. **Evaluate the Board to ensure maximize performance.**
   Board self-evaluation might need just 30 minutes a year from each member in order to complete a questionnaire about the quality of operations of the Board. Results of that self-evaluation usually are extremely useful to the Board.

Consider the free, on-line, self-directed, learning module about Boards at http://www.managementhelp.org/np_progs/brd_mod/boards.htm .

See the topic, "Boards of Directors," in the Free Management Library[SM] at http://www.managementhelp.org/boards/boards.htm .

How to Verify Programs Meet Needs of the Community

Programs are the primary strategies by which a nonprofit meets a specific need in the community. Therefore, Board members must have strong knowledge of programs, especially as to whether they are indeed meeting the specific community needs that the nonprofit was formed to meet.

Guidelines for Effective Board Oversight of Programs and Services

If your Board uses committees, then a Programs Committee would be helpful in this area.

1. **Know what the nonprofit's program are – many Board members often do not.**
   It is amazing how long Board members can serve a nonprofit, but when asked what the programs are, members are not able to identify them. Ask the Chief Executive to describe specifically what the programs are for the nonprofit.

2. **Understand each program, including the need it is to meet in the community and how.**
   This requires that client groups provide continual feedback to the nonprofit about the clients' needs. It also requires that the nonprofit identify certain outcomes, impacts or benefits, among clients that the program will work to achieve among client groups.

3. **Ensure programs are consistent with the mission and goals of the nonprofit.**
   Do not stray into providing programs that seem useful, but that might already be offered by other nonprofits or that might be so outside the nonprofit's focus that the programs would cost far too much in time and distraction to do.

4. **Ensure programs are sufficiently resourced.**
   Resources include people, expertise, funding and facilities. Resources also can include time and attention from Board members and other constituents.

5. **Ensure programs continue to meet the needs of clients – conduct evaluations.**
   This requires ongoing outcomes evaluations that focus on:

   a. Identifying indicators, or measures, that suggest what impacts or benefits (outcomes) the programs are helping clients to achieve.

   b. Collection of ongoing feedback from clients and program staff regarding the achievement of those measures for clients.

   c. Conclusions about the ultimate effectiveness of programs in achieving the desired outcomes for client groups.

6. **Ensure the various programs are highly integrated in purpose and operations.**
   It is not uncommon that various programs almost seem to stand apart from each other, as if the nonprofit is really running various separate other organizations. A tight integration of programs means savings and efficiency from sharing resources.

Consider the free, on-line, self-directed, learning module about marketing at http://www.managementhelp.org/np_progs/mkt_mod/market.htm .

Consider the guidebook, *Field Guide to Nonprofit Program Design, Marketing and Evaluation,* from Authenticity Consulting, LLC. Go to the "publications" link at http://www.authenticityconsulting.com .

How to Ensure Fair Management and Productive People

The way in which a nonprofit utilizes its human resources depends very much on the particular structure of the nonprofit and its Board. In some models, staff work closely with Board members, for example, in a working or collective Board. In other models, such as a policy or Policy

Governance® Board, staff report to a CEO, who reports to the Board. If the nonprofit does have staff, then it is critical that all staff (including the Chief Executive) and volunteers be recruited, trained and supervised according to up-to-date personnel policies and procedures that are approved by the Board.

Guidelines for Effective Board Oversight of Human Resources

If your Board uses committees, then a Personnel Committee would be helpful in this area.

1. **Ensure the nonprofit has up-to-date written personnel policies and procedures.**
    Employee laws today are so numerous and complex that nonprofits have to have written policies and procedures in order to ensure compliance to laws, rules and regulations. An expert on employment laws should review policies on a regular basis. All staff should have copies of the policies and procedures in the form of an employee handbook. The Chief Executive and other management staff, in particular, should be trained to ensure compliance. The Board should formally approve the personnel policies.

2. **Ensure staff are hired according to expertise, not personalities.**
    People should not be hired primarily because they know someone in the nonprofit or because they are likeable. Focus on the requirements of the job and ensure that a job description accurately describes those requirements. Then reference the job description to fill the position.

3. **Ensure all staff and volunteers are fully resourced (trained and equipped).**
    Particularly with volunteers, it is important to give them a brief orientation of the nonprofit program's, other volunteers and/or staff members, and resources available to help the volunteers. Sometimes with paid and unpaid staff members, they might seem like they are poor performers when instead they need better training and resources.

4. **Ensure all staff and volunteers receive regular written evaluations.**
    Too often, nonprofit leaders assume that people are doing fine because they keep showing up for work each day. High-performing people usually want to know how they are doing and how they can improve. The best way to convey that information is to provide written evaluations. Those evaluations also serve as a valid benchmark, or indicator, if leaders need to take some form of performance-related action later on.

5. **Ensure all staff members receive fair and equitable benefits and compensation.**
    There are many online salary surveys that suggest pay ranges for various positions. Even if a nonprofit cannot pay compensation that is well within these ranges, the Board still should approve a formal policy to determine, not only how much staff members should be paid, but to ensure that all staff members are treated fairly when compensation is determined.

Consider the free, on-line, self-directed, learning module about staffing at http://www.managementhelp.org/np_progs/sup_mod/staff.htm .

Consider the guidebook, *Field Guide to Leadership and Supervision for Nonprofit Staff,* from Authenticity Consulting, LLC. Go to the "publications" link at http://www.authenticityconsulting.com .

How to Take the Lead in Fundraising – All Kinds

Fundraising is sometimes a dreaded activity for Board members. However, a recent trend among funders is to expect that Board members take a very active role in leading fundraising, including making their own monetary contributions to the organization. Board members can approach funders, not only to solicit funds, but also to develop relationships with funders. Funders expect nonprofits to present a clear case for the need for funds and clear methods for continuing to verify that funds are spent in an effective fashion. If a fundraiser is hired, Board members should follow sound practices in hiring and supervising consultants. Therefore, Boards and their nonprofits must conduct fundraising activities in a highly focused, plan-based fashion that directly follows from the nonprofit's mission and goals.

Guidelines for Effective Board Oversight of Fundraising

If your Board uses committees, then a Fundraising Committee would be helpful in this area.

1. **Work smarter, rather than harder – do not do the same techniques even harder.**
   Nonprofits often do the same few techniques to raise money, for example, an annual fundraiser that requires an extensive amount of time from Board and staff members, but that generates very little in revenue. Or, they burst out a large number of grant proposals, all with the same wording. They would benefit much more from planning their fundraising.

2. **Ensure prospect research to identify all sources of funding.**
   Prospect research can identify the percentage of funding that a nonprofit with similar nonprofits in your locale might get from individuals, foundations, corporations and government, for example, 30% from individuals, 30% from foundations, 20% from corporations and 20% from government. That sets a benchmark, or measure, at which you can target your expected levels of funding from fundraising efforts. That helps your organization to go beyond doing the same approaches to fundraising (for example, doing annual events).

3. **Ensure development and approval of a comprehensive Fundraising Plan!**
   The Plan should specify:

   a. The fundraising target or amount to be raised and by when.

   b. Percentage to be raised from among the different types of sources, including individuals, foundations, corporations and/or government (that requires prospect research).

   c. Specific sources in each type, for example, names of specific individuals or specific foundations.

   d. How each of those sources will be approached and by whom.

   e. How status of fundraising will be tracked.

4. **Ensure that Board members remain actively involved in fundraising activities.**
   A Board Fundraising Committee or task force should ensure that the Fundraising Plan is developed and implemented – but all Board members should take part in implementing the Plan. Board members should get a short training from staff about programs, including who

is served and what successes have occurred so far, along with providing members a set of talking points so members feel comfortable approaching funders.

5.   **Ensure that funds are spent according to the requirements and specifications of donors.**
Board members must ensure that the funds continue to be spent in the manner that was described in the grant proposals that produced those funds. Otherwise, there can be lawsuits for misappropriation of funds and the nonprofit will lose all credibility with funders.

6.   **If fundraisers are hired, be clear about expectations to them and hire them ethically.**
For example, many experts assert that it is unethical to hire a fundraiser and expect him/her to pay his/her fee or salary with the monies that are raised. Instead, fundraisers should be paid an amount regardless of the amounts raised. Also, distinguish between the type of fundraiser who can help you with your planning and those who primarily write many grants.

 See "Guidelines for Working With Consultants" on page 219.

7.   **Carefully monitor implementation of the Fundraising Plan.**
Is the Plan being implemented? Are you getting the results that you desired? If not, what should be done? Put more priority on implementation? Get more resources? Extend deadlines in the Plan?

8.   **Ensure that all donated funds are reported as required by law and funders.**
Sometimes nonprofits forget about funders once the nonprofits receive the checks. That is a mistake. Usually, foundations, corporate and government funding is accompanied by stringent reporting requirements that the nonprofit report how the funds were spent, including in which programs and what the results were from the expenditures.

 Consider the free, on-line, self-directed, learning module about fundraising at
http://www.managementhelp.org/np_progs/fnd_mod/fnd_raise.htm .

 See the topic, "Nonprofit Fundraising and Grantwriting," in the Free Management Library[SM] at
http://www.managementhelp.org/fndrsng/np_raise/np_raise.htm .

Can a Nonprofit Make a Profit From Programs and Services?

Yes. There is an age-old misconception that "nonprofit" means that the organization cannot make any excess monies – even that nonprofits should only raise monies primarily from fundraising. There is an increasing trend for nonprofits to engage in "earned-income" ventures where they generate significant funds from fees for services or products. They, in turn, use this increased revenue to offset the amounts that they must raise via fundraising. Many foundations and major funders even prefer that nonprofits undertake this "commercial" activity because it results in more financial self-reliance and sustainability on the part of the nonprofit.

Nonprofits that engage in activities where a substantial portion of their revenue is from sales of goods and services that are not directly in regard to their tax-exempt purposes (as described on their

Form 1023 in the USA) have to pay taxes on that portion of revenue, the "unrelated business income." In the USA, that income must be reported on the Form 990-T to the Internal Revenue Service (IRS). If a "substantial" portion (as yet undefined by the IRS) of revenue is from unrelated business income, then the tax-exempt nonprofit could lose its tax-exempt status. If it plans to generate sizeable portions of its revenue from unrelated business income, then it might consider forming a for-profit subsidiary. In that situation, the nonprofit should seek counsel from a tax expert who is well versed in tax-exempt law.

You can benefit from the free advice shared by thousands of members on the free forum at http://www.npenterprise.net .

Nonprofit earned-income ventures are similar to those in for-profits in that they require careful business planning, including market research about the potential products and markets, perhaps feasibility or market testing, product development planning, identifying needed staffing, structuring the approach to managing the venture, and computing final costs to develop and sell the product.

This might seem like a lot of effort, but many nonprofits are probably already doing some form of business planning in order to successfully deliver programs to clients – these nonprofits probably are just not referring to their activities as business planning.

There is more information about earned-income ventures at http://www.managementhelp.org/soc_entr/soc_entr.htm#anchor80808 .

How to Effectively Get the Word Out About the Nonprofit

Those who are new to the nonprofit world might think that nonprofits should not have to "sell" their services. After a few months in a nonprofit, many people realize that "selling" is needed in the nonprofit world at least as much in the for-profit world. However, nonprofit personnel may not be nearly as effective at understanding how to sell.

First, it helps to understand what we are talking about. Advertising and promotions are aimed at continuing to bring a service to the attention of potential and current clients. Successful advertising and promotions depend very much on knowing what groups of clients your program aims to serve, what features and benefits of the program you want to convey to the clients, and what methods of communication will be most effective in reaching those clients. Sales is a "partnership" between the program and the client, geared to explore the client's needs and assess if there is a suitable match or not. If there is a match, the salesperson helps the client to take advantage of the program's services. Public relations might be viewed as advertising and promotions, not of a specific program, but of the entire nonprofit organization.

One of the Board's major responsibilities is to represent the nonprofit to the community. Ideally, the Board is comprised of representatives from the nonprofit's major stakeholders. Thus, Board members are poised to be very effective in advertising, promotions, sales and public relations for the nonprofit. (This activity is sometimes called "outbound marketing.")

Guidelines for Effective Board Oversight of Outbound Marketing

If your Board uses committees, then a Marketing Committee would be helpful in this area.

1. **Be sure that all Board members understand the nonprofit's programs.**
    As mentioned above, Board members often do not know what the nonprofit's programs are. Members should know each program, who it serves, the results that the program aims to achieve, the methods used by the program, and the types of results that have been achieved so far.

2. **Define an overall desired image for the nonprofit – how should people view it?**
    For example, should the nonprofit be known primarily for its strong programs, or its diverse values, or its strong relationships in the community? Should the nonprofit adopt a slogan, or concise phrase, that helps to convey that image? Should the nonprofit standardize on a graphic, or logo, to convey its unique identity?

3. **Develop an overall Marketing (or Promotions) Plan – ideally for each program.**
    In the Plan, for each different, specific group of clients, specify:

    a. The specific benefits that each different group will achieve from the different programs.

    b. The different messages that will be conveyed to each different group. (When selecting the messages, consider the different needs and wants for each of the different groups.)

    c. How each group prefers to get its messages, for example, some prefer television, some prefer the radio, some prefer newspapers, etc.

    d. Who will convey the messages by using the preferred communications approaches with each group.

    e. When those messages will be conveyed.

    f. How implementation of the Promotions Plan will be tracked.

4. **Develop a Public Relations Plan about the entire organization.**
    Whereas a Marketing Plan ideally is about marketing each program, that is, a Plan for each program, a Public Relations plan is about marketing the entire organization. Develop a Plan that specifies:

    a. The unique identity, or branding, of the nonprofit, along with any slogan, mission, etc.

    b. The major stakeholders of the nonprofit, for example, clients, funders, collaborators and community leaders.

    c. What the nonprofit wants each group of stakeholders to believe or feel about the nonprofit.

    d. The communication channels that might be preferred by each group of stakeholders.

    e. The messages to convey to each group via its preferred channel(s).

    f. Who will convey the messages and by when.

5. **Ensure Board members work from a public relations or media kit, talking points, etc.**
    Each Board member is a representative of the nonprofit in the community. Board members

deserve a short training about how to effectively describe each program and the entire organization to the community.

6. **Carefully monitor implementation of the Promotions and Public Relations Plans.**
Are the Plans being implemented? Are you getting the results that you desired? If not, what should be done? Put more priority on implementation? Get more resources? Extend deadlines in the Plans?

Consider the free, on-line, self-directed, learning module about marketing at http://www.managementhelp.org/np_progs/mkt_mod/market.htm .

Consider the guidebook, *Field Guide to Nonprofit Program Design, Marketing and Evaluation,* from Authenticity Consulting, LLC. Go to the "publications" link at http://www.authenticityconsulting.com .

How to Ensure Sound Management of Finances and Taxes

Sometimes Board members prefer to leave the finances up to someone else, like the Board Treasurer, to address. This is unfortunate because financial information can rather quickly convey the "reality" of how the nonprofit is doing. Every Board member is completely responsible to understand at least the basic trends, highlights and issues portrayed by basic financial reports. In addition, even though a nonprofit might be exempt from paying certain federal, state/provincial and local taxes, there still might be certain payroll deductions that need to be withheld from staff paychecks, if staff are employed. Overseeing financial management also means overseeing management of assets, such as facilities, major equipment, etc.

Guidelines for Effective Board Oversight of Finances and Taxes

If your Board uses committees, then a Finance Committee would be helpful in this area.

1. **Develop up-to-date fiscal policies and procedures and have them approved by Board.**
These policies specify how finances and monies will be collected, managed, reported and dispersed in a highly accurate and controlled fashion that conforms to laws and regulations and minimizes the likelihood of loss, fraud or malfeasance. New organizations might obtain sample policies and modify them according to the organization's nature and needs.

Sample financial policies are available at http://www.mncn.org /doc/Sample%20Financial%20Procedures%20Manual.PDF .

2. **Approve an annual operating budget.**
Usually, the budget is developed and approved near the end of the strategic planning activities when planners have identified what resources will need to be obtained and supported in order to achieve the goals in the strategic plan.

3. **Establish internal controls for the handling of cash and the approval of expenditures**.
Fiscal policies and procedures usually specify how cash should be managed, for example, that the person who tracks incoming invoices is not the same person who writes checks to

pay the invoices, thereby minimizing any likelihood that one person could steal funds without getting caught.

4.   **Ensure all federal and state/provincial payroll taxes are paid.**
Tax-exempt nonprofits can avoid paying certain taxes. However, payroll taxes must be paid regarding paid staff members. In the USA, payroll taxes are for Social Security and Medicare. Be sure these taxes are being paid.

5.   **Report and review the trends, issues and highlights regarding key financial statements.**
Instead of Board members reviewing columns of numbers, have the Board Treasurer and/or Chief Executive provide a summary report, in addition to the numbers. The report explains:

a.   Highlights to notice about the numbers, for example, an account that is significantly overspent or underspent.

b.   Trends to notice about the numbers, for example, significant tendencies in certain accounts that might result in overspend or underspend, which might result in an issue later on.

c.   Issues, for example, an account that is so overspent or underspent that Board members need to take action on that item now.

6.   **Review financial reports, especially cash flow and budget-versus-actual reports.**
For new or small organizations, a cash-flow statement is extremely important to review because it shows whether the nonprofit has the funds to pay its near-term bills or not. The Statement of Financial Activities (an income statement) should be reviewed at least quarterly and more often if the nonprofit is struggling financially. A Statement of Financial Condition (balance sheet) should be reviewed at least quarterly, as well.

7.   **Ensure a Form 990 is filed on an annual basis in the USA.**
Tax-exempt nonprofits normally do not have to file if their gross receipts are under $25,000.

To learn about reporting requirements, go to
http://www.irs.gov/charities/article/0,,id=96103,00.html .

8.   **Ensure the nonprofit has adequate insurance coverage.**
For example, the nonprofit might need general liability insurance to cover situations where someone is hurt on the premises, workers compensation if an employee is hurt on the job, property insurance if a major asset is damaged or destroyed or lost, or Directors and Officers (D&O) Insurance for Board members if someone sues the Board for its actions or lack of actions.

9.   **Consider financial audits and/or reviews by external auditors.**
There are different types of audits and reviews. Typically, an audit is verification by an outside expert of the nonprofit's financial management practices and its financial numbers in terms of accuracy and completeness. There are requirements for nonprofits to have an audit under different circumstances, depending on the state in the USA, if the nonprofit raises more than a certain amount of donations/funding or has grants over a certain threshold. Audits are good way to verify that the numbers on the financial reports are accurate – that is always a strong reassurance to Board members. A review is an analysis by an outside expert

on some aspect of financial management, usually of the financial numbers, to report on the quality of that aspect.

10. **Be sure that Board members are trained to analyze and decide on finances.**
     Far too often, only one Board member – the Treasurer – really understands the finances. Some members even pride themselves that they refuse to try to understand finances, it is "just not their thing." Having that stance is irresponsible. Board members' responsibilities for the nonprofit cannot be delegated to anyone else, especially to only one Board member. There should be at least one other Board member who knows the details of the finances, and who probably is on the Finance Committee. All Board members should be trained about how to analyze financial reports, detect where attention is needed, and make necessary decisions to address any issues.

Consider the free, on-line, self-directed, learning module about finance at http://www.managementhelp.org/np_progs/fnc_mod/fnance.htm .

See the topic, "Nonprofit Fundraising and Grantwriting," in the Free Management Library[SM] at http://www.managementhelp.org/finance/np_fnce/np_fnce.htm .

Sample financial policies are available at http://www.mncn.org/doc/ Sample%20Financial%20Procedures%20Manual.PDF .

How to Advocate for Public Needs – and Lobby Legally

Lobbying consists of activities to directly influence a specific piece of legislation (the creating or modifying of a law), for example, by contacting legislators or hiring lobbyists. (This is in comparison to advocacy, which is promoting a position about an issue, for example, sharing information with the public about the need for cessation of smoking.)

Nonprofits exist to serve the general public, not only one specific group of people. In return, the general public grants nonprofits the special rights to avoid paying certain taxes and to collect donations that can be deducted from the donor's tax liabilities. Tax-exempt nonprofits that engage primarily in lobbying can be viewed as working to benefit only one specific group of people, and could lose their tax-exempt status, depending on the amount of lobbying they do and report.

Because of this concern, there is a common misconception that nonprofits should not be engaged in lobbying, lest their organizations lose their tax status. Actually, one of the responsibilities of Board members is to represent the nonprofit to stakeholders, including to enhance conditions for clients of the nonprofit's programs. Board and staff members can, and are expected to, do lobbying. However, there are certain requirements that must be met in order to retain a favorable tax status.

In the USA, the amount of lobbying activities, including preparation, development of an agenda to push to legislators and/or lobbyists, and the dollars spent on these activities, must be "insubstantial" as mentioned in the 1976 Lobby Law. Although "insubstantial" is not quantifiably defined by the Internal Revenue Service (IRS), a general rule of thumb seems to be less than 10% of revenues. Organizations that choose to engage in an amount of lobbying activities over that amount, and wish to retain their tax status, can elect 501(h) status with the IRS by filing Form 5678. Organizations that want to spend an amount of 20% should consider re-filing the Form 1023 with the IRS to apply for 501(c)(4) status, rather than 501(c)(3) status.

Guidelines for Effective Board Oversight of Lobbying

If your Board uses committees, then a Public Policy Committee would be helpful in this area.

1.   **Learn the limitations placed on nonprofits that engage in lobbying.**
      As explained above, nonprofits can – and should – engage in lobbying.

> For more information on lobbying, go to http://www.nonprofits.org/npofaq/11/08.html . Also see the Charity Lobbying in the Public Interest Website at http://www.clip.org .

> An excellent book on this topic is *The Nonprofit Board Member's Guide to Lobbying and Advocacy* by Marcia Avner, (Amherst H. Wilder Foundation, 2004).

2.   **Carefully craft Public Policy Plan with messages and methods to influence legislation.**
      Similar to the design of a Public Relations Plan as itemized in the above section about oversight of outbound marketing, you should clearly identify:

      a.   The specific social issues you want to address.

      b.   The specific results that you want in order to address regarding each issue.

      c.   Who you need to influence in order to get those results.

      d.   How you will influence each of those people.

      It may even be worth hiring a professional in public relations or lobbying to help you because you probably will have a very small amount of time with a legislature. Professionals know how to craft and convey a message in a way that is most powerful in getting the attention and consideration of the decision makers.

3.   **Carefully monitor implementation of the Plan.**
      Is the Plan being implemented? Are you getting the results that you desired? If not, what should be done? Put more priority on implementation? Get more resources? Extend deadlines in the Plan?

> For more information about public relations, go to http://www.managementhelp.org/pblc_rel/pblc_rel.htm .

How to Track Performance of Nonprofit, Board and People

Performance is effectively achieving goals and objectives in a timely manner – goals that are directly aligned with the mission and strategic priorities of the organization. A primary responsibility of Board members is to ensure that the nonprofit remains a high-performing nonprofit. Without specific goals to achieve – or at least monitoring for "best practices" – for the organization, programs and management functions, Board members have little or no reliable means by which to measure performance.

Guidelines for Effective Board Oversight of Performance

If your Board uses committees, then an Executive Committee would be helpful in this area, especially if the Executive Committee is comprised of Chairs of each of the other committees.

1. **Specify goals – what will be achieved, how much, who will achieve them and by when.**
    Attention to specifying goals in plans often is as important – or more important – than extensive attention on the wording used in mission, vision and values statements. Specify goals in strategic plans and especially in plans for Board development, program growth, finances and fundraising. Do not worry about the specification of goals having to be perfect the first time, just do your best for now. The specifications can always be changed, as needed.

2. **Monitor status toward achieving specific goals – and then adjust accordingly.**
    On a regular basis, monitor whether the goals are being achieved or not. If goals are not being achieved, then increase priority on achieving the goals, allocate more resources to achieve them, or extend the deadlines to reach the goals.

3. **Monitor for "best practices" in different governance and management functions.**
    As mentioned in this guide, there can be wide disagreement about what constitutes "best practices." However, particularly for new or struggling nonprofits, they are much more likely to benefit from at least monitoring whether the best practices are being followed rather than ignore the best practices altogether.

     See "How to Regularly Measure Overall Health of the Nonprofit" on page 118 for more guidelines to monitor the health of the organization.

4. **Invite each Board member to evaluate his/her performance on the Board.**
    This can include each member privately using a basic self-assessment tool that asks the member questions about the quality of his/her participation on the Board. Members could be invited to share the results of their self-evaluations in order to get help to improve their participation.

     See "Sample Board Member Self-evaluation Form" on page 272.

5. **Ensure all Board members formally evaluate the entire Board, at least annually.**
    This includes all members privately completing an assessment tool that asks questions about the quality of the overall Board operations. These Board evaluations often can be done very quickly and conveniently.

    See "Sample Board Self-evaluation Form" on page 273.

6. **Ensure annual, formal evaluation of the Chief Executive (if a CEO role is on the staff).**
    Board members should ensure the CEO has certain responsibilities to carry out, as specified in the CEO's job description. Also, the CEO should have certain annual goals to achieve (performance goals) and these goals should closely align with those in the strategic plan.

    See "Sample Executive Director Evaluation Form" on page 269.

7. **Ensure evaluation of staff, according to procedures in personnel policies.**
    All staff, including the CEO, deserve feedback about the quality of their performance. That feedback, including in the form of performance evaluations, should be done according to guidelines in up-to-date personnel policies.

8. **Most important, evaluate programs to verify they are meeting community needs.**
    This means ensuring that outcomes-based program evaluations occur to verify that each program is indeed meeting the needs that the nonprofit was formed to meet.

    Consider the free, on-line, self-directed, learning module about evaluation at http://www.managementhelp.org/np_progs/evl_mod/evl_mod.htm .

    Consider the guidebook, *Field Guide to Nonprofit Program Design, Marketing and Evaluation,* from Authenticity Consulting, LLC. Go to the "publications" link at http://www.authenticityconsulting.com .

How to Identify and Avoid Risks to the Nonprofit

Board members are responsible to ensure the reliable, ongoing and effective operations of their nonprofit. That includes ensuring that the most critical assets and functions are protected from sudden loss or significant damage. It also includes ensuring the means to quickly recover from those unfortunate situations. Most nonprofits have very limited resources, so damage or loss to any of them usually means a significant – even traumatic – loss to operations. Therefore, risk management is an extremely important topic for Board members to address.

Guidelines for Effective Board Oversight of Risk Management

If your Board uses committees, then a Finance Committee or Audit Committee would be helpful in this area.

Avoiding Sudden Loss or Damage

1. **Compensate the CEO commensurate to his/her capabilities and responsibilities.**
    One of the most frequently cited reasons that CEOs of nonprofits leave their jobs is because of significantly low pay. Very often, they could make 30% to 50% more in the for-profit sector or in working independently, for example, as a consultant. Board members must recognize this situation and not rely on CEOs working for low pay because "we're a nonprofit."

2. **Undertake ongoing CEO succession planning**
    If the CEO suddenly left that position because of illness, death, firing or other reasons, it would be traumatic for the nonprofit. Board members are responsible to minimize that affect on the nonprofit, as much as possible.

     See "How to Quickly Replace Your CEO (CEO Succession Management)" on page 166.

3. **Ensure up-to-date job descriptions for all Board members and critical staff members.**
    In case any of their positions needs to be filled soon, at least there will be general description of the responsibilities so that others can more quickly understand the positions in order to help fill them as soon as possible.

4. **Ensure protected and stable facilities.**
    Computers and peripherals should have consistent levels of electrical protection, so that electrical surges do not damage them. Facilities should have adequate fire protection, including water sprinklers that would not damage critical electrical components. All important information and materials should be locked, including password protection on computer files.

Avoiding Damaging Acts

1. **Have up-to-date, Board-approved personnel policies for paid and volunteer staff.**
    Personnel policies specify how personnel should be hired, supervised and fired in accordance with employment laws that ensure fair, equitable and legally compliant treatment of others. Personnel, especially those who supervise others, should be trained on the policies.

2. **Conduct background checks on hires.**
    Background checks can detect if a person has committed crimes, major or minor in nature, that might suggest tendencies for how the person will act in the workplace. These checks also ensure the public that the nonprofit's Board and staff members are suitable for working with the public.

3. **Conduct Board orientations once a year for members.**
    Board orientations make members aware of the unique aspects of the Board and nonprofit, including the Board's policies, for example, about ethics, conflict-of-interest, whistleblowers and document retention/destruction.

4. **Establish a Whistleblower Policy.**
    The policy should specify how Board members, staff and others can safely report an alleged or actual organizational behavior, practice or event which is illegal, unethical or inappropriate, without retaliation to the whistleblower.

     See "Sample Whistleblower Policy" on page 277.

5. **Establish a Board Ethics Policy.**
    The policy should specify the types of behaviors to conduct and/or to avoid in order to ensure that Board members conduct themselves in a manner that treats others fairly, equitably and that is legally compliant.

     See "Sample Board Ethics Policy" on page 267.

6. **Ensure accurate and Board-approved meeting minutes.**
    The minutes formally document Board members' deliberations, decisions and actions and, thus, serve as an accurate record to explain or justify to others the intentions, participation and actions of Board members.

7. **Establish up-to-date, Board-approved fiscal policies and procedures.**
    These procedures ensure that the activities in financial management are conducted in a highly thorough, accurate and useful manner that also minimizes the likelihood of malfeasance, including theft, fraud or misappropriation of funds.

8. **Annually conduct a financial audit and/or review.**
    The audit or review verifies the usefulness and accuracy of some or all aspects of financial management and, thus, greatly increases the likelihood that financial numbers and reports are indeed accurate.

Recovering from Loss

1. **All major functions should have written plans that specify current goals and priorities.**
    Organizations can more quickly recover if plans are documented so that personnel can quickly reference them to continue addressing important priorities. These should include the strategic plan, program plans, staffing plans, marketing plan and fundraising plan.

2. **Establish written procedures for routine tasks in the workplace.**
    These procedures can be referenced by personnel to quickly restore and resume the practices, thereby reducing adverse impact on operations as a result of a major interruption in operations. Procedures might in regarding, for example, to ordering supplies, operating facilities, bringing clients into a program, delivering services and evaluating services.

3. **Keep contact lists of personnel and major stakeholders.**
    Document their names, the role that the personnel have with the nonprofit, and contact information so they can be contacted, especially to help restore operations.

4. **Have suitable insurance coverage.**
    Consider general liability insurance in case someone sues because of workplace injury.

Consider property insurance in case property is damaged or lost. Consider professional liability insurance in case someone sues as a result of what he/she perceives as malpractice in programs. Consider Directors and Officers Insurance to pay any lawsuits lost by Board members when someone sues the Board, alleging damage because of members' actions or inactions. Consider workers' compensation insurance in case someone is injured on the job.

5.   **Establish a Document Retention/Destruction Policy.**
      The policy should specify which documents are retained for how long before they can be destroyed. It also should specify how the nonprofit will completely cooperate if any documents are required by agencies investigating the nonprofit or its affiliates.

> See "Sample Document Retention/Destruction Policy" on page 278.

> More information and materials on risk management are available from Nonprofit Risk Management Center at http://www.nonprofitrisk.org .

How to Ensure Sustainability of Nonprofit, Programs, People and Money

Sustainability often is misunderstood. It is more than generating enough money to keep paying the bills. True long-term, organizational sustainability for an organization involves four dimensions, including strategic, programs, personnel and finances. If sufficient attention is given to the first three dimensions of sustainability, then financial sustainability is much more likely to occur – and much easier to accomplish. The following guidelines help Board members ensure sustainability in each dimension.

Guidelines for Effective Board Oversight of Sustainability

If your Board uses committees, then an Executive Committee would be helpful in this area, especially if comprised of Chairs of other committees, because that form of Executive Committee is more likely to have representatives from each of the four dimensions of sustainability as listed below.

Strategic Dimension of Sustainability

1.   **Ensure realistic vision and strategic goals for the organization.**
      If these are not realistic, then the organization will be trying to do too much. As a result, it will very likely run out of resources, including money and people.

2.   **Ensure realistic strategies to achieve the vision and goals.**
      Even if the vision and goals are realistic, if the efforts to achieve them are unrealistic, then the organization will have the same problems as mentioned above.

3.   **Modify the vision, goals and strategies to remain realistic when implementing plans.**
      One of the most important parts of a plans is often forgotten – procedures for how to change the plans. Consider extending deadlines to achieve goals or dropping them altogether if that is what it takes to ensure long-term sustainability.

Program Dimension of Sustainability

1. **Verify what clients truly need, versus what they only want – or programs will fail.**
    Clients will come to programs based on what they want, and they will stay based on what they need. If programs are not meeting the true needs of clients, then programs will fail. Consider basic market research to verify what the clients really need.

2. **Evaluate effectiveness and outcomes of programs to verify they are meeting needs.**
    Effectiveness is in regard to the quality of program's processes for delivering services as well as outcomes. Outcomes are in regard to the actual changes in clients as a result of participating in programs. Consider doing process and outcomes evaluations for each program.

3. **Change program methods, if needed, to improve quality in order to meet client needs.**
    Programs should undergo continuous improvement in order to remain effective. Listen to the opinions of the clients about the program. Consider results of program evaluations. Then make changes to the programs accordingly.

Personnel Dimension of Sustainability

1. **Ensure staff has sufficient expertise, training and resources to provide programs.**
    Even if the vision, goals and strategies are realistic and the programs are designed well, staff members have to continue to operate high-quality programs. Often, that is a matter of staff members having strong expertise, getting training and having sufficient resources.

2. **Ensure staff members are using all of their resources to provide programs.**
    This is a matter of effective supervision. Ensure there is effective delegation to staff members (setting goals, sharing feedback, adjusting performance) and evaluation of staff such that members are always doing their best.

3. **Ensuring redundancy and succession planning for staff in case people leave.**
    In a typical nonprofit, programs and other operations would be damaged significantly if involved staff members suddenly were no longer available. Ensure that key staff members have suitable "backup" personnel who also can do much of their jobs, and that guidelines and procedures exist for jobs, as much as possible.

Financial Dimension of Sustainability

1. **Identify how much funding (fees and/or fundraising) is needed to offset expenses.**
    Develop an annual budget and especially identify any deficits to know how much funding is needed, so that fundraising targets and/or fees can be adjusted accordingly to rid those deficits.

2. **Do adequate prospect research to identify *all* likely sources in fundraising.**
    Do not do the same fundraising activities, but even harder. For example, fundraising events often require a substantial amount of time and often do not generate much in funds. Research all sources among individuals, foundations, corporations and government.

3. **Allocate sufficient funding to administration and programs.**
    Know how much money each program needs. To do that, develop program-based, or functional, budgets. Those budgets identify the expected revenues and expenses associated

with each program, along with a percentage allocation of overhead (expenses common to all programs, for example, the salary of the Chief Executive, facilities, costs, etc.) to each.

4.   **Track expenditures and revenues to promptly address financial priorities and issues**. Make sure the numbers on the reports are accurate, via financial reviews and audits. Make sure more than one Board member is able to understand the finances. Two reports are useful in particular, a budget-versus-actual report and a cash-flow report.

5.   **Follow policies to establish adequate reserves and to do contingency planning.** Establish a policy to set aside some percentage of your revenue, for example, 10% to be available in case of emergency. When budgeting, plan a couple of scenarios, one where all expected revenue arrives and another where, for example, only 70% of revenue arrives. Then, if there is a shortage of revenue, the nonprofit can reference the latter scenario to more quickly respond.

How to Regularly Measure Overall Health of the Nonprofit

One of the biggest questions that lurk – consciously or unconsciously – at the back of Board members' minds is "How's our nonprofit really doing? Are we verifying that we're effectively and efficiently meeting specific needs in the community?" Despite the importance of this question, nonprofit leaders rarely pursue means to measure the overall health of their nonprofit, even though there are a variety of free, easy-to-use tools available. The tools are usually comprehensive questionnaires that ask about the occurrence of certain "best practices" in the organization or the tools suggest standards of excellence for the nonprofits to pursue in their operations. (This guide has mentioned that there are a variety of views on what constitutes "best practices" – the same is true about what makes for "organizational effectiveness.") The tools might ask questions or suggest standards for operations, including about Boards, strategic planning, programs, staffing, finances, fundraising, facilities and evaluations.

Use of the tools, especially questionnaires, can take as little as 30 minutes from each Board member and senior staff member, and the analyses and reporting of results can take 2-3 hours – this is time very well spent for the health of the organization.

Guidelines for Effective Board Oversight of Organizational Assessments

If your Board uses committees, then a Planning Committee would be helpful, for example, if the assessment is being done as part of the strategic planning process.

1.   **Annually, do the quick assessment near the beginning or middle of the fiscal year.** This timing is intended to produce results of the assessment that can be considered during strategic planning (strategic planning often is best to do in the middle of the fiscal year in time to produce an approved budget for the next fiscal year).

2.   **Or do the assessment whenever the nonprofit seems to have many chronic struggles.** For example, struggles might include financial shortfalls, or high turnover or frequent conflicts among Board and staff members. The assessment is a great way to identify the "root causes" of issues (usually lack of plans and policies), rather than blaming each other.

3.   **Be careful not to consider the tools as if they portray the "perfect" nonprofit.**
The practical purpose of these tools is to identify the most important functions or practices
that need to be improved in the nonprofit for now, not to identify each and every little issue.
Answers to the questions should be informed by leaders understanding of their nonprofit.

4.   **Appoint a small group of Board and staff members to oversee assessment activity.**
The group would identify which tool to use, notify others about the purpose of the tool and
how to use it, and coordinate the analysis and reporting of results.

5.   **If it is the nonprofit's first time to do an organizational assessment, consider help.**
You might hire a consultant to work with the group, including to recommend a tool, guide
the planning and communication about use of the tool, analyze and report the results, and
generate recommendations to address any issues found in the results.

6.   **Include recommendations from the assessment in the strategic and Board plans.**
Be sure that the recommendations somehow are captured in other plans, which greatly
increases the likelihood that the recommendations will be followed. The best plans
(strategic plans, Board development plans, marketing plans, program plans, etc.), include
specification of who will do what and by when, and also a means to track implementation.

See "Tools to Measure Health of Nonprofits" on page 227 for a variety of
free, online organizational assessments, and the complete content of one
such tool.

How to Ensure Transparency and Accountability

Nonprofits are entrusted by their communities to be successfully meeting a variety of public and
social needs in the communities. In return, the public grant the nonprofits tax-exempt and/or
charitable status. The communities expect the nonprofits to continually prove that the work they are
doing is really meeting the needs of the community – the communities want to know what the
nonprofits are really doing. The nonprofits need to be transparent and accountable to the public.

Board transparency means Board members always providing full disclosure and explanation of the
nonprofit's governance, finances and affects on communities, and also willingly supporting
stakeholders' efforts to understand that information. Board accountability means members
continually making the nonprofits and themselves responsible to meet the expectations of
stakeholders, and verifying with those stakeholders that their expectations are indeed being met.

The Sarbanes-Oxley Act of 2002 in the USA (commonly referred to as SOX) instituted certain
requirements to make publicly traded companies more legally and ethically compliant, especially in
financial practices, including by increasing transparency and accountability of governance. For
example, some requirements include: establishing a skilled and independent Board Audit Committee
(a Board committee comprised of independent Board members); the CEO and financial officers
certifying accuracy of financial statements; and instituting policies for avoiding conflict of interest,
having whistleblower protection and for retention/destruction of documents. Although the
requirements apply primarily to publicly traded companies, the policies on conflict of interest,
whistleblower and document retention/destruction can apply to nonprofit corporations, as well.

There is more information about *Sarbanes-Oxley* at
http://www.abanet.org/abastore/books/inside_practice/july_2005/oxley.htm

Guidelines for Effective Board Oversight for Transparency and Accountability

If your Board uses committees, then a Finance Committee or Audit Committee would be helpful in this area.

1. **Recruit independent Board members.**
    These are members who are not staff members, have no other business affiliation with the nonprofit and are not very close and personal friends of any executives in the nonprofit. Independent Board members are much more likely to challenge opinions and decisions offered by the CEO and other Board members.

2. **Establish a Board Conflict-of-Interest Policy.**
    The policy should explain conflict of interest, give examples, and specify what Board members can do to report and avoid apparent or real conflict-of-interest situations.

    See the "Sample Board Conflict-of-Interest Policy" on page 264.

3. **Establish a Whistleblower Policy.**
    The policy should specify how Board members, staff and others (the Whistleblower) can readily report apparent or actual events of illegal, unethical or inappropriate behaviors and practices, without retribution to the Whistleblower.

    See "Sample Whistleblower Policy" on page 277.

4. **Establish a Document Retention/Destruction Policy.**
    The policy should specify which documents (hardcopy and computer-based) are retained and for how long, how documents are protected, and how documents are made readily available in the event of potential or actual criminal proceedings that might involve those documents.

    See "Sample Document Retention/Destruction Policy" on page 278.

5. **Establish a Board ethics policy.**
    The policy should suggest behaviors for Board members to follow and/or avoid in order to ensure legally compliant, fair and equitable dealings when acting as members of the nonprofit's Board.

    See "Sample Board Ethics Policy" on page 267.

6.   **Utilize financial audits and/or reviews.**
        The reporting of accurate financial information to the public is a strong requirement for
        achieving transparency and accountability. One approach to verifying financial accuracy is
        via reviews and/or audits. Not all nonprofits are required to undergo annual financial audits.
        (Nonprofits should identify requirements for audits by contacting the appropriate
        government agency, for example, the Attorney General's office in their states in the USA.)
        There are different types of financial analysis and services related to audits and reviews,
        ranging from a basic review of financial practices, to the auditing for financial practices and
        their resulting financial data. A significant benefit of a review, especially an audit, is having
        an outsider's objective conclusions and recommendations regarding financial practices
        and/or information.

7.   **Review and approve the annual filing to the appropriate tax agency.**
        Certain charitable organizations in the USA must file an IRS Form 990 (or Form 990-EZ or
        Form 990-PF) to the Internal Revenue Service. Board members must be sure that the
        information in the Form is complete and accurate. Members must also formally approve the
        Form, thereby, indicating that each member is aware of the information and asserts that it is
        accurate.

8.   **Train Board members how to analyze and make decisions about finances.**
        Frequently, nonprofit Boards have one member – the Treasurer – who is comfortable dealing
        with "the numbers." Each and every Board member is responsible to ensure that the
        numbers are accurate and that the nonprofit is making the best decisions about those
        numbers. Therefore, all Board members should receive relevant, up-to-date and accurate
        financial information, and all should be trained how to understand and respond to that
        information.

9.   **Make publicly available, information about finances, governance and operations.**
        For example, on the nonprofit's Website, provide: Articles of Incorporation, By Laws, most
        recent strategic plan, annual report, list of Board members, Board policies, Form 990s,
        recent audited financial reports and a list of funders.

10.   **Finally, be accountable to verify that programs are meeting community needs.**
        Accountability is about more than efforts to avoid losing lawsuits – it is about Board
        members doing their primary job to verify that their nonprofit is indeed meeting the need in
        the community that the nonprofit was formed to meet.

How to Have Productive Board Meetings

How to Design Successful Board Meetings

Most of the work that gets done by Board members gets done in their meetings, held usually once each month or every other month, depending on the preferences of Board members. Successful Board meetings are critical to the effectiveness of a Board. There are key steps that go a long way toward ensuring that Board meetings are highly productive.

1. **Establish means by which Board members make decisions in meetings.**
    Members might choose to make decisions by vote or by consensus, as discussed in the previous section, "Board Decision Making."

2. **Establish ground rules that guide members' participation in the meeting.**
    Consider the following as ground rules:

    a. Meetings start and stop on time.

    b. Focus on priorities, not on personalities.

    c. Everyone participates.

    d. All opinions are honored.

    e. No interruptions.

    f. No sidebars (or conversations not involving the main group).

3. **Carefully prepare the Board agenda with topics, types of actions and timing per topic.**
    Typically, the Board Chair and the Chief Executive (if the nonprofit has a CEO) prepare the Board agenda. The agenda should be carefully designed to include:

    a. Items that are strategic (unless the Board is a working or collective Board, in which case, the agenda might include day-to-day matters).

    b. What kinds of actions are sought from Board members regarding each item, for example, to make a decision, inform members, consider a resolution, etc.

    c. Estimated time to attend to each item. An example of a useful agenda is included in the next section.

4. **Board Chair, CEO and committee Chairs should prepare for the upcoming meeting.**
    People in these roles should prepare for succinct presentation and support of discussion in the meeting.

5. **Provide meeting materials to all Board members before the Board meeting.**
    Board members need time to sufficiently review materials for the meeting. This is critical. (Often, the hallmark of a good Board is that materials are provided in advance of the Board meeting.)

6. **All Board members should review materials before the meeting.**
    They should come prepared to deal with each topic on the agenda.

7. **The Board Chair should diligently facilitate according to the agenda.**
    The Chair watches the clock, guides discussion to closure and action, and starts and stops the meeting on time. The notion of stopping a Board meeting when it is scheduled to stop might seem heavy-handed to some. On the other hand, the notion of extending a meeting until every Board member feels that an issue has been adequately addressed, usually extends meetings far past when planned. That extension is often one of the biggest causes of Board member burnout. Therefore, facilitate according to the time planned on the agenda, and if a topic has not been suitably addressed within that time, then identify means to get more information for a later discussion, vote on the topic now or dismiss the topic.

The following agenda should be modified by the nonprofit according to its own nature and needs.

Table III:3 – Sample Board Meeting Agenda

[Name of Agency]
Board Meeting Agenda
[Month Day, Year] [Location] [Planned Starting Time to Ending Time]

Activity	Required Action	Allotted Time
Call to order		9:00 – 9:05
Approve minutes from previous meeting	Approval	9:05 – 9:10
Review status of implementation of strategic plan	Recognize effort well done	9:10 – 9:30
Chief Executive Officer's Report	Review highlights, trends and any issues	9:30 – 9:45
Finance Committee's Report - Review monthly financial statements	Review highlights, trends and any issues	9:45 – 10:05
Fundraising Committee's Report - Present Fundraising Plan for coming fiscal year	Approve Fundraising Plan	10:05 – 10:25
Board Development Committee - Present Board Development Plan for coming fiscal year	Approve Board Development Plan Approve Plans for Retreat	10:25 – 10:40
Review of Actions from This Meeting	Establish action plan	10:40 – 10:45
Roundtable Evaluation of Meeting	Record evaluations	10:45 – 10:55
Adjourn		11:00

Questions Your Board Members Should Always Ask

Board members must not be afraid to ask the hard questions of the Chief Executive and each other. That is always better than just "numbing out" and only focusing on whatever is put in front of them during Board meetings. If you ever really want to make a strategic impact on the nonprofit, then start asking some of the questions in Table III:4. This page could be in front of the Board members during their meetings to encourage strategic questioning.

Avoid "Sidebar Meetings"

A "sidebar meeting" occurs when two or more Board members convene without adequate notice to other Board members and end up addressing a matter that should be brought before the entire Board. Sidebar meetings do not provide fair and equitable discussion on matters – matters about which all Board members are legally responsible to address. This practice can be quite destructive to the sense of trust and decorum necessary to effectively operate as a Board of Directors.

If a Board member finds him/herself discussing a Board matter with another member outside of a formal Board meeting, the member should acknowledge to others present that the discussion should be brought to the entire Board. At this time, the member should offer to notify the Chair so that the matter can be placed on the agenda for the next meeting.

Roberts' Rules of Order – The 20% Used 80% of the Time

These rules lend some sense of order and efficiency to the exchange between members during Board meetings. The Robert's Rules can seem exhaustingly detailed and tedious, particularly for small- to medium-sized organizations. There are a few rules that apply the vast majority of the time. It is useful to know at least these rules. They include:

1. **Calling the meeting to order.**
   This formally starts the meeting.

2. **Making a motion.**
   This is done by a member who wants all Board members to direct attention to a specific topic in order to take a specific action regarding that topic. A member makes a motion by saying "I make a motion to …". Common motions must be seconded by another Board member in order to initiate the motion, for example, to start discussion.

3. **Calling the question.**
   The Board Chair makes this formal gesture to end the discussion about a specific matter.

4. **Adjourning the meeting.**
   This formally ends the meeting.

There are practical references to a variety of Roberts Rules at http://www.jimslaughter.com/robertsrules.htm . Also consider Roberta's Rules of Order at http://www.robertasrulesoforder.com/book/articles .

Table III:4 – Strategic Questions for Board Meetings

Programs and Services

1. What are the different programs? Who does each serve? How? For what desired results?
2. How do we know who really needs our programs? Have we verified our impressions?
3. Who are our collaborators? Who might be? Have we reached out to them? Should we?
4. What are the results of each program? How do we know? Are those results acceptable?
5. Are programs really meeting the community need that we were formed to meet?

Board Operations and Meetings

1. Do all Board members know their roles? How do we know?
2. Are all Board members participating actively in Board operations? If not, what do we do?
3. Are the agenda topics the topics that we should be addressing? How do we know?
4. Are all pertinent topics being addressed effectively? How do we know?
5. Are all Board members attending meetings?
6. Are all members actively taking part in deliberations and actions?
7. Are meetings very effective? How do we know?
8. Are we doing our job to verify that the nonprofit is meeting a specific community need?

Personnel (Chief Executive Officer, Paid Staff and Volunteers)

1. Do we have the best people for the jobs? How do we know?
2. Are they doing their jobs well? How do we know?
3. Are all personnel policies up-to-date and adhered to? How do we know?
4. What if the CEO suddenly left the organization? What would we really do?

Fundraising

1. How much money do we need from fundraising? How do we know?
2. Have we identified all of the possible sources of funding from individuals, foundations, corporations and the government? How do we know that we identified all sources?
3. What is the best way to approach each of the sources? How do we know?
4. Are all the sources being approached effectively? Is the Board involved?
5. Are all Board members making a contribution to the organization? How do we know?

Promotions and Public Relations

1. What different groups of stakeholders do we have? Clients? Funders? Collaborators?
2. What image do we want each to have about our nonprofit? Do they have it? Really?
3. Are we clearly conveying the benefits of each of our programs to stakeholders? Really?

Finances, Rules and Regulations

1. What are the most recent highlights, trends and issues depicted by recent financial reports?
2. Are the financial numbers really accurate? How do we know?
3. Are all taxes being paid? How do we know?
4. Are all rules, regulations and fiscal policies being followed? How do we know?

If Your Gut Tells You "Something Is Not Right," Then SAY SO Now!

What to Document In Your Board Meeting Minutes

Meeting minutes are documented descriptions of the key activities and decisions made by Board members during a certain, regular Board meeting, for example, the meeting held each month. Minutes can be considered legal documents by the courts, and they represent the official actions of the Board. Many assert that if it is not in the minutes, it did not happen.

There is no standardized level of content and format for Board minutes. In courts, as important as what you did is that you were reasonable when you did it. Therefore, sufficient information should be included to describe how Board members reasonably came to reasonable decisions.

On your minutes, include at least: the name of the organization, date and time of meeting, who called it to order, who attended and if there is a quorum, all motions made, any conflicts of interest or abstentions from voting, when the meeting ended and who developed the minutes.

Usually, the Board Secretary drafts the minutes during meetings, but this can be done by anyone else in the meeting who is willing, as long as other members agree that the person is charged to write the minutes. Soon after the meeting, the minutes are distributed to Board members for their review and approval in the next meeting. The unapproved minutes should be marked "draft," until approved. In the next Board meeting, any changes should be amended to the minutes and a new version, still marked "draft," should be submitted until the Board approves the minutes. Approved minutes should be retained in a manual and shared with all Board members.

The following sample represents the typical format and content of a Board meeting minutes report. This sample should be customized to the particular culture and purpose of the organization.

Sample of Board Meeting Minutes

Name of Organization

(Board Meeting Minutes: Month Day, Year)
(time and location)

Board Members:
Present: Bhata Bhatacharia, Jon White Bear, Douglas Carver, Elizabeth Drucker, Pat Kyumoto, Jack Porter, Mary Rifkin and Leslie Zevon
Absent: Melissa Johnson
Quorum present? Yes
Others Present:
Executive Director: Sheila Swanson
Other: Susan Johns, Consulting Accountant

Proceedings:
Meeting called to order at 7:00 p.m. by Chair, Elizabeth Drucker
Reviewed minutes from June 12, Board meeting. APPROVED.

Chief Executive Officer's Report
- Recommend that if we are not able to find a new facility by the end of this month, the organization should stay where it is in the current location over the winter. Board discussion, Moved by Johns to extend facilities study by three months, seconded by Porter. APPROVED.
- Staff member, Jackson Browne, and Swanson attended the National Practitioner's Network meeting in Atlanta last month and gave a brief extemporaneous presentation. Both are invited back next year to give a longer presentation about our organization. Staff requested Board approval of $1,500 expenditure for next year's trip. Drucker asked if funds were available, and Browne explained funds were available. Moved by Johns to approve funds, seconded by Bhatacharia. APPROVED. Drucker asserts that our organization must ensure its name is associated with whatever materials are distributed at that practitioner's meeting next year. Board briefly discussed Drucker's assertion. Drucker also recommended organization should generate revenues where possible from the materials, too. NOTED
- Swanson mentioned that staff member, Sheila Anderson's husband is ill and in the hospital, and requests agency send a gift of no more than $25 to Anderson's husband, expressing the organization's sympathy and support. Moved by Browne to send gift, seconded by Porter. APPROVED.

Finance Committee Report Provided by Chair, Elizabeth Drucker
- Drucker explained that consultant, Susan Johns, reviewed the organization's bookkeeping procedures and found them to be satisfactory, in preparation for the upcoming yearly financial audit. Johns recommends that our agency ensure the auditor provides a management letter along with the audit financial report. Moved by Browne to request management letter from auditor, seconded by Porter. APPROVED.
- Drucker reviewed highlights, trends and issues from the balance sheet, income statement and cash flow statement. Issue includes that high amounts of accounts receivables require Finance Committee attention to policies and procedures in order to ensure our organization receives more payments on time. Brief discussion of the issues and suggestions about how to ensure receiving payments on time. MOTION by White Bear to accept financial statements, seconded by Porter. APPROVED.

Board Development Committee's Report Provided by Chair, Douglas Carver
- Carver reminded the Board of the scheduled retreat coming up in three months, and provided a drafted retreat schedule for Board review. MOTION by Drucker to accept the retreat agenda, seconded by Zevon. APPROVED.
- Carver presented members with a draft of the reworded By Laws paragraph that would allow members to conduct Board meetings via Webcast. Carver suggested review and a resolution to change the By Laws accordingly. Kyumoto suggested that Swanson first seek legal counsel to verify if the proposed change is consistent with state statute. Swanson agreed to accept this action and notify members of the outcome in the next Board meeting. MOTION to accept the retreat agenda pending outcome of verification with statute, seconded by Zevon. APPROVED.

Other Business

- Porter noted that he was working with staff member, Jacob Smith, to help develop an information management systems plan, and that two weeks ago he (Porter) had mailed Board members three resumes from consultants to help with the plan. In the mailing, Porter asked members for their recommendation for a consultant from among the list of resumes. (NOTE: Zevon noted that she was also a computer consultant and was concerned about conflict of interest in her Board role regarding this selection, and asked to abstain from this selection. Members discussed and agreed. Zevon ABSTENTION .) After extended discussion, motion by Kyumoto to hire Lease-or-Buy Consultants, second by Drucker. APPROVED.
- Swanson announced that she had recently hired a new Secretary, Karla Writewell. NOTED.

Assessment of the Meeting

- Kyumoto noted that the past three meetings have run over the intended two-hour time slot by half an hour. He asked members to be more mindful and focused during discussions, and suggested that the Board Development Chair take an action to identify solutions to this issue. Drucker AGREED.

Meeting adjourned at 9:30 p.m.
Minutes submitted by Secretary, Bhata Bhatacharia.

When to Have an Executive Session (in camera)

An Executive Session (sometimes called *in camera*) is a meeting of the Board without the CEO and staff in attendance. (Do not confuse Executive Session with Executive Committee, which is a type of Board committee.) Reasons to have an Executive Session include, for example, to discuss evaluation and compensation of the Chief Executive, conflicts between Board members, or to address pending or current lawsuits against the organization and/or its members. Different applications of Boards, for example, Church Boards or School Boards, might have different requirements about when to use Executive Sessions. School Boards might meet in Executive Session if members are discussing the purchase of land. Meeting minutes should reflect that the Board met in Executive Session and mention the general topic.

It is always a good idea to have an Executive Session at least once a year. With only the Board members in attendance, they often feel more freedom to share opinions, for example, about the performance of the Chief Executive. Also, without the Chief Executive in attendance, members often take more control over their agenda – they address matters they feel are important, rather than matters driven by the Chief Executive.

When to Have Open Board Meetings

An open Board meeting is a meeting in which anyone can attend. The law is not universal or consistent about which Board meetings always have to be open for all nonprofits, although there is strong public opinion that all Board meetings of nonprofits should be open in order to ensure strong transparency and accountability. Organizations where open meetings might be required are those with a large government contract, a charter school or an association. Contact your Attorney General in the USA, or provincial agency in Canada, to verify your local requirements.

There is more information about open meetings at http://www.idealist.org/if/idealist/en/FAQ/QuestionViewer/default?section=03&item=07 .

How to Measure the Quality of Each Board Meeting

It is not uncommon to hear a Board member lament that the Board meetings are a major waste of time. Usually that lament is made outside of the meetings when not much can be done about it. This is very unfortunate, considering that it does not take much time at all to conduct a very effective evaluation of the meeting – and to do so in the meeting when useful discussion can occur about the results of the evaluation.

There are a variety of approaches to evaluating meetings, some as simple as asking all the Board members a question or two about the quality of the meeting. Other approaches include having members complete a checklist of important aspects of a Board meeting, and then discussing results in the next meeting.

One of the most powerful approaches to evaluating a meeting is the following procedure, which is facilitated by the Board Chair right before adjourning the meeting. Proceeding around the table, each Board member, out loud to other members:

1.   Rates the quality of the meeting from "1" (lowest) to "5" (highest).

2.   Explains why he/she gave the rating that he/she did.

3.   Explains what he/she could have done *during that same meeting* for the meeting to be getting a rating of 5 now from him/her.

The above procedure helps to ensure that, during the meeting, all Board members take strong ownership in ensuring a high-quality meeting.

For more information, see the topic "Meeting Management" in the Free Management Library[SM] at http://www.managementhelp.org/misc/mtgmgmnt.htm .

How to Ensure a High-Quality Board

One Set of "Best Practices" for Your Board

"Best practices" are practices conducted by individuals, groups or organizations that are widely respected for some particular expertise or activity that involves those practices. For example, highly respected Boards often are perceived as conducting certain practices, such as those practices listed below. Best practices are increasingly being questioned as credible for assessing performance or competence because identification of best practices can be a highly subjective activity. In addition, the concept of high-performance is a highly subjective concept, as well. Best practices are often very dependent on who is concluding the best practice and on the particular context in which the performance or competence is being assessed. (There is evidence that a nonprofit can provide very useful services to the community, despite having a highly ineffective Board. However, there is great risk in these situations, for example, if the CEO suddenly leaves the organization or the nonprofit undertakes robust fundraising efforts – funders want to see evidence of a strong Board.)

As a potential benefit to you, the following is offered as one set of best practices that is likely to produce a high-performing Board. In this context, high-performing might be very concisely interpreted as a Board with members who consistently enact plans and policies that produce programs and services which effectively and efficiently meet the needs of the public that the nonprofit serves. Certainly there are other traits of a high-performing Board, for example, strong planning, respected by stakeholders, effective evaluations, independent thinkers, and ability to manage conflict and achieve consensus. The following list is about the core, or most important, best practices – practices that, if followed, usually will result in other best practices being followed, as well. The following list suggests the order in which to do the practices.

Note that the following list is focused on actions, not on grand outcomes. Many experts and articles provide very good suggestions about the overall outcomes that high-performing Board members should have, for example, accountability, transparency, legitimacy and credibility. The following list is about practices, or actions, that can help to achieve those overall outcomes. The list applies to any model of Boards.

1. **Adopt a Board calendar of annual activities that has many best practices in it.**
   Members' reference to the calendar will ensure that the Board does all of the most important Board activities and when to do them, for example, staffing the Board, evaluating the Board, evaluating the Chief Executive, strategic planning, reviewing By Laws, etc. The calendar is probably one of the most important policies for Board members.

 See the sample Board calendar on page 257.

2. **Conduct a brief Board training annually.**
   This can be a 20-minute review of the responsibilities of any nonprofit governing Board. (Do not confuse this with Board orientation, which is all about the unique aspects of the nonprofit, for example, its programs, Board members, staff, when and where to meet, etc.)

See "How to Train Board Members on Their Roles" on page 73.

3.   **Do a Board orientation to new members or when the organization changes.**
     Orient members to the unique aspects of the nonprofit, including to fellow Board members, and the nonprofit's history, programs and staff members. Discuss major accomplishments achieved by the nonprofit. Mention its major funders.

See information about Board orientation on page 72.

4.   **Do strategic planning at least yearly – include stakeholders' input.**
     Be sure the strategic plan includes an action plan of who will be doing what and by when – do not do only the top-level mission, vision and values – be specific. Many times, this is even more important than having a very inspirational and well-crafted mission statement. Do the 20% of effort that generates 80% of a relevant, realistic and flexible plan.

5.   **Use committees (or task forces), each with charters and work plans.**
     Ensure that each committee or task force has a work plan that specifies what that group is to be doing and when. Some Boards prefer not to use committees, which is fine, but then there should be some means to occasionally focus Board resources specifically on a current priority when needed.

See "How to Organize Committees (If You Use Them)" on page 82.

6.   **Ensure that each member is on at least one committee (task force) with specific goals.**
     The best way to keep good Board members is to be sure they have something to do – the best way to get rid of inactive members is to make sure that they have something to do and then making an issue if they are not doing it. Do not be reluctant to make sure each member has specific assignments and deadlines to complete them, for example, is on a committee with a work plan – that approach gives them straightforward means to bring value to the organization and the community.

7.   **Review meeting materials at least one week before the Board meetings.**
     One of the best ways to ensure that a Board is not effective is to overwhelm members during meetings with materials that they have not seen before. A mark of a very good Board is each member getting the materials in time to review them before meetings.

8.   **Facilitate meetings to an agenda with topics and times – discuss, decide and move on.**
     The agenda should include important topics, the amount of time allotted for discussion of each topic, and the kind of action that is needed regarding that topic, for example, an action to make a decision. If a decision had not been reached within the time allotted on the agenda, then the Board should delegate the topic to a committee or staff member for further research so that a decision can be made in the next meeting. Ineffective Boards too often address the first topic on the agenda until all members are so tired and frustrated that they ignore the rest of the topics on the agenda and then they just leave the meeting.

9.   **Produce approved meeting minutes.**
      Experts often assert that "if it ain't in the minutes, then it didn't happen." Although minutes can sometimes seem to be an administrative irritation to complete and approve, the minutes ultimately can cultivate a strong sense of accomplishment among Board members. Also, if and when Board members decide to improve their operations, they often can clearly see the symptoms of their problems in the minutes of their meetings, for example, too many members missing meetings, discussions that do not lead to decisions, members often straying from the agenda, etc.

10.   **Train all members about how to analyze – and make decisions – about finances.**
      Rather than providing massive amounts of numbers to Board members, provide reports with "highlight, trends and issues." Highlights are important points to notice, trends are tendencies that could become issues later on, and issues are priorities that need decisions now. Do not count on just one Board member (the Treasurer) to do all of the financial analysis and decisions for the Board.

11.   **Conduct a brief Board self-evaluation yearly**.
      Have each Board member privately complete a simple questionnaire about the quality of Board operations – the questionnaire could ask about the occurrence of the best practices on this list in this guide. It should ask if members are verifying that community needs are being met. Then compile the results of the questionnaires and share them with the entire Board.

See "Sample Board Self-evaluation Form" on page 273.

12.   **Remove "dead wood" per the By Laws and a Board attendance policy.**
      One of the most destructive tendencies of ineffective Boards is the tolerance of poor attendance or participation among Board members. That tendency indirectly conveys to all members that it is permissible to not be effective. To very busy volunteer Board members – members who might already be on several other Boards – it can be very seductive to become less effective on the Board. Instead, if members miss meetings without notifying members beforehand, then enact a Board attendance policy to remove those members. If members sit in meetings and do not speak up, then contact them privately to help them assess how they can become more active. Realize that you deserve – and will significantly benefit from – a Board with active members.

See "Sample Board Attendance Policy" on page 275.

How to Conduct Board Retreats For Planning and Renewal

A Board retreat is a special-purpose meeting scheduled other than during the regular (usually monthly) meetings. Retreats are used for a variety of applications, including for Board members to reflect on the quality of their Board and how to improve it.

Common Uses of Board Retreats

▪   **Conduct Board member orientation and training.**
     Members learn about the nonprofit and their roles as members of a governing Board.

- **Team building**
  Members become more acquainted, and build strong structures and relationships.

- **Strategic planning**
  Board and staff members, and stakeholders, clarify the mission and organizational priorities.

- **Deal with a specific challenge**
  For example, retreats might be used to consider a merger or reorganization.

Designing Retreats

Like any other substantial meeting, it is important to follow sound principles of meeting management, including:

1. **Clarify what outcomes the Board wants as a result of the retreat.**
    Include Board members and staff in this decision.

2. **Design an agenda that will guide the group to achieving those results.**
    Include:

    a. Opening and welcome to participants.

    b. Specification of results desired from the retreat.

    c. Major topics to be addressed.

    d. Time allotted to each topic.

    e. The desired result from each topic, for example, a decision or resolution.

    f. Who will lead that section of the retreat.

    g. Evaluation of the retreat.

3. **Have the agenda and invitation list reviewed by several of the intended participants.**

4. **Invite everyone who is critical to achieving that result, including key staff members.**

5. **Send a written invitation them well in advance of the meeting.**
    Include a cover letter and the agenda. Require them to call ahead to say they are coming or not. Be sure you let everyone know who else will be at the meeting.

6. **A week before the retreat begins, call attendees to remind them of attendance.**

7. **During the meeting, select a recorder who documents discussions and decisions.**

8. **At the end of the retreat, review all action items – who is to do what and by when.**

9. **Immediately after the retreat, disseminate written minutes from the Board retreat.**

Where to Conduct Retreats

Attempt to locate the Board retreat somewhere other that at the nonprofit's place of business or operation. Possibilities are:

- Board member's houses

- Corporate (for-profit) Boardrooms

- Community centers

- Public libraries

- Retreat centers

How to Help Board Members "Diagnose" Nonprofit's Problems – Rather than Focus on Symptoms

Board members are charged to make very important decisions about their nonprofits. In their roles, they often hear about major, ongoing problems. Often, they do not fully understand the situation and so they end up making the wrong decisions. Staff members also do not understand how to identify the true causes of problems. So everyone ends up focusing on the symptoms of the problems, rather than solving the problems. Here are some common examples:

- Board members show up at Board meetings, but do not seem to get anything done. Members and the Chief Executive continue to blame each other for not "doing their jobs" – but nothing changes.

- The nonprofit keeps running out of money. Board and staff members continue to believe that the solution to their problems is to keep doing more fundraising – but the cash crises continue to occur. So the Chief Executive blames the Board for not doing enough fundraising.

- Programs have very poor attendance from clients. Board members continue to tell the Chief Executive that he/she must do a better job of getting the word out – but increased advertising is not making any difference. So the Board blames the Chief Executive.

- Board members continue to hear about increasing conflicts and high turnover of staff. Board members tell the Chief Executive to get some leadership training. The Chief Executive does, and later tells the Board members that the staff problems are also caused from 1) no clear direction in the nonprofit as a result of no strategic planning; and 2) insufficient resources, especially from the ineffective fundraising of Board members. Board members disagree and lose confidence in their Chief Executive.

In these examples, the Board and Chief Executive are dealing with the symptoms of the problem, rather than the real causes. A high-quality Board of Directors can see beyond the symptoms to get at the real solutions. Table III:5 and the rest of this section describe one way to understand the inner workings of nonprofits and how to be more successful at resolving problems for the long-term. Notice how the functions in a nonprofit seem to occur in a cycle, from top to bottom and back to the top again. As you read the rest of this section, notice how problems often show up as symptoms in functions near the bottom of the table, but are resolved by addressing functions at the top.

Table III:5 – Cycle of Important Functions in Nonprofits

Inputs: Unmet community needs, input from stakeholders, funding, laws and regulations, etc.		
System Loop	**Major Functions**	**Comments**
Planning	Strategic planning for organization (mission? vision? values? goals?)	▪ All activities are integrated with each other.
	Planning for programs (similar to business planning) (clients? outcomes? services? Marketing? costs?)	
	Resource planning (people? fundraising/revenue? technologies? other?)	▪ Driving force behind all activities is leadership among Board and staff.
Developing	Revenue / fundraising development (for major activities)	
	Board, staff and volunteer development (recruiting, training, organizing)	
	Development of other resources (facilities, supplies, policies, procedures, etc.)	▪ Leadership sets direction, guides resources toward the direction, and makes adjustments to keep resources on track.
	Supervision and teamwork	
	Program operations	
	Advertising and promotions	
Operating	Facilities management	
	Financial management	▪ Strategic vision and goals set the direction for the organization and suggest the performance goals for Board and staff.
	Administration	
	Board	
	Individuals	
Evaluating	Programs	▪ Communicating about these goals is key to achieving them.
	Processes	
	Organization	
Outputs: community needs that were verified to have been met by the nonprofit, for example, by conducting market research and also program outcome evaluations		

Table III:5 includes the roles and the integration of standard management functions, including the planning, implementation and evaluation of programs, staffing, marketing, finances, fundraising and facilities. The relationships between these functions and the symptoms of issues are described here.

Planning

1. **Poor strategic planning causes symptoms throughout the organization.**
   During strategic planning, members of the Board and staff determine the overall purpose (mission) and direction (vision and goals) for the nonprofit, as well as the methods (values, strategies and programs) for the nonprofit to work toward the purpose and direction. The strategic planning process provides direction and efficiency to all other major functions in the organization. Thus, if strategic planning is not done well, symptoms of the problem can show up in Board operations, programs, staffing, fundraising and finances. To address these symptoms, strategic planning must be improved.

2. **Poor program planning causes symptoms, especially in finances and fundraising.**
   During program planning, the marketing research (or "inbound marketing") activities are conducted to identify: specific community needs for the nonprofit to meet, what outcomes are needed to meet those needs, what specific groups of clients to serve, and how to serve them to achieve those outcomes. Thus, if program planning is not done well, programs will not be targeted where they are needed or will not be meeting the needs of clients. This will result in poor participation of programs and also in decreased revenues and ineffective fundraising. Many problems commonly associated with financial shortfalls and fundraising are really the result of poor program planning. Until program planning is improved, attempts to improve fundraising and financial management are likely to be ineffective.

3. **Poor resource planning causes symptoms, especially in staffing and funding.**
   During resource planning, planners identify what resources (the best Board and staff members, money, trainings, facilities, etc.) are needed to most effectively work toward the mission and to provide the best programs. Thus, if resource planning is not done well, the Board and staff members might not be the best for the nonprofit, and funding might be inadequate because the funders are not convinced of the need for specific resources. Facilities might be insufficient, as well. This can cause related symptoms, such as conflicts and burnout among Board and staff members. Many problems commonly associated with Boards, staffing and funding are really the result of poor resource planning, which, in turn, needs good strategic and program planning.

Developing

4. **Successful fundraising needs good strategic, program and resource planning.**
   Strategic and program planning clarifies what programs are needed and identifies budgets for the coming years. Program planning specifies how much money the programs might earn (expected revenues), how much money they might cost (expected expenses) and if there are any deficits (expenses exceeding revenue) for the programs. The deficits often are addressed by fundraising. If the planning for fundraising is not based on good strategic and program planning, then the fundraising target (the amount to raise by fundraising) will always be vague and changing, resulting in much frustration among those doing the fundraising. In addition, funders will quickly recognize that the nonprofit has not been doing the right kind of planning, so they will not be likely to invest in the nonprofit. Problems associated with fundraising often are symptoms of problems in strategic and program planning.

5. **Board, staff and volunteer development needs good strategic and program planning.**
    Members of the Board and staff are developed first by identifying what expertise is needed to achieve the goals in the strategic and program plans. Then the best Board and staff members are recruited, trained and organized in a manner that best achieves the goals in the strategic and program plans. If those plans are not done well, then ongoing confusion, conflicts and inefficiencies can occur, resulting in high turnover and poor performance of the Board and staff. Program and administrative operations can suffer. Problems with Board and staff members can be symptoms of poor overall planning and resource development, including poor recruitment, selection, organization and development of members.

6. **Successful operations require clarification of roles, and some policies and procedures.**
    There are a variety of types of resources (other than money and people) that need to be obtained and developed, for example, facilities, equipment, roles, policies and procedures. Perhaps most important among these resources are roles, policies and procedures. They form the "glue" that aligns and integrates the resources of money and people. If they are not established, they can cause significant symptoms, such as increasing inefficiencies, conflicts and turnover. The best solution to these conflicts might be to clarify roles, policies and procedures, rather than chastising people to make them get along better with each other.

Operating

By now, you understand that problems that show up in the day-to-day activities (for example, in supervision, program operations, financial management, fundraising, advertising, etc.) are often symptoms of larger problems in planning and resource development. Thus, to address those symptoms for the long-term, Board and staff members must ensure that planning and resource development are done well. Without that understanding among Board and staff members, they will likely continue to focus primarily on the symptoms, making things much worse in the long term.

Below, are descriptions of other major functions in nonprofits and how they are integrated and related to each other.

7. **Supervision and teamwork**
    A supervisor is someone who oversees the progress and productivity of people who report directly to the supervisor. Thus, a Board supervises the Chief Executive Officer, and a CEO supervises, for example, the Program Director (if the nonprofit chooses to have a CEO or any paid staff at all). Teamwork is about how people work together to coordinate goals, roles, leadership and communications. The activities of supervision and teamwork are critical to the success of a nonprofit because those activities ensure that goals are established in accordance with strategic and program goals, progress toward the goals is monitored, and adjustments are made among individuals to more effectively achieve the goals. Many times, recurring problems in other types of operating activities are really symptoms of poor teamwork.

8. **Program operations**
    This includes the ongoing activities that provide services directly to the clients. The nature of these activities depends on the types of needs met by the program. For example, health services often require highly trained program staff and technologies. Food shelves require large facilities to store groceries. The success of programs depends a great deal on the effectiveness of strategic and program planning and of teamwork in the organization.

9. **Advertising and promotions**

   These "outbound" marketing activities are geared to inform stakeholders (clients, funders, community leaders, etc.) about new and current programs, and also to keep those programs in the minds of stakeholders. Many times, problems in advertising and promotions are the result of poor program planning, such as unclear identification of what specific groups of clients should be served, the needs of each group and how the programs meet each need.

10. **Facilities management**

    This includes identifying what major facilities will be needed, such as buildings, equipment and computer systems, and ensuring those facilities are optimized for the most effective use. The need for major facilities is identified during resource planning. Thus, problems caused by lack of facilities often are a result of poor resource planning. Ineffective use of facilities might also be a symptom poor staff development.

11. **Financial management**

    Activities of financial management include documenting financial transactions (bookkeeping), generating and analyzing financial statements, and making management decisions based on the financial situation. This is usually done according to Board-approved fiscal policies and procedures. Many times, people report problems with finances when they really mean problems with inadequate funding. Those problems are often caused by ineffective program planning, resource development and/or fundraising activities. Problems that are truly about financial management often can be addressed by training personnel about bookkeeping, and about generating and analyzing financial statements.

12. **Administrative activities**

    This includes the extensive range of detailed activities that must be coordinated and conducted on a daily basis to ensure the efficient operations of the nonprofit. Many people think of these activities as clerical, or "paperwork." Problems with administrative tasks often are the result of poor resource planning and staff development, or lack of appreciation for policies and procedures.

Evaluating

13. **Board self-evaluation**

    Members of the Board of Directors should regularly evaluate the quality of their activities on a regular basis. Activities might include staffing the Board with new members, developing the members into well-trained and resourced members, discussing and debating topics to make wise decisions, and supervising the CEO. Probably the biggest problem with Board self-evaluation is that it does not occur frequently enough. As a result, Board members have no clear impression of how they are performing as members of a governing Board. Poor Board operations, when undetected, can adversely affect the entire organization.

14. **Staff and volunteer (individual) performance evaluation**

    Most of us are familiar with employee performance appraisals, which evaluate the quality of an individual's performance in their position in the organization. Ideally, those appraisals reference the individual's written job description and performance goals to assess the quality of the individual's progress toward achieving the desired results described in those documents. Continued problems in individual performance often are the results of poor strategic planning, program planning, staff development and communications. If overall planning is not done effectively, individuals can experience continued frustration, stress and low morale, resulting in their poor overall performance. If goals that result from planning are not clearly communicated, the individual may not understand how to succeed or perform effectively. Experienced leaders have learned that continued problems in performance are not always the result of a poor work ethic – the recurring problems may be the result of larger, more systemic problems in the organizations.

15. **Program evaluation**

Program evaluations have become much more common, particularly because many donors demand them as evidence that their investments are making a difference in their communities. Program evaluations are typically focused on the quality of the program's process, goals and/or outcomes. An ineffective program evaluation process often is the result of poor program planning – programs should be designed so they can be evaluated. It can also be the result of improper training about evaluation. Sometimes, leaders do not realize that they have the responsibility to verify to the public that the nonprofit is indeed making a positive impact in the community. When program evaluations are not performed well, or at all, there is little feedback to the strategic and program planning activities. When strategic and program planning are done poorly, the entire organization is adversely effected.

16. **Evaluation of cross-functional processes**

Cross-functional processes are those that span several functions, such as financial management across the central operating activities and all programs. Other common examples include information technology systems and quality management of services. Because these cross-functional processes span so many areas of the organization, problems in these processes can be the result of any type of ineffective planning, development and operating activities.

17. **Organizational evaluation**

Ongoing evaluation of the entire organization is a major responsibility of all leaders in the organization. Leaders sometimes do not recognize the ongoing activities of management to actually include organizational evaluations – but they do. The activities of organizational evaluation occur every day. However, those evaluations usually are not done systematically. As a result, useful evaluation information is not provided to the strategic and program planning processes. Consequently, both processes can be ineffective because they do not focus on improving the quality of operations in the workplace.

This section stressed the importance of having good strategic planning. Consider the book, *Field Guide to Nonprofit Strategic Planning and Facilitation*, from Authenticity Consulting, LLC. Go to the "publications" link at http://www.authenticityconsulting.com .

This section also stressed the importance of having good program planning. Consider the book, *Field Guide to Nonprofit Program Design, Marketing and Evaluation*, from Authenticity Consulting, LLC. Go to the "publications" link at http://www.authenticityconsulting.com .

How to Match Board's Priorities to Life Cycle of Nonprofit

Organizations go through different life cycles just like people do. Experienced leaders have learned to recognize the particular life cycle that an organization or program is currently going through. They understand the types of problems faced by the organization or program during its current life cycle. That understanding gives them a sense of overall perspective on the situation. It helps them to decide how to respond to current decisions and problems in the workplace. It helps them to focus on instilling practices to resolve problems and not on blaming personalities.

For example, many nonprofits are started by very visionary, inspirational leaders. However, as the nonprofits continue to expand in size and programs, visionary leaders might struggle to attend to the more operational practices that form the foundation for continued growth. As a result, there might be increasing confusion and conflicts about roles in the organization at the same time as increasing pressures to provide more services. Board members and other leaders might tend to blame the founders for these increasing problems. However, resolution often comes from recognizing that these are common symptoms of organizations going through transitions in life cycles. The cause is broken systems, not broken people.

 See "Recovering From Founder's Syndrome" on page 192.

There are various views on life cycles. Usually, the cycles are highly integrated and not always sequential in order. Table III:6 depicts a perspective on life cycles that is straightforward to understand and describe to others. From this perspective, the phases include infancy, growth and maturity. Decline, stagnation or growth can occur between the infancy, growth and maturity phases. Board members might attend to different priorities, depending on the particular life cycle of the organization.

In the Infancy Phase, priorities for Board members would be to:

- Gain a clear understanding of the mission and programs of the nonprofit.

- Learn the roles and responsibilities of a governing Board of Directors.

- Develop Board policies about By Laws, staffing, making decisions, etc.

- Organize into standard committees or task forces, for example, Finance and Fundraising.

In the Growth Phase, priorities for Board members would be to:

- Ensure that strategic planning occurs, including goals to manage growth.

- Decide if more resources, including staff and funding, are needed.

- Expand the Board with necessary skills or representation to address each strategic goal.

- Systematize Board functions, for example, financial analysis and fundraising.

Table III:6 – One Perspective On Nonprofit Organizational Life Cycles

Infancy Phase	Growth Phase	Maturity Phase
• Clarify mission, vision and values	• Focus on effectiveness of programs and services	• Sustain momentum in progress and operations
• Firm up the leadership systems, including Board and CEO role	• Focus on efficiencies through policies and procedures	• Focus on innovation
• Identify clients and stakeholders	• Expand programs and services, especially current services to new clients	• Cultivate renewal among Board and staff members
• Clarify desired outcomes from programs and services	• Accomplish diverse fundraising streams for increased sustainability	• Focus on succession planning and risk management
• Clarify best methods to deliver programs and services	• Document successful operations	• More diversification of funding streams
• Build a strong, positive image in the community	• Attend to longer-range planning	• Share learning with other people and organizations
• Build infrastructure and lay groundwork for future sustainability	• Implement and refine plans and policies	• Expand services, especially new services to new clients
	• Expand evaluations and accountabilities, and capture learnings	• Seek to successfully duplicate model elsewhere
	• Systematize major functions, including systematic plans	• Attend to even longer-range planning
		• Successfully manage change and transformation

In the Maturity Phase, priorities for Board members would be to:

• Renew Board operations with new members and stronger self-evaluations.

• Diversify funding sources among individuals, foundations, corporations and government.

• Increase effectiveness through innovation in program methods and collaborations.

• Explore whether to expand or duplicate programs elsewhere.

 An excellent resource about nonprofit life cycles and what Board members should do in each life cycle, is *The 5 Life Stages of Nonprofit Organizations* by Judith Sharken Simon (Amherst H. Wilder Foundation, 2001).

How Board Members Can Evaluate Their Board

Board members are accountable to the public to ensure that their nonprofit is indeed meeting the specific community need that the nonprofit was formed to meet. It is not unusual for members of a Board to fall into the same old way of doing things, an approach that becomes quite stale and even ineffective. One of the ways to quickly identify this problem is for the Board to conduct a self-evaluation.

But a Board should be evaluating itself once a year, whether there are apparent major problems or not. Members contribute a great deal of time, energy and expertise to the workings of their Board. They deserve to know how they are doing overall. Besides, it is a little hypocritical for Board members to evaluate the CEO and programs without evaluating the Board itself.

Board evaluation need not take substantial time and energy. Often a little bit of effort can reveal a lot of information about the quality of the Board. The "Sample Board Self-evaluation Form" referenced below can be used by all Board members and the Chief Executive (if the nonprofit has a CEO) to get an impression of how well the Board is doing in meeting its duties. This is a rather basic form for Board evaluation. But, if the evaluation is conducted open and honestly, the form should indicate how well the Board is doing in conducting its role of governance.

Each member (and the CEO, if the nonprofit has a CEO) should complete the form about four weeks before a Board retreat. They attach suggestions about how the Board could get higher ratings for any or all of the 20 considerations in the sample form.

Ideally, someone from outside the organization receives the completed forms, collates the results, and writes a report indicating the number of respondents and the overall ratings for each of the 20 categories. The report also conveys comments provided by respondents, unless they request their comments to be confidential.

See "Sample Board Self-evaluation Form" on page 273.

How to Ensure Full Participation of Board Members

To increase attendance and/or participation by Board members, consider some or all of the following ideas – the ideas are a compendium from the guidelines listed above. Realize that some Boards are not configured to have committees, so comments specific to committees may not apply.

1.   Require Board members to sign a contract that specifies what they are committing to, in their role as Board members.

See "Sample Board Member Contract" on page 266.

2.   Provide adequate orientation that describes the organization and its unique services. Be sure each committee has a clear charter that specifies how members are to participate in the committee.

3. Remember that the organization and its committees deserve strong attendance and participation. Do not fall prey to the perspective that "we're lucky just to get anyone at all." Set a standard for a strong level of participation.

4. Have ground rules that support participation and attendance. List them at the bottom of agendas and quickly mention them in every meeting.

5. Develop a Board attendance policy that specifies the number of times a member can be absent in consecutive meetings and in total meetings per time period.

 See "Sample Board Attendance Policy" on page 275.

6. In Board and committee meeting reports, list who is present and who is absent.

7. Monitor quorum requirements for the entire Board (the quorum is the minimum number of Board members who must be present for the Board to officially enact business, as listed in the By Laws). Repeated lack of a quorum is a clear indicator that the Board is in trouble.

8. Generate minutes for each Board or committee meeting in order to get closure on items and to help members comprehend the progress made by the Board or the committee.

9. Remove "dead wood" – inactive Board members. Potentially active members will appreciate the elimination of perpetually inactive members. Remember: one of the best ways to get and keep good Board members is to give them something to do; one of the best ways to get rid of "dead wood" is to give them something to do.

10. Consider using committees and subcommittees to more clearly organize individual Board member's responsibilities and to help them to more efficiently focus on achieving goals.

11. Ensure each committee Chair understands and can clearly convey the role of the committee to its members.

12. In the committees of Programs, Finance, Marketing and Fundraising, have at least one staff member participate to help with administrative support and providing information.

13. Conduct yearly committee evaluations that include a clear evaluation process in which each committee member evaluates the effectiveness of the committee, and receives a written report about its strengths and weaknesses and also how it can improve.

14. Consider having low-attendance Board members involved in some other form of service to the organization, than in the governing Board. For example, they might join an Advisory group or attend to special events rather than ongoing activities.

15. Have a "summit meeting" with committee members to discuss any attendance or participation problems and use a round-table approach so each person must speak up with their opinions.

16. Rotate in new members every year.

Field Guide to Developing, Operating and Restoring Your Nonprofit Board

PART IV:

BOARD AND

CHIEF EXECUTIVE

How to Hire Your Chief Executive Officer

Role of Typical Nonprofit Chief Executive Officer

Not all nonprofit Boards choose to utilize the role of Chief Executive in their organizations. When they do, the Chief Executive officially reports to the Board of Directors and often is referred to as the "Executive Director." It is the Board's officially responsibility to hire and supervise the Chief Executive, though the Board and CEO often work together in a "strategic partnership," as discussed in the next major section. The Chief Executive is a very important position in the nonprofit – the CEO is the person who often knows the most about the nonprofit's services and clientele. The first Chief Executive of the nonprofit is also commonly the founder of the nonprofit. Therefore, the Chief Executive plays a major role in first organizing the Board and helping members to do their job as Board members. Here is an overview of the CEO's role. Note that the description is provided in the context of a policy governing Board structure.

Board Administration and Support

Theory and law assert that the Board oversees and governs the nonprofit organization. Many experts assert that it is the CEO who actually facilitates the Board to do that job. The CEO often knows much more about the nonprofit organization than do the members of the Board. Consequently, the CEO must continually update Board members about the nonprofit organization, often by providing written reports that are reviewed during Board meetings. The CEO often helps with Board development and administration, sometimes in a Board Development Committee.

Program, Product and Service Delivery

The CEO is an expert on the nonprofit's programs and the needs of the nonprofit's clientele, including who they are, what their needs are and how those needs should be met. The CEO oversees design of programs to ensure that the organization continually meets the needs of clients in a highly effective fashion. Programs must be advertised and promoted to community stakeholders, particularly clientele and funders. The CEO works with the Board in this regard, often in a Programs Committee, to ensure that Board members are up-to-date about programs and their effectiveness.

Financial, Tax, Risk and Facilities Management

The CEO works with the Board Treasurer, or with a Finance Committee, to develop the yearly budget. The budget should be derived from results of the Board's yearly strategic planning. Once the budget is established, the CEO must operate the nonprofit in accordance with the strategic plan, and in a manner that is consistent with various laws and regulations, and also the policies of the Board. This includes ensuring that all relevant taxes are paid. It also includes managing the facilities of the organization in an efficient and safe fashion. The CEO works with the Board in this regard, often in a Finance Committee.

Human Resource Management

The CEO leads the effort to specify organizational roles and responsibilities among staff. Ideally, these roles and responsibilities are derived directly from results of regular strategic planning. The CEO oversees staffing, training and supervision of personnel. These activities must closely conform to up-to-date personnel policies and procedures that are reviewed on a regular basis by an employment law expert and also are approved by the Board. The CEO works with the Board in this regard, often in a Personnel Committee.

Community and Public Relations

The CEO often takes the lead in ensuring that the community continues to have a strong positive image of the nonprofit and its services. It is often most effective if the CEO works from a comprehensive marketing plan that is developed in conjunction with a Board Marketing Committee and that is approved by the Board.

Fundraising

One of the primary responsibilities of a nonprofit Board of Directors is to actively participate in fundraising activities. Unfortunately, many Board members do not assume this full responsibility. In any event, the CEO usually leads the fundraising efforts including: clarifying the amounts of monies needed to reach strategic goals, where to go to appeal for those monies, how to make those appeals, and making the appeals themselves. It is often most effective if the CEO works from a comprehensive fundraising plan that is developed in conjunction with a Board Fundraising Committee and that is approved by the Board.

See "Sample Executive Director Job Description" on page 256.

What Title Should We Use for Position?

New nonprofits might wonder what title to use to refer to its most senior staff position. Here are the most frequently considered titles.

Executive Director?

This is the traditional title and it is still used widely. It is clear to most people when they encounter the title that it refers to the "boss" of all of the staff members in a nonprofit. So it usually is not confusing to people who, for example, are referencing the title on salary surveys, searching for senior-level nonprofit jobs, or using to send correspondence to nonprofits.

Chief Executive Officer?

The trend is for nonprofits to choose this title more frequently. Organizations might choose it because it somehow conveys more stature than "Executive Director" or because it is more consistent with the title in the for-profit business world. Large nonprofits seem to use the title more than smaller nonprofits. This title is used much more in for-profits than nonprofits.

President?

This also seems to be used more frequently, and probably to convey stature in the position. However, it can be confusing because the role of Board Chair often is also referred to a "President." A related issue is that the title might somehow convey that the most senior staff position (President) is also a Board position (Board Chair) – many experts and stakeholders would rather not see the senior staff position also as a Board member.

Administrator?

This title is used particularly in hospitals. Similar to "President," it can be confusing because senior clerical staff members are sometimes referred to as "administrators," as well.

Wrong Reasons to Hire Chief Executive

There are several wrong reasons to hire a CEO, including:

1.   **To do fundraising right away.**
      If your organization does not have funds sufficient to pay at least the first six months of the CEO's salary, then you very likely have more important challenges to address than hiring a CEO. Taking on the challenge of adding a CEO role to the organization may make things worse. For example, you probably want to figure out why you do not have the needed funds in the first place. Is your Board entirely ineffectual at raising funds? Have you tried to raise funds, but funders do not find your appeals credible? Do you expect a new CEO to do the fundraising by him/herself? A good CEO will not join an organization that is already in a big financial crisis. A good CEO probably will not join an organization where he or she immediately has to start out trying to raise his or her own salary.

2.   **To provide overall direction to the nonprofit.**
      An organization gets its direction from formal or informal strategic planning. It is the job of the Board to ensure that strategic plan is implemented effectively. A good CEO will wonder why the Board has not been effective in establishing the direction for the organization.

3.   **To provide direction to the Board or help members to get unstuck.**
      If a Board lacks direction, then a new CEO role will probably only make things worse. A Board is not lacking direction or getting stuck because the nonprofit has no CEO. Rather, the Board lacks its own leadership. Or, perhaps there really is no reason for the nonprofit to exist in the first place – maybe there is no strong community need that could be met by the nonprofit's programs.

4.   **To expand skills on the Board.**
      The Board should expand its skills by bringing in new Board members, Board training, or by reducing its workload, including by reducing its expectations. Adding a CEO to the organization will likely increase demand for new skills on the Board and make things worse.

5.   **To manage Board details.**
      The last thing a good CEO will be interested in is managing the details of the Board. Instead, the Board members should recruit a volunteer Secretary or take turns managing details. Perhaps the Board needs a more efficient method of tracking its details. For example, perhaps the Board's member have not been recording all the meeting minutes that tracked planned activities and progress, or have not been using Board committee work plans to track assignments to committees, etc.

6.   **To energize Board members.**
      Adding a new CEO might cause even more fatigue or disinterest among Board members because the new role will require more time, energy and attention to define the new CEO role, hire a new CEO, orient the new CEO, supervise the CEO, etc.

7.　**To try to get volunteers.**
Often, it is much easier for a group of people (a Board) to recruit volunteers, than for one person (a CEO) to recruit volunteers. The way to get and retain good volunteers is to give them something to do. Someone has to decide what they are going to do. A new CEO will not know right away what to assign to volunteers. So, sooner or later, the Board members will have to get involved in the volunteer effort anyway.

Right Reasons to Hire Chief Executive

1.　**Nonprofit has sufficient funds to pay at least first six months of the CEO's salary.**
Some new CEOs might be interested and confident enough in their own fundraising ability that they would accept a job where they soon need to raise the rest of their salary. Although, many funders will question that approach, believing that it is somewhat of a risk for the nonprofit. However, some nonprofits might have sufficient short-term funds and strong enough programs that they can "jump start" further growth by adding a new CEO role. In that case, the nonprofit should have clear strategic goals and have been operating in a highly effective fashion.

2.　**To achieve strategic goals.**
The job of CEO should be geared primarily toward implementing the Board's plans and policies for the organization (especially in a policy governing Board). If the organization has done a good job of strategic planning and its programs are focused on meeting verified and clarified needs among clients (and there is sufficient funds for at least the first six months salary for the new CEO), then the nonprofit might be in a fair position to hire a CEO.

3.　**Nonprofit already has successful ongoing programs and projects.**
If those programs and projects are bringing in sufficient revenue to pay for a new CEO role and/or to warrant funds from a donor, then it might be a good idea to add a new CEO role to the organization in order to ensure effective leadership and management of the programs.

4.　**To meet long-established expectations of adding more staff.**
If the Board has been supervising staff, for example, in a working Board or collective Board arrangement (and the preceding criteria have been met), then it might be wise to add a new CEO role to the organization to supervise staff.

How to Determine Compensation for Your Chief Executive

The position of CEO is one of the most critical assets in the nonprofit. It is very important that the CEO's compensation be sufficient to attract, keep and help motivate a highly competent CEO. Determination of compensation is one of the most important activities of the Board. Much of that activity should be done even before a new CEO is hired. Unfortunately, there is no specific procedure that accurately and reliably computes exactly what you should pay your CEO. Instead, the process is one of addressing certain general and specific considerations (listed below), referencing some salary surveys to identify suitable pay ranges for the CEO role in the nonprofit and locale, and then making a best estimate on what might be a reasonable salary and set of benefits. This section explains major considerations and also suggests additional resources for salary and benefits information.

Board members' explanation of how they addressed each consideration can pose strong explanation and justification to stakeholders (for example, the Internal Revenue Service in the USA) for the compensation and benefits selected for the CEO. That explanation might be useful if, for example, the nonprofit was ever challenged about its compensation to the CEO. A team, or committee, of Board members, for example, a Personnel Committee, should address the considerations and make recommendations. However, the Board as a body (with at least a quorum) should approve the approach to determining compensation and benefits, and the resulting amount and benefits.

The following information is not offered as legal or tax advice. Nonprofits would benefit from consulting authorities in the related fields to gain the most up-to-date and thorough advice and materials. In addition to considering the information in this section, Board members would benefit from consulting a local specialist who has expertise in benefits and compensation for nonprofit executives. Any final compensation and benefits decisions should be carefully described in updated personnel policies.

Broad Considerations – Societal, Public and Community

1. **Consider the strengths of the economy, local and national.**
    For example, a lower unemployment rate might be reason to offer a higher salary in order to be more competitive with other jobs that the CEO might be able to get. A weak economy, for example, a rate of slow spending or low confidence in the economy, might suggest offer a lower salary.

2. **Consider public perception.**
    The public believes that nonprofits should be dedicated to meeting the needs of the public, not to making certain people rich. The public already has strong distaste for the seemingly exorbitant salaries of for-profit CEOs. Consequently, nonprofit executive compensation is increasingly under public scrutiny. So be very careful when determining compensation that the public does not perceive the compensation as being too high.

3. **Consider pay for similar positions in local nonprofits with similar nature of services.**
    For example, if yours is a social service agency, then consider the salaries of other social service agencies in your area. This consideration is one of the strongest to address when determining salary. (A list of sources of salary surveys is included later on in this section.)

Considerations – Organizational and Personal

1. **Consider the organization's personnel policies.**
    Personnel policies should have up-to-date guidelines about how to hire, manage and fire personnel in a fair, equitable and legally compliant manner. The guidelines should be reviewed annually by an expert on employment laws and then approved by the Board. Guidelines in the policies should be referenced in case they provide any direction about determining salaries.

2. **Consider the CEO's match to the requirements in the job description.**
    This consideration is probably the strongest when determining the CEO's salary. The job description should specify the duties and responsibilities of the position, along with ideal and minimal requirements for the position. The closer the match between the CEO's expertise and the requirements in the job description, the higher the salary that you would offer.

3. **Consider the match between the CEO's expertise and current strategic priorities.**
For example, if the nonprofit has strategic goals to build a firm foundation for further growth by instilling strong management systems, then a CEO with that kind of experience would warrant a higher salary.

4. **Consider the culture and values of the nonprofit.**
For example, if the culture values a highly inclusive and participatory management style, then a CEO with experience of working according to those values would warrant a higher salary. In contrast, some members of the Board and organization might strongly believe that nonprofits should always pay below-market rates because that is the duty of a nonprofit.

Nonprofits are strongly discouraged from a strategy to compensation that is based on offering the CEO a specific amount of money that greatly exceeds what the organization can actually afford, and then expecting the CEO to do robust fundraising to "earn" the remainder of his/her salary. The nonprofit should already have sufficient revenue from fees for services and/or fundraising to comprise much of that salary amount – and all Board members should participate in fundraising, not just the CEO. CEOs should be paid based on their expertise and performance, not primarily on the success of their fundraising.

Considerations – Some Restrictions and Limitations

1. **Consider expectations of donors and funders.**
For example, some foundations prefer that administrative costs (costs that are not specific to one program, such as the CEO's salary, facilities costs and general supplies) be under a certain threshold, for example under 20% of the operating budget. The higher the CEO's salary, the greater the likelihood that the nonprofit will exceed that threshold.

2. **Consider concerns and priorities of governmental agencies.**
For example, the Internal Revenue Service (IRS) in the USA poses excise taxes on tax-exempt nonprofits whose Board and staff members receive "excess benefit" from the nonprofit. Compensation should be "reasonable" and approved by the Board of Directors. The Board's deliberations and decisions about compensation should be fully described in the minutes of the Board meeting. The Board's approach to determining compensation for staff should be explained in the personnel policies, which also should be approved by the Board. If a Board member has a conflict of interest in the consideration, then he/she should abstain from that matter. Reasonable compensation might be determined by using salary surveys that depict salaries for similar positions in similar types of nonprofits in the locale. The IRS's Executive Compensation Compliance Initiative reviews compensation practices and identifies any areas of abuse. Nonprofits found to be paying unreasonable salaries can be exposed to an excise tax.

 There is more information about the IRS's concerns at
http://www.irs.gov/newsroom/article/0,,id=128328,00.html .

3. **Consider requirements for fair and ethical treatment.**
Compensation should not be based on the CEO's personal features, including age, race, gender, sexual orientation or physical disability. Compensation should be based on the person's expertise and match to the job requirements.

Forms of Compensation and Benefits

Although nonprofit Board members and executives are required by law not to receive stock as compensation, there are a wide variety of ways to compensate and reward nonprofit personnel (Board members are not to be paid, but can be reimbursed for expenses). Consider the following:

Payments

1. **Salary**
    This is the most common form of compensation. Executives in the USA usually are classified by the government as "exempt" (rather than "non-exempt"), meaning they usually should be paid a certain amount (a salary), regardless of the hours worked (within reason). Non-exempt personnel usually are paid by the hour (wages). Salary surveys are extremely useful when determining salary (there is more information about surveys later on in this section).

2. **Incentive-based compensation (bonuses)**
    Bonuses seem to be used increasingly as means to reward CEOs for his/her, or the organization's, performance. Ideally, the performance is measured in reference to pre-established and specific goals that were discussed with the CEO before this form of compensation is determined and issued.

3. **Salary adjustments**
    These are sometimes used when nonprofits do not have the funds to pay all of a salary payment. Instead, the nonprofit might issue a payment near the end of the year in order to make up for the amount that was not afforded and paid earlier. Sometimes these are paid as means to compensate a CEO who wanted other forms of benefits, such as a certain form of insurance, which the organization was not able to provide.

Benefits

4. **Insurances**
    The most common forms of insurance in benefits include life insurance, medical insurance, disability insurance and dental insurance. In the USA, costs of insurance have increased dramatically, resulting in organizations dropping forms of insurance from benefits or expecting employees to pay an increasing percentage of the costs of their insurance.

5. **Pensions and individual retirement plans (deferred compensation)**
    Pensions are not as important as they were decades ago when an employee was expected to remain with an organization throughout his/her entire career. There are a variety of individual retirement options for individuals, such as 401(k) and Roth IRA plans, to which organizations can contribute amounts. Sometimes the organization provides a "matching" amount, meaning they contribute a certain percentage of the amount contributed by the employee on a regular basis.

Other Forms of Reward

6. **Professional development (and/or tuition reimbursements)**
    This is one of the most important forms of reward and for providing value to the CEO because it helps him/her, not only to enhance competence and credibility, but also to provide more value and performance to the organization. Many would argue that professional development should not be means of compensation and benefits, but rather should be a right for the CEO within an organization.

7. **Flexible time or compensation time**
    This might be particularly valuable to a CEO who has worked a large number of hours in a certain month or who needs a particular schedule for personal needs, such as family responsibilities.

8. **Lodging and meals**
    This would apply especially to nonprofits that have substantial facilities, for example, churches and camps. Many times, lodging and meals are extremely important to the CEO because related costs can be quite high. Yet, lodging and meals might be a much lower cost for the nonprofit. The employee or staff member should be careful to specify on his/her personal tax forms whether lodging and meals are a form of compensation.

Using Salary Surveys

It is extremely useful to reference salary surveys when determining salaries. The surveys lend tremendous credibility and fairness to the process of determining compensation. Be sure that surveys are somewhat current. Reference them to find the salaries for the job roles that are the closest match to your CEO's. Unfortunately, many surveys use job classifications only, for example, they might refer to "Chief Executive" in the category of "Nonprofit". Ideally, the classifications also are matched to the nature of the nonprofit (for example, "social services") and its locale. Note that some types of nonprofits tend to have higher-than-usual CEO compensation, including educational institutions and hospitals. The closer you can match your CEO role to the type of services, locale and job title, the more useful the survey is likely to be to you, especially if the survey was generated in the past five years or less.

The following reference is to a list of nonprofit surveys. You might also contact your local United Way or nonprofits similar to yours to ask them for references to specific surveys.

Idealist.org has a list of nonprofit salary surveys at
http://www.idealist.org/en/career/salarysurvey.html .

Use an Employment Contract With Your Chief Executive?

Before hiring a new CEO, it is useful to consider how to retain the person in that role. Many organizations directly hire the CEO as an employee. However, some organizations are now considering use of an employment contract instead.

Rather than the standard employee-nonprofit relationship that is usually entered into when an employee accepts a letter of offer, an employment contract is like hiring a contractor to do the job of CEO. However the nonprofit might still withhold payroll taxes – consult a tax specialist about this specific matter because the appropriate governmental tax agency (for example, the Internal Revenue Service in the USA) might be particularly concerned about organizations hiring contractors to avoid paying payroll taxes. The terms of the contract supercede standard personnel requirements as specified in personnel policies and any state laws about "at will" employment. Contracts can bring an extra level of specificity, clarity, credibility and focus to the agreement between the CEO and the nonprofit. Contracts might decrease the likelihood of lawsuits about unfair employee termination because contracts can specify specific start and stop dates of service, so Board members can simply choose not to renew the contract as means to remove the CEO.

Contents of the contract might be the following (the following is not offered as legal advice):

- Name of the organization
- Name of the CEO
- Date the contract went into effect
- Date service starts and stops
- Duties and responsibilities to be met (for example, those in a job description)
- Performance goals
- Contractor's conformance to mission, vision, values, plans and policies

- Non-compete and confidentiality requirements
- Specification of compensation and benefits
- Specification of termination (with cause, without cause)
- How the contract can be amended
- Terms of mediation, if needed
- Signatures of all parties

See "Guidelines to Working With Consultants" on page 219.

How to Recruit and Select Your Chief Executive

1. **Form a Board Search Committee?**
    It is extremely useful if the Board can delegate the following activities to a subgroup of Board members. Ideally, the group includes at least one member who has some expertise in human resources or who has been involved in carefully hiring new staff members.

2. **Advertise the position, by referencing the CEO's job description.**
    Post ads in classified sections of local major newspapers and appropriate alternative press. Consider placing ads in online listings. In the ads, include the job title, general responsibilities, minimum skills and/or education required, and whom they should send a resume to if they are interested and by when. Mention the preferred culture of your organization.

    Mention the role to customers. Send cover letters and job descriptions to professional organizations. Be sure to mention the role to all staff to hear if they have any favorite candidates.

3. **Current employees should be able to apply for the job.**
    You may need to repeat a similar process to fill their job, if the employee is currently in a critical role in the organization and accepts the CEO role.

4. **Applicants to the Chief Executive role deserve complete confidentiality.**
    Make every effort not to expose applicants' names to the public or staff. If certain staff are selected to interview the candidates, they should be coached not to reveal candidate names to the rest of staff. This confidentiality is not a matter of secrecy to be manipulative, rather it is a matter of protecting candidates who may not want it publicly known that they are looking for a new job. Of course, this matter of confidentiality is ultimately up to the Board, but if confidentiality is not assured, it is very likely that the number of candidates will be less.

5. **Screen resumes.**
    Often, the Board Search Committee will screen the first round of candidates, including to review resumes and conduct first-round interviews. When screening resumes, notice:

a. The candidates' career objective – or the lack of it. If not specified, the candidates may not have considered what they want to do in the future, which may impact their commitment to your new role.

b. Have they stayed at jobs long or did they leave quickly?

c. Are there holes in their work history? If so, are the explanations satisfactory?

d. Is their education and training appropriate for the new role?

e. Consider what capabilities and skills are evidenced in their past and current work activities. Interview all candidates who meet the minimum qualifications. (At this point, be sure that you are not excluding candidates because of unfair biases.)

f. Do they seem to match the preferred culture of your organization? For example, if the culture is highly egalitarian and participative, will that person thrive in that type of culture?

6. **Interview candidates**.

a. Select the interviewer team. Consider having multiple people at the interview. Have the same people as interviewers in all of the interviews. If staff participate in the interviews, make sure they realize they are advisory in capacity. Board members have the legal responsibility to select the new Chief Executive. Although this can be intimidating to the interviewee, this practice can ensure them a much more objective and fair presentation.

b. Send the job description to candidates before they come to the interview meeting.

c. Send the candidates' applications and resumes to the interviewers, along with the interview schedule.

d. Prepare questions in advance of the interview. Following are some guidelines regarding interview questions:

i)   Attempt to ask open-ended questions and avoid "yes-no" questions.

ii) Include some challenging questions such as: Why do you want the job? What skills do you bring to this job? What concerns do you have about filling this role? What was your biggest challenge in a past job and how did you meet it? Do you have a preliminary vision (for the nature of your nonprofit's services)? Describe your ideal process for operations of: Boards, fundraising, budgeting, personnel management or program management.

iii) Questions should be in regard to performing the duties of the job. Do not ask questions about race, nationality, age, gender, disabilities (current or previous), marital status, spouses, dependents and their care, criminal records or credit records.

iv) Ask about their compensation needs and expected or needed benefits.

v)   Find out when they can start if offered the job.

vi) While interviewing candidates, always apply the same questions to all candidates to ensure fairness.

e.   During the interviews, follow these guidelines:

i)   Do not rely on your memory – ask permission from the interviewee to take notes.

ii) Talk for, at most, 25% of the time – listen the rest of the time.

iii) Ask if you can get and check any references.

iv) Be sure to tell candidates of any relevant personnel policies terms, such as probationary periods.

v)   Explain to the candidates that you will be getting back to them soon (and remember to do so).

f.   Have all interviewers share/record their impressions of the candidates right after the interview meetings.

g.   Always check references and share them with the interviewers.

h.   If practical, or if it is especially relevant for the nature of the work in your nonprofit, look into the candidates' background to ascertain if they have a criminal record.

7.   **Select the candidate.**
Usually, the Board Search Committee recommends the top two or three candidates to the entire Board for discussion and selection. Often, this is not as easy as one would like because two or three candidates come in close. This may require another round of interviews, this time including more/other Board members.

Following is a suggested procedure to arrive at a recommendation and/or short list.

a.   Have a highly focused meeting with all interviewers. (Again, note that staff members can provide input to the selection of the new Chief Executive, but should not be involved in voting.)

b.   Have each interviewer suggest his/her favorite candidate.

c.   If there is disagreement, focus discussion to identify the one or two areas in which interviewers disagree about the candidates. Then have each interviewer explain his/her impressions.

d.   The best way to deal with a poor performer is not to hire him or her in the first place. Therefore, be sure that the interview team is very comfortable with the selection process and final decision.

e.   At this point, interviewers usually come to consensus and agree on one candidate.

8.   **Send an offer letter to the selected candidate.**
Specify the compensation, benefits, and starting date, and reference an attached job description. Ask him/her to sign a copy of the offer letter and return it to you.

9.   **If the person accepts the job, then start a personnel file**.
Include: the signed offer letter, tax withholding forms, the job description and any benefits forms. Then follow the guidelines in the next section about orienting the new CEO.

10.   **If there does not seem to be a suitable candidate**:

   a.   Consider if the job requirements are too stringent or are an odd mix.

   b.   Or, consider hiring the candidate who came in closest and plan for dedicated training to bring his/her skills to the needed levels.

   c.   Or, re-advertise the position.

   d.   Consider getting advice from a human resources professional. At this point, your need for him/her is quite specific, so they might provide services on a pro bono basis.

   e.   Or, consider hiring a consultant on a short-term basis, but only as a last resort as this may be quite expensive.

11.   **If everyone turns down the job, determine what you should change**.

   a.   The best strategy is to ask the candidates why they turned the job down. Usually, you will hear the same concerns, for example, the pay is too low or the benefits incomplete, the organization seems confused about what it wants from the role, the interview process seemed hostile or contentious, etc.

   b.   Reconvene the interviewers and consider what you heard from the candidates. Recognize what went wrong and correct the problem.

   c.   Call back your favorite candidate, admit the mistake and what you did, and why you would like to make an offer to him/her again.

12.   **Consider hiring an interim Executive Director?**
Use of interim directors is an increasingly popular consideration because it quickly and temporarily fills the gap left by the out-going CEO. Ideally, an interim CEO has previous experience as a nonprofit CEO. The interim should be able to at least ensure that operations continue and do not deteriorate. You should develop a careful contract with the interim.

See "Use Employment Contract With Your Chief Executive?" on page 154.

How to Orient Your New Chief Executive

Develop an orientation procedure and consider the following activities for inclusion on the list. The following activities should be conducted by the Board, especially a Personnel Committee, if possible.

1. **Before the CEO begins employment, send a welcome letter.**
   In the letter, verify his/her start date and provide a copy of the employee policies and procedures manual. (This can be included in the offer letter.)

2. **At this point, the Board may send a letter to stakeholders.**
   The letter would announce the new CEO, report when he/she is starting, provide something about his/her background, etc., and invite stakeholders to call the Board Chair if they have any questions or concerns.

3. **Meet with the Chief Executive to brief him/her on strategic information.**
   Review the organization chart, last year's final report, the strategic plan, this year's budget, and the employee's policies and procedure manual. In the same meeting, explain the performance review procedure and provide him/her a copy of the performance review document.

4. **When the CEO begins employment (or before if possible), introduce him/her to staff.**
   If the organization is small enough, have all staff introduce themselves. If the organization is larger, invite all managers to the meeting and have each manager introduce him/herself.

5. **Ensure the CEO receives necessary materials and is familiar with the facilities.**
   Ensure an assistant gives them keys, and gets him/her to sign any needed benefit and tax forms. Review the layout of offices, bathrooms, storage areas, kitchen use, copy and fax systems, computer configuration and procedures, telephone usage and any special billing procedures for use of office systems.

6. **Schedule any needed training.**
   This might include, for example, computer training, including use of passwords, overview of software and documentation, location and use of peripherals, and where to go to get questions answered.

Review any policies and/or procedures about use of facilities.

7. **Assign a Board member as his/her "buddy."**
   The buddy remains available to answer any questions over the next four weeks.

8. **Have someone take him/her to lunch on the first day of work.**
   Invite other staff members along. Select a restaurant where people will actually be able to hear each other, so they can learn more about the CEO.

9. **During the first six weeks, have one-on-one meetings with the CEO.**
   Discuss the new CEO's transition into the organization, hear any pending issues or needs, and establish a working relationship with him/her.

How to Work With Your Chief Executive

Your Board and CEO Are Really In Strategic Partnership

Although theory and law assert that the CEO works for the Board, the working relationship and mutual support between the Board and CEO is critical to the success of a nonprofit. There might be an impression that the traditional structure of Boards, with its conventional job descriptions and committees, is somehow a rigid, top-down hierarchy, but this often is not the case. In many nonprofits, it is actually the CEO who facilitates and guides the Board members to do their jobs. Many nonprofits have the CEO and other staff members on certain committees. The CEO has strong input to the deliberations and decisions of Board members. Research suggests that a successful working relationship – a "strategic partnership" – between the Board members and CEO is one of the most important criteria for a high-performing nonprofit organization.

Descriptions of the traditional policy Board often portray the Board members as the "bosses" of CEOs, handing down directives and then "policing" the CEOs to ensure that those directives are followed. CEOs with that perspective often are confounded to understand why they must report to a group of people (Board members), many of whom do not seem to understand much, if anything at all, about the nonprofit and its programs. Consequently, these CEOs struggle to accept the credibility and directions from Board members. New or struggling CEOs can even resent and disrespect Board members to the extent that the CEOs ignore the members altogether.

Many experts assert that one of the reasons that a Board might struggle to be effective is because the CEO really does not want an effective Board and, therefore, does not help members to realize their roles and does not provide needed information to the Board members. Seasoned CEOs have learned that their jobs can be enhanced considerably with the additional guidance and resources from a highly effective Board of Directors – but the CEOs realize they must help the Board members to be that effective. CEOs can support the development of a Board by:

- **Helping Board members to understand their roles as members of a governing Board.**
  The CEO often has more interest and resources to fully understand the role of a nonprofit Board and, therefore, can be extremely helpful to Board members' learning their roles. The CEO can work with the Board Chair or Chair of a Board Development Committee to design and conduct the first several Board trainings.

- **Suggesting people to recruit as Board members.**
  As much as possible, these people should be independent Board members – people who have no other strong, vested interest in the nonprofit, for example, people who are not staff members, or who are not very close and personal friends of the CEO.

- **Training Board members about the nonprofit and its programs.**
  Frequently, members can serve on a Board for years and still not really know what programs are offered by the nonprofit. CEOs can significantly increase the effectiveness of Board members, and their contributions to the nonprofit, by orienting members about the nonprofit, including its history, programs, collaborators and successes.

- **Playing a strong role in strategic planning discussions and decisions.**
  Boards that view members as attending primarily to top-level policy will sometimes make the mistake of determining mission, vision, values and top-level goals without the input from

the CEO and senior staff members. That is a mistake. The most useful strategic planning sessions often involve information, discussions and suggestions from staff members.

- **Participating in Board committees.**
  The CEO can provide great value to committees, especially Fundraising, Finance, Personnel (except when the Board is evaluating the CEO and determining his/her compensation), Programs and Marketing. A trend is for other staff members to be on some of the Board committees, as well.

- **Provide useful information to Board members in time for their review before meetings.**
  Some CEOs have learned that one of the best ways to incapacitate a Board is by giving them new materials during a Board meeting, so that members are quickly overwhelmed and confused. As a result, members end up listening and agreeing with whatever the CEO suggests. Seasoned CEOs share materials well before Board meetings.

An excellent resource that researched and explained the value of this partnership is *Executive Leadership in Nonprofit Organizations: New Strategies for Shaping Executive-Board Dynamics* by R.D. Heimovics and R.D. Herman (Jossey-Bass, 1991).

How to Ensure Effective Board and CEO Relations

If a Board chooses to use a structure that includes use of staff, for example, a working or collective Board, there may be occasional confusion and frustration between the roles of the Board and staff (the Chief Executive Officer is a staff member). Staff might view Board members as having undue power and being aloof from the day-to-day realities of running the organization. Board members might view staff as not needing to be involved in determining strategic purpose and direction – or even forget about staff altogether. This likelihood of these unfortunate situations can significantly be reduced by first getting very clear on the role of the Board members as compared to staff members.

See "Sample Comparison of Board and Staff Roles" on page 258.

The following list describes the most important tactics for avoiding ineffective coordination between Board and staff. Note that the resolution to such problems is usually to ensure that the Board is adhering to the basic practices of a governing Board – the practices specified in this guide. One of the most important outcomes from adhering to the basic practices in this guide are effective planning and communications between Board and staff members.

Basic Practices to Ensure Effective Coordination

1. Board members must know their roles and responsibilities, including how they differ from those of the Chief Executive and staff. Board training should be conducted at least once a year to ensure all Board members and the Chief Executive clearly understand each other's roles and responsibilities.

2. The Chief Executive and other staff should be aware of the Board's roles and responsibilities, including how they differ from those of the Chief Executive and staff.

3.   Board, Chief Executive and staff members should engage in yearly strategic planning activities. Board and Chief Executive should be involved primarily in determining the organization's mission, vision, goals and strategies. Chief Executive Officer and staff might be involved primarily in defining action planning, including who will do what and by when in order to implement the strategies. The resulting strategic plan should be provided to everyone in the organization.

4.   Board members should have regular Board meetings, usually once a month during the first several years of the organization's life. Thereafter, have Board meetings at least every two or three months, ideally with committee meetings between Board meetings that are every other month.

5.   Chief Executive Officer and Board Chair design the agenda for Board meetings, and the agenda is sent to Board members at least one week before the Board meeting.

6.   The Chief Executive Officer should provide regular, written reports to Board members, usually on a monthly basis.

7.   The Chief Executive Officer and Board Chair should have a strong, ongoing, working relationship. Useful pointers are in the next section of this guide, "How to Ensure Strong Relationship Between Board Chair and Chief Executive."

8.   The Board should conduct regular, at least annual, formal evaluations of the Chief Executive Officer.

9.   There should be clear Board policies regarding the roles and coordination of Board members and staff, including:

   a.   Staff participation on Board committees.

   b.   Ensuring that the Chief Executive Officer approves Board member contacts to staff (unless a current, major issue suggests the Chief Executive Officer should not be involved).

10.   Board members and staff should meet each other at least once a year in a rather casual environment focused on celebrating the accomplishments of the organization.

11.   Staff should be allowed to make occasional presentations at Board meetings regarding program activities and how they are carried out.

Most Common Coordination Issues and How to Address Them

Note that the following issues are addressed, in large part, by implementing the above-listed basic practices.

1.   The Board automatically follows the direction of the Chief Executive and staff, rather than the focused direction from the organization's mission. (This is sometimes called Founder's Syndrome.) PART V of this guide includes guidelines to avoid this situation.

2.   The Board micromanages, or is deeply involved in the day-to-day activities of the organization, rather than focusing on strategic direction and policies. Guidelines in PART V can help avoid this situation, as well.

3.   Interpersonal conflicts between Board members and the Chief Executive can occur. To avoid this situation, see the guidelines in this guide's section, "How to Ensure Strong Relationship Between Board Chair and Chief Executive."

4.   The Chief Executive and/or Board members avoid each other. Resolving this situation requires strong leadership from the Board Chair and/or the Chief Executive. That leadership must first be applied to acknowledge the issue and then guide the Board back to conducting its formal role in governing the organization, with ongoing coordination with the Chief Executive. Guidelines in PART V can help avoid this situation, as well.

5.   Board members do not attend Board meetings. The Board must develop an effective Board Attendance Policy and enact that policy.

See "Sample Board Attendance Policy" on page 275.

How to Ensure Strong Relationship Between Board Chair and Chief Executive

Inherent Struggles Between Both Roles

Many experts assert that one of the most important ingredients to a successful corporation (nonprofit or for-profit) is a high-quality relationship between the Board Chair and the Chief Executive. However, this relationship has several inherent struggles to overcome. The Chief Executive was usually in the organization before the Chair was appointed and will be around after the Chair will be gone. In addition, the Chief Executive is also much closer to the day-to-day activities in the organization. Lastly, the Chief Executive usually knows far more about the organization's customers. Consequently, the Chief Executive may feel that he or she knows far much more about the organization than the Board Chair. Yet, the Board Chair is responsible to provide leadership to the Board to whom the Chief Executive is accountable. The Board Chair leads the Board, which evaluates the performance of the Chief Executive. Maintaining a high-quality relationship between the two roles requires a high level of maturity and understanding from both people filling those roles.

Practices That Can Minimize Destructive Conflict

Conflict is inherent in groups where diverse members are participating in deliberations and decisions about very important matters, especially where each member is sharing his/her beliefs and opinions. Conflict itself is not bad – conflict becomes destructive when it is prolonged about the same issue or decision, involves members openly making judgments about a member's character or personality, or involves escalating emotions to the extent that some members are shouting or otherwise impeding the group process.

One of the most effective means to minimize destructive conflict between both roles is to set up formal practices or procedures that help both people in the roles discern between an organizational issue and a personal issue. The following suggestions are provided to help ensure a high-quality relationship between the Board Chair and the Chief Executive by establishing formal practices and procedures.

1.   **Have clearly written and approved procedures for evaluating the Chief Executive**.
     Ensure the procedures include getting strong input from the Chief Executive.

2.   **Have regular Board training sessions**.
     They should include overviews of the roles of Board Chair and Chief Executive.

3.   **Board Chair and Chief Executive meet to discuss how they can work together.**
     They should focus on ideas about how they work together as a team.

4.   **Board Chair and Chief Executive jointly design Board meeting agendas.**
     This helps to ensure that all important matters of the Board and staff are included.

5.   **Board Chair can consult with the Chief Executive when appointing Committee Chairs.**
     Many times, the Chief Executive has a clearer understanding of who knows what on the Board.

6.   **Have clearly written guidelines about the roles of staff.**
     This is especially important when staff provide ongoing support to Board committees.

7.   **Get a new person in the Board Chair position at least every few years.**
     This helps to ensure new and fresh perspectives in the role.

8.   **Consider developing Board Chairs by having Vice Chairs.**
     The Vice Chair gets a year to "shadow" the Chair to really learn the role.

9.   **Have a Board discussion about meetings between the Chief Executive and Board Chair.**
     Get all Board members' ideas about when and why the Board Chair and Chief Executive should meet – do not make the meeting a matter of only those two people.

10. **Avoid frequent, one-on-one meetings that only include those two people.**
     Involve other Board members or other staff.

11. **Always write and share highlights of meetings of Chief Executive and Board Chair.**
     Otherwise, other Board members forget about these meetings.

12. **Ensure all Board members are trained about the role of the Board.**
     That way, all Board members know what to expect from the Board Chair and CEO roles.

13. **The Chief Executive and Board Chair should never conceal information.**
     CEO and Board Chair information is Board business – all members should know about it.

14. **Celebrate accomplishments.**
     All Board members should recognize and appreciate the hard work of the Chair and CEO.

Personal Practices to Minimize Interpersonal Conflicts

In addition to formal practices to minimize conflicts as listed above, the two people in these two roles can follow certain practices themselves.

See "How to Manage Interpersonal Conflicts" on page 188.

If Worse Comes to Worst

Obviously, the course of action for a situation such as this depends to a great extent on the nature of the organization and the two people involved. If you are a Board Chair or Chief Executive who continues to feel conflict in working with the other person, then consider:

1.   **Approach the other person and ask for five minutes of uninterrupted time.**
Explain your concern, what you see and hear that leads you to believe there is continued conflicts between both of you, what you would like to see or hear between both of you in the future, and why continued conflict can be so destructive to the organization.

2.   **If the other person says there is no conflict, then assert what you want from him/her.**
He/she either will change behaviors, in which case things should improve, or he/she will not. In that case, you can escalate the issue up the organization (for example, present the matter to entire Board), if appropriate, or seek additional assistance about how you plan to handle the problem: avoid it, confront it further, negotiate further, etc.

3.   **If the problem persists, ask to have time with the Executive Committee.**
If this is not appropriate, consider approaching two to three Board members one-on-one. At this point, it is critical to remember that any "badmouthing" or "conspiring" against the other person will only end up hurting the entire Board and organization. Therefore, talk with a friend or take careful time to reflect about what you want to say and how to say it to the other Board members. Explain the situation in terms of the behaviors in the issue, not the personality or character of the other person. Explain what you have done so far to address the issue. Describe your perception of the results of your efforts with the other person – note that it is your perception. Ask for specific advice to address the issue. At the end of the meeting, echo back to them what you hear them suggesting. Attempt to follow their advice. Commit to follow up with them about the results of your following their advice.

4.   **If the problem persists, you might consider getting outside help.**
This may be more constructive than posing the problem to the entire Board where it may cause great confusion and unease with little or no clear course of action to resolve the issue.

How to Evaluate Your Chief Executive Officer

Many Benefits of Formal Evaluation

Evaluating the Chief Executive Officer is a primary responsibility of the Board. There are several key benefits from this evaluation, including that the process:

1.   Ensures the Board is meeting its duty to effectively lead the organization.

2.   Ensures organizational goals are being met.

3.   Ensures continued development of the Chief Executive to more effectively conduct his or her role.

4.   Ensures a formal and documented evaluation process that meets standards of fairness and practicality.

5.   Ensures the Chief Executive values his or her role, is benefiting from it and therefore is more likely to stay (finding good Chief Executives seems increasingly difficult).

6.   Leaves written record of the Board's impression of the Chief Executive's performance in case this record is needed for future verification, for example, for salary increases, probationary activities, firing, etc.

See "Sample Executive Director Evaluation Form" on page 269.

How to Quickly Replace Your CEO (CEO Succession Management)

It is the Board's job to ensure that the nonprofit continually has high-quality operations. If the Board chooses to have a CEO or Executive Director role in the nonprofit, then it is extremely important that that role be filled reliably with a high-quality person. CEOs leave their jobs on an unplanned or a planned basis. Unplanned termination occurs because of sudden illnesses or death, or poor performance on the part of the CEO.   Planned termination occurs because the CEO is making a career or life change.

For a very interesting report about nonprofit executives, and their intentions to stay in their jobs, see *Daring to Lead 2006* at http://www.compasspoint.org/assets/194_daringtolead06final.pdf .

Research indicates that most of the nonprofit CEOs will leave their jobs within the next five years. Also, demographic trends indicate that there are not sufficient numbers of next-generation leaders to replace retiring baby-boomers in nonprofits. Thus, succession management is an increasingly important priority for Board members. (Various phrases are used to refer to aspects of ensuring a complete and successful transition to a new CEO, for example, succession planning, succession management and transition management.)

Principles for Successful Succession Management

-   **Do not wait until the CEO will be terminating employment. Start planning now.**
    Succession management is a matter of strong practices in ongoing governance and management, not a matter of sudden crisis management. Start attending to those practices now.

-   **Focus on practices, not on personalities.**
    Succession management is re-filling a role, not replacing a certain person. Be sure the CEO

position is defined well, then look to find the best person to fill the position. Do not look for someone who is just like, or a lot different from, the previous CEO.

- **Succession management is a responsibility of the Board and the CEO.**
  The best succession management results from a working partnership of Board members working to understand and define and fill the CEO role, and the CEO ensuring that Board members have the information and resources to refill the role.

- **Succession management is leadership transition, and staffing and risk management.**
  Leadership is ensuring clear direction and creating the environment so that others are motivated to follow that direction – that function must continue during a transition. The CEO is a staff role and, therefore, must be filled by using up-to-date personnel policies to ensure fair, equitable and legally compliant employment practices. Activities must minimize the risks from lapses in poor management and any undue fears among stakeholders.

- **Quality in managing succession is often proportionate to the quality of the new CEO.**
  The best way for Board members to convey their expectations of high quality in the CEO role now, is to have the CEO perceive a high-quality succession management process. The more thorough and careful that Board members are during succession, the more likely that the nonprofit will get a new CEO who successfully fills the position for the long-term.

Key Governance and Management Practices in Succession Management

If Board members have already established strong practices in governance and in management, then succession management often is a matter of using current practices, rather than establishing many new ones. Key practices include having:

1. A strategic plan that clearly conveys the nonprofit's mission and current strategic priorities. Ideally, that plan also includes specific action plans that specify who is going to do what and by when in order to address each priority.

2. Up-to-date and Board-approved personnel policies about hiring, supervising and firing personnel in a fair and equitable manner, and that also are in compliance with employment laws.

3. An up-to-date job description for the Executive Director role that explains the general duties and responsibilities of the position.

4. Suitable compensation for the CEO role (very often this is a major challenge for nonprofits because they have very limited resources).

5. An annual calendar of the CEO's most important activities, for example, when the CEO: evaluates personnel, does any staffing analysis, updates job descriptions, evaluates programs, participates in certain Board committees, etc.

6. Regular reports from the CEO, especially reports to Board members during Board meetings, and about the trends, highlights and issues regarding the CEO's activities.

7. Evaluation of the CEO on an annual basis, including in reference to the CEO's job description and any performance goals established for that role.

8.   Arrangements with the CEO where he/she goes on vacation so Board members and staff have an opportunity to effectively replace the CEO if only for a temporary period of time.

9.   A complete list of major stakeholders. Get a list of donors, including contact information, how each is approached and who does that (ideally, there is some form of Fundraising Committee or task force that has been heavily involved in fundraising with the CEO) in case that information is needed when/if the CEO goes. Get a complete list of other stakeholders, including collaborators, suppliers, facilities management contacts, etc.

10.   Fiscal policies and procedures to ensure strong Board oversight of finances, including that financial numbers are correct and tracked accurately, and also that there are sufficient funds to pay near-term expenses.

11.   At least annual discussions with the CEO regarding succession management, including how management can be done effectively in the CEO's absence. (Be careful about raising this topic with the CEO so that he/she is not overly concerned that Board members somehow want a change now). This discussion can be an opportunity to hear about the CEO's career plans and desires, too.

12.   At least annual discussions, not only about CEO succession, but about other critical positions in the staff, for example, program directors and development (fundraising) officers.

Replacing an Outgoing CEO

If the nonprofit has regularly been conducting succession planning with the current CEO, then it could be a straightforward matter to replace the CEO in a relatively low-risk and smooth manner. The following guidelines assume that the CEO has given sufficient notice that he/she is leaving soon. Otherwise, some of the guidelines in the following section will need to be modified if the CEO is suddenly leaving, for example, is fired, seriously ill or deceased.

CEO's Notification to Board

1.   **Typically, the Chief Executive will notify the Board Chair or other Board member.**
The Chair should immediately notify the rest of the Board members in the next Board meeting.

2.   **Ask the Chief Executive to document his/her decision in writing to the Board.**

3.   **Attempt to negotiate a four-week-notice period from the Chief Executive.**
It is not unlikely that there will be a period without a new Chief Executive. This procedure will minimize disruption through that period.

Maintaining Confidentiality During Transition

1.   **All Board members should be apprised as soon as possible.**
Occasionally, members believe that transitions should be handled so cautiously that even some Board members should not hear about the transition. This is the wrong approach. Each Board member is legally responsible for the leadership of the organization, and deserves to know about all matters when they occur.

2.   **Discuss how to handle public relations.**
The community will soon hear or read that the Chief Executive is leaving. Agree on how

this message will be conveyed to the community. If the transition is expected to take over a month (and they often do), consider sending a letter to the major stakeholders (advisors, suppliers, collaborators, funders, etc.) notifying them of the transition and assuring them that transition planning is being carried out thoroughly. Invite them to contact the Board Chair if they have any concerns or questions.

Board Activities During Transition

1. **Start activities to recruit and hire new CEO. Appoint an ad hoc Search Committee?**
   The Board might choose to form an ad hoc Board Search Committee (or task force) now, in which case that Committee could handle the search activities, too. The Committee will manage the transition, including developing a transition plan. This Committee role could be assumed by the current Executive Committee or a Personnel Committee. Committee members should commit to availability over the next four to eight weeks. The Search Committee should focus on:

   a. Identifying desired skills of the new Chief Executive.

   b. Verifying the accuracy of the job description of the Chief Executive.

   c. Conducting the recruiting and selection activities itemized in this section.

 See "How to Hire Your Chief Executive Officer" on page 147.

2. **Develop a written transition plan and have the Board approve it.**
   The contents of this section about succession management could comprise much of the transition plan, but responsibilities and deadlines would need to be added to the plan.

3. **As soon as the transition plan is developed, promptly notify staff of the transition.**
   A Board member should attend the staff meeting where notification is given and the staff should be assured that the transition is being carefully planned and carried out. The plan might be reviewed in the staff meeting. A copy of the transition plan should be shared with all staff members.

4. **Identify any necessary funding for the transition.**
   For example, are any funds needed for a national search, to move the new candidate, for training the new candidate, for consultants on interim basis, etc.?

Administrative Activities During Transition Before New CEO Arrives

1. **Establish an interim staff structure.**
   Consider appointing an acting Chief Executive from staff reporting to the current Chief Executive. If this course is followed, ensure the job description is well understood by the acting Chief Executive, and the acting arrangement is documented in a letter between the acting Chief Executive and the Board. Send a memo to all the staff, indicating this interim appointment and how the acting Chief Executive will work with the staff until a permanent Chief Executive is identified. (Be very careful with this type of temporary arrangement as it can lull Board members into believing the transition is complete, which it is not.)

2. **Update the administrative calendar for the organization.**
    Ask the outgoing Chief Executive to make a schedule of all major recurring activities during the year (for example, performance reviews, special events, staff meetings, one-on-one meetings, lease/contract expiration dates, when paychecks come out, etc.).

     See "Sample Annual Calendar of Board Activities" on page 257.

3. **Get a list of key stakeholders from the outgoing CEO.**
    Have the outgoing Chief Executive make a list of all community key stakeholders whom the new Chief Executive should know about, for example, funders, advisors (legal, accounting, real estate), collaborators, etc.

4. **Review outgoing Chief Executive's office facilities.**
    Ask the outgoing Chief Executive to document the status of his/her office, for example, ensure there are labels on all documents and drawers. Appropriate staff and at least two Board members should meet with the Chief Executive to review where he/she keeps files and major documents. Staff should retain a key to the office and appropriate Board members should retain keys to the desk drawers and file cabinets.

5. **Review personnel status with the outgoing CEO.**
    Two or more Board members should meet with the outgoing Chief Executive to review personnel files, for example, if there any current personnel issues, if some personnel will be leaving/retiring or have performance issues, etc.

6. **Outgoing CEO should complete performance reviews on all personnel.**
    This ensures that the outgoing Chief Executive's important feedback to personnel is collected before he/she goes, gives personnel a fair opportunity to reflect their past performance to the new Chief Executive, and gives the new Chief Executive the input he/she deserves about each employee to ensure effective supervision.

Interim Coordination Between Board and Staff During Transition

1. **Get emergency contact information for each of the staff members.**
    Staff should be given names and phone numbers of at least two Board members who can be contacted if needed. These two members should brief the entire Board on the nature of any emergency calls from staff, if calls were made.

2. **Have weekly meetings with staff until the new CEO arrives.**
    Depending on the size of the organization, have weekly meetings of full staff (if small) or all managers (if large) during the transition until a new Chief Executive is hired. Have a Board member attend the meetings. Have a staff member (acting Chief Executive, or the current top reports, or rotate among top reports) attend portions of the Board meetings.

3. **Come up to speed on outgoing CEO's current activities in the organization.**
    Have the current Chief Executive ask all staff members to update a "to do" list of their current major activities over the past month, planned activities over the coming two months and any major issues they are having now. These "to do" lists will serve to coordinate work details during the transition and help the new Chief Executive come up to speed.

4.   **Develop any authorization lists.**
        Decide who will issue paychecks and sign off on them during the transition. Often, the
        Board Treasurer and/or Secretary will conduct this sign-off role.

5.   **Board members should meet with the outgoing CEO once a week until he/she goes.**
        Review status of work activities, any current issues, etc.

PART V:

RESTORING

STRUGGLING BOARDS

Context for Successfully Restoring Your Board

Issues to Always Watch For On Your Board

Here is a listing of the most common problems that can arise in Boards. Usually, these problems are really symptoms of larger, underlying problems that we will address in this section. Often, a "broken" Board has several of the following symptoms and the symptoms can be highly integrated with each other.

- **Burnout**
  Board members feel that their activities are not productive or that they are overwhelmed with responsibilities and workload, resulting in decreasing attendance and increasing conflict among members.

- **Conflict among Board members**
  Some or all members cannot come to agreement, frequently interrupt each other during deliberations, and sometimes make unfair conclusions about each other's personalities or natures.

- **High turnover**
  Members frequently quit the Board and are replaced by new members who, in turn, quit the Board, usually well before their membership terms expire.

- **Low attendance**
  Members struggle to achieve a quorum, that is, to achieve a sufficient number of Board members in attendance at a Board meeting, such that their activities and decisions can become official. (The quorum number is specified in the Board's By Laws.)

- **Low participation**
  Even though members attend meetings, they do not participate in discussion and decisions. Perhaps only a few members take part, resulting in a lack of robust diversity, perspectives and "voices" in Board deliberations and decisions.

- **Micro-management**
  Members spend most of their time and concerns focusing on the day-to-day activities of the organization, with great concern and some skepticism about staff, usually because members lack trust in the ability of staff. As a result, Board members also neglect attention to top-level plans and policies.

- **No planning**
  Members might participate in meetings, but their communications tend to be about the latest crisis or about whatever documents are placed before them in their Board meetings. They do not proactively attend to the most important priorities.

- **Poor decision making**
  Members might come to consensus or agreement on an issue or goal, but they frequently change their minds, or they later realize that their decisions did not solve the problems or achieve the goals that they had intended.

The above issues are specific to Board operations. However, if a Board is not effective, then there can be a wide range of other problems that can occur throughout the organization, especially in strategic planning, staffing, finances and fundraising. Ironically, nonprofits that have very strong programs (programs proven to be very successful at meeting specific needs in the community) can often survive – but not thrive – despite having very poor Boards.

Similar to people, it is difficult to "diagnose" whether a Board is having minor or major problems, just based on the types and number of issues that it has. Different Boards have different tolerance for issues. For example, nonprofits that need strong strategic direction cannot tolerate prolonged conflict and poor decision making on the Board because the nonprofits need well-designed strategic plans and policies – those plans and policies require high-quality deliberations and decisions. Similarly, nonprofits with little or no staff cannot tolerate low participation and high turnover of Board members because members often help with activities that staff otherwise would do.

Common Types of "Broken" Boards

Nonprofit Board members should work together as a strong team to verify that the nonprofit is effectively and efficiently meeting a certain public need. Here are four types of "broken" governing Boards where members are not effectively doing their job. Perhaps the best way to recognize each type is to listen to what Board members talk about in each type.

Problematic Board: Detached Board

In the detached Board, members might not even remember that they are on the Board. In a detached Board, you might hear members having the following exchanges:

- When the member is called to go to a Board meeting and reminded about the purpose of the meeting, the member responds, "Why are you calling me? I forgot that I was even on that Board."

- When called to attend a meeting, many members often respond, "I'm too busy to attend. I'll try to make the next meeting, though."

- Board members often think to themselves and say to each other, "I've not heard from the Executive Director. Therefore, everything must be fine. Don't worry about it."

Members of a detached Board were often recruited because of the members' stature, not because the nonprofit wanted the members to actually participate on the Board. Many times, the Chief Executive and staff members do not want a governing Board anyway – they want to run things without what they perceive as the necessary evil of dealing with a Board. Strong, charismatic founders often do not want Board members involved in the nonprofit, other than to do fundraising for the founder. As a result, nonprofits in these situations often have detached Boards.

Problematic Board: Servant Board

This is a very common type of Board. Members are very passionate and dedicated. They are there to do whatever is helpful. In their actions, they informally "report" to the Chief Executive, rather than the other way around. Here is how Board members might talk in a servant Board:

- "I'm here to help the Executive Director in any way that I can. All he/she has to do is just ask me and I'll be there."

- "What would you like me to do? Just tell me."

- "I'll agree with ['rubber stamp'] whatever the Chief Executive or Board Chair wants."

That approach works until one of the Board members or the Chief Executive attends a training session about Boards and realizes that his/her Board is not functioning well. It works until a funder realizes that the nonprofit really does not have a governing Board, and demands that the Board members undertake Board development.

Problematic Board: Personalities Board

In this type of Board, the members usually have not done any strategic planning, formal or informal, so they do not know what types of expertise would be useful on the Board. Also, they do not know their governing roles at all, so they have resorted instead to using Board members based on their personalities. Usually, they seek members who seem "passionate" about the mission, and members who might even come to meetings. Members of these Boards often feel lucky if they get any participation on the Board at all. Here is what members might say:

- "Let's get Jim on our Board. He's such a nice guy!"

- "Let's get Jane on the Board. At least she'll come to meetings."

- "Let's get Jack on the Board. He's got 'deep pockets'."

Problematic Board: Micro-Managing Board

Micro-managing Boards often are in response to a crisis in the nonprofit. Many times, the members were another type of Board before the crises. Now, members are operating in strong fear that another crisis might occur or that they might get sued so they have resorted to exerting strong forms on control. Here is what members might say:

- To the Executive Director, "Give us your to-do list!"

- To other staff members, "How's the Executive Director doing – really?"

- "When did you come to work today? We'd like to get a time report each day."

Although the micro-managing at least gets members involved, it often is to the detriment of their attending to more strategic matters, and so matters regarding the nonprofit's mission, and top-level plans and policies are neglected.

Healthy Board: Strategic Board

In a healthy governing Board, members might be a "working" governing Board where they sometimes do "hands-on" activities, such as fixing the fax; they might be a collective where Board and staff members work together in a seamless team; or they might be a policy governing Board primarily attending to top-level policies and plans. Regardless of the personality of the governing Board, members would always be asking the following types of questions in addition to their other activities:

- "Where's our Strategic Plan? How are we doing in implementing that Plan?"

- "What's the status of each Committee's work plan?"

- "Are we sticking to the agenda, the topics and timing for the topics, in our meeting?"

- "Is this discussion really strategic, or should we delegate the topic for further research?"

- "Are our programs really making an impact? How do we know?"

- "We've got some 'dead wood' on this Board. Are we going to tolerate that?"

General Principles for Restoring Your Board

Changing the nature of how a Board works is like changing the nature of a person – it takes clarity, consistency, persistence and time, but it can be done. Fortunately, over the past few decades, we have a learned a great deal about how to successfully change other types of systems, including organizations and Boards. If you are working to restore a struggling Board, then you should work according to the following principles. The upcoming section, "Procedures to Restore Your Board," follows these principles. (These principles come to us from Peter Senge's book, *The Fifth Discipline* (Doubleday, 1990), and are applied here in slight variation for use in restoring Boards.)

Structures Determine Behaviors, Which Determine Events

An example of the application of this principle is two Board members, Tom and Sally, who keep arguing with each other. Board members might try to solve the problem simply by telling Tom and Sally not to argue anymore. Other members might try to work with Tom and Sally to make them appreciate each other more, to feel better about each other. Wiser Board members would also consider the structures (roles and policies) in the Board that might be causing Tom and Sally to argue. For example, Tom and Sally might not be clear on what their roles and responsibilities are in the Board. Or, they may have conflicting roles and responsibilities because the Board has no clear work plans. Or, Tom and Sally might be lacking the resources required to effectively carry out their jobs as Board members because they received no orientation or training about their roles. Rarely is the problem simply that Tom and Sally like to argue with each other.

There Is No Blame

When major issues recur in a Board, it usually is the fault of a dysfunctional structure (roles and policies), rather than the fault of the Board members who are struggling to operate within that dysfunctional structure. One of the ways that ineffective nonprofit leaders try to motivate Board members is by using guilt and blame. They remind members that the nonprofit will shut down if members do not raise more money. Then, if the nonprofit continues to have major struggles, leaders blame those Board members even more. Soon the guilt and blame no longer motivate members, at all. Too often, the leaders cannot change their ways and, as a result, the Board members quit the Board. These leaders need to recognize that the problem is not caused by some amazing coincidence that all of the Board members are lazy and inept, but rather by larger problems in the Board itself. For example, members might not have been trained how to participate in fundraising. Or, members might not have confidence in the fundraising plans. Or, the problems might be that there is insufficient strategic and program planning, resulting in ineffective fundraising proposals to funders. (Ineffective planning also is not the fault of nonprofit leaders – they did the best they could with what they had at the time. Now, they should learn from the problems on the Board and investigate if planning could be done better.)

Today's Problems Are Yesterday's Solutions

Many times, nonprofit leaders attempt to get Board members more involved by making the experience of Board membership more pleasurable. For example, they schedule Board meetings to occur less frequently and/or they make Board meetings shorter. Ironically, while this might make Board members more involved in meetings, the nonprofit really is getting less value from Board members because, overall, they are now much less involved than before when meetings were longer and more frequent. Sometimes, to address this new problem, leaders will begin working with only a few of the more active Board members, with hope to get at least some involvement from at least some of the Board members. So now, the effectiveness of the Board is worse than ever before. Instead, leaders need to be clear to themselves and the Board members about what kind of Board the nonprofit needs and requires. If the nonprofit needs more attendance among Board members, then enact a Board attendance policy that removes members who do not attend.

Easy Way Out Usually Leads Back In

When a few Board members continue to complain that the Board and nonprofit need to do a better job, then other members – usually those who are completely content with the status quo – might blame the few members as being "bad apples" and want those few members to just leave the Board. The more those few members complain, the more that other members blame the complainers. Eventually the Board Chair confronts the complainers, who become even more frustrated and eventually just quit the Board. Then new members come on the Board – often members who have had some Board training so they expect a high-quality Board. Soon the new members start sharing the same complaints, and so they eventually are asked to leave the Board, too. The cycle continues several times until an outside stakeholder, for example, a funder, asserts that the Board needs help.

Faster Is Slower

If Board members do not take the time and energy required to develop and implement Board roles and policies, then they might enjoy the benefit of having fewer Board meetings to work on these matters. However, they will soon realize that they seem to be attending to the same Board problems over and over again – for example, Board members' complaining that discussions never lead to decisions, decisions do not get implemented, only some members participate and some members do not come at all. Hopefully, they will realize that they have to take the time to work smarter, rather than harder. They will identify the causes of these complaints, for example, that agendas are poorly designed, they need a policy for making decisions and they need a Board attendance policy.

Come "From" Them, Not "At" Them

It can be extremely difficult to change a Board merely by preaching at members about how they have to change. For example, it usually does little good to tell frustrated and conflicted Board members that they need to "suck it up" and "do what they are supposed to do." Their performance will just get worse. They will feel more frustration, anger and despair. Rather than coming *at* them with dire warnings, listen *to* their side of the story. Do a quick Board self-evaluation to get each member's feedback about how the Board could be improved.

Behavior Grows Better Before It Grows Worse

Usually, quick fixes to the symptoms – rather than real fixes to the real causes – of a problem will make things better, but only for a while. For example, if Board members have continued conflicts amongst each other, then members might resort to team building. Poorly designed team building might help Board members to temporarily feel better about themselves and each other. But if the team building did not attend to the underlying structures that caused the conflicts in the first place, then team building can actually make things much worse. (See the section immediately below.)

Why Board Training or Team Building Alone Seldom Restores Boards

Why Board Training Alone Seldom Restores Boards

It is not uncommon that Board members want a "quick fix" to their issues merely by undertaking a short Board training session. They have the illusion that their problems are the result of members not knowing their jobs. That is like believing that you can stop people from arguing merely by telling them not to do that anymore. If a training session was the solution, then members could easily solve their issues merely by downloading free Board job descriptions from the Web. Besides, if members are not coming to Board meetings, they probably will not attend a Board training either.

Board members rarely struggle because members lack understanding of their legal roles and responsibilities. New information in members' heads is rarely enough to make a major difference. Instead, members need ongoing guidance, support and accountabilities to actually use that new information. That comes from a combination of activities, for example, evaluating the health of the Board, helping members understand what is required for long-lasting change, Board orientation and Board training for members, refining the organization of the Board, coaching the Board Chair and other leadership roles to drive changes, and then re-evaluating the health of the Board.

Why Team Building Alone Seldom Restores Boards

Team building is conducted to improve the performance of a team, or small group of people. There are a wide variety of approaches to team building. Too often, the approach is to improve performance primarily by trying to improve team members' feelings, beliefs and perceptions about themselves and each other. That approach rarely works for Boards that have major, ongoing struggles. Actually, that approach to team building can make the situation much worse when the good feelings from team building quickly encounter the same dysfunctional structures on the Board, resulting in even more frustrated – and now cynical – Board members.

We have learned a great deal about what makes for high-performing teams. In addition to respecting themselves and each other, all team members need to have the same clear understanding of certain structures, including:

1.   The purpose of the team.

2.   How decisions are made and problems are solved, and how communications will be done.

3.   Each member's current roles and responsibilities.

4.   What authority and resources the team has to work with.

Lack of the above structures often is the primary cause of prolonged frustration, blaming and conflicts among team members. Teams can be formed to be self-organizing, self-directed or self-managed, but to be successful, they must ensure that they have the above-listed structures in whatever form the team decides to take.

Specific Principles for Restoring Your Board

A previous section explained general principles for long-lasting, successful change in organizations and Boards. This section provides additional principles that are aimed specifically at restoring a struggling Board.

Focus On "Human" Side – and on Changing Structures

There are probably as many different approaches to addressing Board issues as there are experts trained to do so. Consultants who specialize in human relations (for example, coaches, human resource personnel and leadership developers) might focus primarily on the interpersonal relationships among Board members, especially on their feelings, beliefs and perceptions about each other. Other types of consultants might focus primarily on "structural" approaches, especially on plans, policies and practices used by Board members.

It is the belief of this author that the most effective approaches to restoring a Board are to combine both the human relations and the structural approaches. However, when Boards become dysfunctional, members often resort to blaming each other and their issues can become deeply interpersonal. Therefore, to restore these Boards, it often helps to balance members' perspectives, especially by focusing them more on the structures of the Board. This might mean modifying their Board model somewhat, for example, to become more of a traditional policy Board, with its seemingly distinct roles and lines of authority – at least until the Board improves significantly. The author has used the following approach many times to successfully and significantly improve the operations of a nonprofit Board of Directors.

Focus On "Broken Systems," Not On Broken People

It is extremely important to adopt the philosophy that Boards are not broken because of broken people – they are broken because of broken systems. Members are missing the systems – the plans, policies and practices – to:

- Accomplish a common purpose, roles and procedures for the Board.

- Effectively staff and equip Board members.

- Make useful decisions and to closely monitor implementation of those decisions.

- Evaluate the quality of their planning, decisions, meetings and members.

When these systems are not in place, Board members often struggle to remain effective. Not knowing what the causes of their issues are or what to do to resolve them, Board members sometimes turn on each other – they start blaming each other. However, few Board members get out of bed in the morning intent on destroying their Boards. Often, the Board members who are perceived to be the least effective or the most destructive are the Board members who most passionately want to help the nonprofit – they just are not sure how to do that. So they are passionately resorting to whatever they believe will work for now, including blaming others who do not seem to be doing their jobs.

To resolve chronic issues on a Board, it is important to focus on instilling the systems whereby members can move away from blaming each other, and can instead focus on practicing the policies and procedures that will help them all get back "on the same page."

Pull – and Push – Board Members

As previously mentioned, it is common for nonprofit leaders to attempt to increase the participation of Board members merely by enhancing the experience of being a Board member. For example, leaders might schedule Board meetings to be much less frequent or they might reduce the length of Board meetings, thereby reducing the demand on Board members' time such that they are more likely to attend meetings. In the case of a broken Board, this approach to pull members into increased performance rarely works. In some cases, Board members are not effective because the CEO perceives the members to be a hindrance more than a help. In those cases, the CEO might try to reduce the number and length of meetings primarily to reduce the participation of Board members.

When a Board has been struggling, it is often far more useful to mix strategies to both pull and push the Board members to increase their effectiveness. Pull them along by sharing appreciation for their participation and contributions. But push them along by setting clear expectations of what they should be doing and then "policing" them to be sure that they are doing it.

To Keep Good (Or Get Rid of "Bad") Board Members, Give Them Something to Do

Good Board members join Boards to contribute to the health of their communities, develop themselves personally, and cultivate relationships with other leaders in the community. They do not join a Board primarily to go to meetings. The best way to retain these good Board members is to be sure that they have clear opportunities to make a positive difference on the Board and in the nonprofit. Give them the resources (orientation, training, information and assignments) to make that positive difference. Good Board members actually appreciate having assignments that help them to contribute value to the nonprofit and its community.

In contrast, Board members who skip meetings, or who go to meetings and rarely provide value, often do not appreciate having specific expectations placed on them. If you have resolved that your community deserves an active Board, then you do not need this type of Board members. You are not benefiting from having them and usually they are not really benefiting from being on your Board, as well. Often, the best way to get rid of them is to ensure that they get specific assignments to do by a certain time. They will either become more active or they will leave the Board. If these efforts result in them becoming more active, then the problems they had before were probably just because they were struggling and frustrated about not being able to contribute value on the Board.

Procedures to Restore Your Board

One Set of Proven Steps to Restore Your Board

If people do certain "best practices" (for example, eat well, and get enough exercise and sleep), they can often minimize or remove many different illnesses commonly associated with stress and poor physical health. The same is true for Boards, as well. Instilling a set of best practices can produce breakthroughs that solve many of the Board's problems. The process to restoring a Board is not quick – it can take from six to nine months, but each month results in a stronger Board than before.

Sometimes, the following steps result in 10%-15% of the Board members leaving the Board because they perceive that the changes will result in more demands being placed on them. (Actually, the changes usually result in the same amount of work for them as before because all members end up working smarter, rather than harder.) It is important not to blame these members – they are actually doing themselves and the Board a favor by leaving the Board. However, the "worst" Board members – those who complain or do not participate in meetings – often become the best Board members during the process to restore the Board because they now have clear means to really make a difference in their communities and the Board.

The following steps are in accordance with the general and specific principles for successful change as described in the previous sections. Be sure to read those sections if you have not yet done so. Ironically, the more struggles that your Board is having, the more likely that all members will cooperate in the following procedure because members will want very much to relieve their discomfort. The following steps should be followed sequentially.

Start With Quick, Practical, Non-Threatening Board Evaluation

One or more Board members can administer the evaluation, or you can use an external consultant. Ideally, more than one member is involved in administering because that lends more credibility to the activity, so that other members are not as likely to "shoot the messenger."

1. **Suggest a quick, convenient Board self-evaluation, as a "best practice."**
   Suggest to other Board members that they do a quick self-evaluation, an evaluation that will take about 10-15 minutes per member. Do not suggest it because the Board is in trouble, rather suggest it because it is a "best practice" among Boards, it can be quick and easy, and it gives one more perspective on how members are doing.

   The purpose of the evaluation for now is not to identify every issue and its cause, rather it is to focus and mobilize Board members to improve their Board operations. Do not worry about doing a scientifically accurate, valid and reliable analysis. Instead, just focus on doing a quick, practical evaluation.

   Select an assessment questionnaire that asks about whether certain actions have occurred on the Board or not, not primarily about members' feelings. For example, the tool should ask "Is a quorum regularly attained in Board meetings?". It should not ask "Are enough Board members in attendance in meetings?"

See "Sample Board Self-evaluation Form" on page 272.

Then hand out the simple questionnaire to show how simple it will be to complete it. Mention that it could be completed anonymously. Explain that a few Board members could look at the results and report back to the Board.

An option is to hire or recruit a volunteer outside expert to do the evaluation, analyze the results and report back to the Board. See "Guidelines to Working With Consultants" on page 219.

2.   **Analyze the results of the self-evaluation in preparation for sharing with Board.**
Before the next meeting, add up the number of "yes"s and "no"s for each question and collect the comments made by members onto one summary report, but do not associate names to the comments unless a member has insisted so. Share the results with members via email or postal mail shortly before the next Board meeting so that they have time to analyze the results. When preparing to discuss the results, it often is useful to share a list of best practices with members to help them get perspective about what the results of the evaluation should be. Ask for 30 minutes on the agenda for all members to discuss the results.

See the list of best practices on page 130.

Suggest Realistic Vision of Health for the Board

3.   **In next Board meeting, review results. Decide: what kind of Board do members want?**
In the next meeting, first answer any questions about the evaluation methodology. Then open up discussion about the results. Ask, "Are there issues that we want to improve on? Are our Board issues hurting our service to our community?" Mention that issues on Boards seldom have clear, rational causes and that it is more important to just move forward to make things better. Suggest to the members that they move forward by instilling the "best practices" in how they operate. Explain how that will better help the community.

When establishing a vision of health with Board members, it will be useful to look at "What Does a Healthy Board Look Like?" on page 29 and "How to Match Board's Priorities to Life Cycle of Nonprofit" on page 140.

It also might be helpful for members to get quick perspective by considering types of "broken" Boards as listed on page 176.

It also might be helpful for members to quickly consider if the results of the assessment indicate that they have Founder's Syndrome. See the section starting on page 192.

It might be useful to share the general and specific guidelines for changing Boards (listed in the previous sections) with the members, especially if they start suggesting that all they need is Board training.

If members struggle to make a decision about the results of the evaluation, it might be useful to call for a vote. In that case, be sure that you know what constitutes a quorum (reference your By Laws), so that you can make sure that their decision was official.

Assign Committee (or Task Force) to Guide Board Changes

4.   **Start Board Development Committee (or task force), start Board Development Plan.**
You could make this suggestion during the Board meeting in which the evaluation results were shared. Explain that the role of the Committee is to ensure that the operations of the Board are always high quality. Many experts assert that this Committee is the most important Committee on a Board. If members are concerned about starting another committee, mention it could be ad hoc (or temporary).

See "Goals and Objectives for Board Development Committee" on page 243 for suggested goals, and associated objectives and responsibilities for this Committee.

The Committee should include 2-3 people, including the Board Chair and ideally 1-2 other Board members who have either been on a very good Board or who have the time and energy to participate on the Committee. Do not include the Chief Executive on the Committee – that often continues to cultivate passive Board members who look to the Chief Executive for direction, rather than to each other.

Draft a 1- to 2-page Board Development Plan that lists the best practices and any other changes that the Board members wanted to implement. Be sure that Board members formally approve the charter of the Board Development Committee and approve the Board Development Plan.

Get Members Re-Focused on Roles and Responsibilities

5.   **Do a one-hour Board training session about Board roles and key Board policies.**
The training should be about the roles and responsibilities of a governing Board of nonprofit corporation. (Do not confuse this with a Board orientation.) In this training, be sure to review the following Board policies: roles of Board versus staff, annual calendar of Board activities (for example, when to do strategic planning, Board self-evaluation, evaluation of the CEO, etc.), policy for how decisions are made, and the attendance policy.

See "Sample Board Policies," starting on page 249.

Be sure they come to agreement on Board and staff roles. See the suggested roles on page 258.

For Now, Re-Organize Board Members Around Committees (or Task Forces)

6. **For now, establish standard committees (or task forces) and ensure all members are on.**
    Even if the nonprofit prefers not to use committees, the Board needs some well-organized approach now to depersonalize issues and to focus members on achieving clear and specific best practices. Committees or task forces are often a good way to do that. They can be dissolved later on, if needed. When restoring a Board, the best committees or task forces to form usually are in regard to finance, fundraising, programs and personnel. Struggling Boards often result in poor financial oversight and ineffective fundraising. The Program Committee is to ensure that Board members engage around whether the nonprofit is really meeting needs in the community. The Committee also ensures that members truly understand the programs. The Personnel Committee is needed to coach the Chief Executive to adapt to the changes on the Board (more on that later in this section).

Ensure All Members Have Specific Assignments

7. **Be sure that each committee (or task force) has a work plan to instill best practices.**
    Each committee should be assigned the standard goals and objectives necessary for that committee to instill best practices regarding the function associated with that committee. Associate objectives with achievement of each goal and then associate deadlines with each objective. Do not be overly concerned about identifying the best objectives or deadlines – at this point, the priority is for each committee to have something specific to work on. The work plans can be changed as necessary.

> For ideas for goals and objectives of each committee, see "What Each Committee Typically Does" on page 85. Also see the suggested list of best practices for each area as contained in the assessment tool that starts on page 230.

> For ideas about how to format goals and objectives onto work plans for each committee, see "Goals and Objectives for Board Development Committee" on page 243.

Establish Leadership Structures to Guide and "Police" Change

8. **Reorganize the Executive Committee to be comprised of Chairs of Committees.**
    This is in contrast to organizing the Executive Committee to be comprised only of officers. That new organization, with members from each Committee, makes sure that the members of the Executive Committee always know what is going on in each of the other Committees and, thus, becomes a very effective central "policing function" to monitor and ensure that the other Committees are making progress in instilling best practices into Board operations.

Adopt Board Policies for High-Quality Participation and Meetings

9. **Enact a Board calendar that makes sure best practices are done regularly.**
    The calendar is an extremely important tool to refocus Board members on effective Board operations. Members can reference the calendar to know when to do strategic planning, evaluate the Board, evaluate the Chief Executive, staff the Board, approve the budget, etc.

See the "Sample Annual Calendar of Board Activities" on page 257.

10.   **Enact a policy for making formal decisions so members do not get bogged down.**
In struggling Boards, members often do not know how to efficiently address a decision or problem and then move on. They usually talk endlessly about the topic until conflict or fatigue overcomes them, and so they either drop the topic or they quickly make any decision just to get away from their increasing discomfort.

 See "Sample Board Decision-Making Policy" on page 268.

11.   **Enact a Board attendance policy.**
This is important because it is not uncommon that one or more Board members might decide that, if they are to become more participative in an improved Board, then they do not have the time to do so and so they should quit the Board. Often, this is not their fault – they might already be on several others Boards and so they are already too busy.

 See "Sample Board Attendance Policy" on page 275.

Conduct Highly Focused Board Meetings

12.   **Meet every month, facilitate to timed agendas and use ground rules.**
The Board needs to meet every month in order to maintain focus and momentum on making new changes. Agendas should include topics and suggested times to address each topic. If a topic has not been addressed in that time, then delegate to a subgroup of members to get more information to help the Board with the topic in the next meeting. Use ground rules to keep focus. If conflicts occur, use guidelines in the follow sections about managing conflict.

 For guidelines about agendas and ground rules, see "How to Have Productive Board Meetings" on page 122.

Ensure Strategic Priorities Are Addressed

13.   **During meetings, practice focusing on strategic questions.**
Even if your Board is a working governing Board or a collective governing Board, the strategic questions still need to be addressed by Board and staff members. The questions are an opportunity for Board members to practice being strategic.

 See "Questions Your Board Members Should Always Ask" on page 124.

Ensure Each Committee (or Task Force) is Active

14. **Executive Committee, comprised of committee Chairs, "polices" work plans.**
    By now, each Committee (or task force) has a work plan with goals and associated
    objectives, along with timelines to achieve each objective. The Executive Committee has
    the Chair of each Committee and, therefore, should easily be able to get status on
    implementation of each Committee's work plan. If plans are not on schedule, then the
    Executive Committee should raise the issue. Should priority be increased on the work plan?
    Should timelines be moved out? What should be done?

Coach Board Chair and Chief Executive During Change

15. **Board Development Committee coaches the Board Chair.**
    It is extremely important that the Board Chair understands, supports and guides the new
    changes in Board operations. It is the Board Development Committee's job to suggest those
    new changes, so it also is the best Committee to help the Board Chair to fully understand the
    changes and to facilitate according to the changes, as well.

16. **Personnel Committee coaches the Chief Executive.**
    The Chief Executive will very likely be undergoing major stresses as the Board members
    start to become more involved and operating in a manner that the CEO is not used to. Also,
    the new Board operations often result in various changes in the role of the CEO. Therefore,
    the Personnel Committee should be supporting and guiding the CEO to adjust to the
    changes, as well.

Re-Evaluate Board Health to Measure Success of Change

17. **Repeat the Board self-evaluation in six to nine months.**
    Use the same assessment tool that you used when you started the activities to restore the
    Board. This evaluation measures the progress made so far and can be used to update the
    Board Development Plan for the next round of Board development activities.

How to Manage Interpersonal Conflicts

If two Board members seem to be in continual conflict in a meeting, then facilitate the following
quick conversation with them. The following is the quick, powerful technique of reflective listening.
It can be done in 10-15 minutes during a break from the Board meeting. While it probably will not
result in both members really liking each other, it will call attention to the fact that they are being
disruptive to the Board and that they both need special attention. Usually, that situation is enough to
make members work harder at resolving their conflict.

1. **Move the discussion with the two members to a private area, if possible.**
   This is helpful if one or both of the members seem upset. Perhaps do this during a break.

2. **Share with them what you are seeing or hearing that is destructive to the Board.**
   Do not attempt to "diagnose" or analyze reasons for their behavior – focus on their actual
   behaviors, what you are seeing or hearing from them. Take one minute to do this.

3. **Ask one person (Member A) to speak and the other (B) to just listen.**
   Do this for 2 (at most 3) minutes. Dissuade any interruptions from B.

4. **When A is done, ask B to say what he/she heard from A, and no more.**
    Take one minute for this. Do not interrupt.

5. **If A says that B did not really hear what A said, then repeat steps 3 and 4 once.**
    Usually, this results in B hearing much more of what A actually said.

6. **Repeat steps 3 through 5, with A and B switching roles.**
    Again, do not interrupt. Watch the timing carefully.

7. **Suggest where they might seem to agree. Seek common ground.**
    Now you can intervene for one minute to share what you are hearing and what seems to be in common to what each has said.

8. **If there is no common ground, then ask both specifically how to move forward.**
    Remind them that their agreement is critical to the success of the Board and its role to serve the community. Ask them to say what they personally will do to get the Board's discussions back on track. Let one person speak for a minute, then the other.

9. **Thank them for explaining their opinions.**
    Mention that you appreciate their passion for the Board and their willingness to support the Board and the community.

> For more information and guidelines about addressing interpersonal conflict, see the topic "Addressing Interpersonal Conflict" in the Free Management Library at http://www.managementhelp.org/intrpsnl/conflict.htm .

How to Manage Board Conflict and Come to Decisions

If there seems to be prolonged conflict among several people on the Board, consider the following guidelines:

1. **First, verify if members indeed are in conflict. Ask the members. Listen for 3 minutes.**
    They might not be in destructive conflict, at all. Name or describe what behaviors you are seeing that might indicate destructive conflict. Do not try to "diagnose" causes of those behaviors, just name what you are seeing or hearing. Acknowledge that conflict is natural in healthy groups, but why you conclude that conflict has become destructive.

2. **If members are in destructive conflict, then select approaches to resolve conflict.**
    Take a 5-minute break. Ask two other members to step aside with you. Ask them to suggest the best approach(es) to address the conflict, and then read the ideas listed immediately below. Ask them to suggest which approach(es) would be most likely to move things along.

3. **Use the approaches, selected by the subgroup, with the Board.**
    Explain that the approaches were selected by several of you, not by just one person. Ask that members set aside 10-15 minutes on the agenda to try them out. The more the members are in destructive conflict, the more likely they will be willing to try out the approaches.

Possible approaches that Board members can use to resolve destructive conflict:

- Focus on what members agree on, for instance by posting the mission, vision and/or values statements to remind people of why they are there.

- Ask members, "If this disagreement continues, where will we be? How will it hurt our community?"

- Have members restate their position. If it will take longer than three minutes, allow opportunities for others to confirm or question for understanding.

- Shift to prioritizing alternatives, rather than excluding all alternatives but one.

- Take a 10-minute break in which each member quietly reflects on what he/she can do to move the Board members forward.

- Take 5-10 minutes and in groups of two, each person shares with the other what they are confused or irritated about. The other person in the pair helps the speaker to articulate his or her views to the larger group. Then, reverse the roles, so each person has the opportunity to express him/herself.

- Propose an "agree to disagree" disposition.

- If disagreement or lack of consensus persists around an issue, have a committee select options and then report back to the full Board.

- Tell stories of successes and failures in how Board members operate, including how members got past their differences and reached agreement.

- Call for a vote on a stated question or decision.

How to Get Your Board Members Unstuck

Sometimes, even if there is a lot of participation from members and no prolonged conflict, a group might not seem to be making any progress. They may simply be stuck, for example, during planning or when needing to make a major decision. Consider a similar process as when a group seems in prolonged conflict. The Board Chair or another Board member could:

1. **First, verify if members indeed are stuck. Ask the members. Listen for 3 minutes.** They might not be stuck, at all. Name or describe what behaviors you are seeing that might indicate they are stuck. Do not try to "diagnose" causes of those behaviors, just name what you are seeing or hearing.

2. **If members are stuck, then select approaches to move the Board forward.** Take a 5-minute break. Ask two other members to step aside with you. Ask them to suggest the best approach(es) to move things along, and then read the ideas listed immediately below. Ask them to suggest which approach(es) would be most likely to move things along.

3. **Use the approaches, selected by the subgroup, with the Board.** Explain that the approaches were selected by several of you, not by just one person. Ask that members set aside 10-15 minutes on the agenda to try them out. The more the members are stuck, the more likely they will be willing to try out the approaches.

Possible approaches that Board members can use to become un-stuck:

- Ask the group, "If we continue to be stuck, where will we be? How will we be hurting our community?"

- Take a five-minute break to let members do whatever they want.

- Resort to some movement and stretching.

- Ask for five examples of "out of the box" thinking.

- Resort to thinking and talking about activities in which resources do not matter.

- Play a quick game that stimulates creative thinking.

- Use metaphors, such as stories, myths or archetypal images. For example, ask each person to take five minutes to draw or write a metaphor that describes his/her opinions, and position in the meeting.

- Have each or some of the planners tell a story and include some humor.

- Use visualization techniques, for example, visualize reading an article about the organization's success some years into the future. What does the article say about how the success came about?

- Play reflective or energizing music (depending on the situation).

- Restructure the group to smaller groups or move members around in the larger group.

- Have a period of asking question after question after question (without answering necessarily). Repetition of questions, "why?" in particular, can help to move planners into deeper levels of reflection and analysis, especially if they do not have to carefully respond to each question.

- Establish a "parking lot" for outstanding or unresolved issues, and then move on to something else. Later, go back to the issue on which the group seemed stuck.

- Ask key questions, for example, "How can we make it happen? How can we avoid it happening?"

- Focus on what the group agrees on, for instance by posting the mission, vision and/or values statements to remind people of why they are there.

Recovering From Founder's Syndrome

What is Founder's Syndrome?

Blindly Following the Leader – Not Mission, Plans and Policies

Often the first major challenges in the "maturing" process for a Board – or for an entire organization – is to move away from always following the nature of certain personalities in the organization and instead work according to its mission, plans and policies. That challenge is common to any type of Board model, whether it is a working Board, policy Board, Policy Governance® Board or collective Board. The maturing process does not mean that members cannot choose any of these models. It means that members must use the model for the betterment of the nonprofit, not for the betterment of the leader.

It is common for members of new Boards to follow the lead of whoever seems to be the most persuasive person in the organization. Often that person is the founder of the organization and the person who goes on to become its first Chief Executive, Board Chair or both. Other times, it can be a variety of people on the Board and/or staff. In any case, the Board is not referencing the mission, policies and plans to guide the organization, rather it is just playing "follow the leader."

The problems inherent in working according to personalities, rather than according to the mission, have become so common, especially in new and small organizations, that some experts refer to the problems collectively as Founder's Syndrome. That phrase can be misleading, though, because the people having undue influence are not always the founders of the organizations. The "founder" can be one person on the Board or staff or, at times, a certain group of people in the organization.

Typical Problem in New and Small Organizations

To continue to reliably meet the needs of their customers (or clients), organizations must evolve through a particular life-cycle change, just like people must do in order to mature. This change is usually from a highly reactive and seat-of-the-pants approach to growth to a well-planned and managed approach. Plans do not have to be constricting plans that are full of unnecessary paperwork – the nonprofit does not have to become highly bureaucratic. However, there should be enough plans and policies to provide a stable and efficient infrastructure from which to continue to grow.

This necessary evolution often requires a change in the nature of leadership from a highly reactive, individualistic style to a more proactive, consensus-oriented style. Many charismatic and visionary leaders cannot make this transition – whether the founder is the CEO, someone on the Board or a group of people on the Board. They might have more confidence in their own grand plans and intuition than in what they often perceive as unnecessary "paperwork." As a result, more detailed plans and policies are not made, if at all.

As these nonprofits continue to grow and the demand for their services continues to grow as well, the need for more efficiency and resources continues to increase. As a result, the leader demands that people work even harder to take on more roles and that Board members get even more money. Yet, the problem is not from lack of effort and money. It is from people's confusion about their purpose, direction and roles. It is from constant pressure from the leader – pressure that does not really seem to be solving any of the problems in the organization. Soon, Board and staff members become so frustrated that they leave – and the organization continues to struggle from one crisis to another.

No one really seems to know what is going on. Those who remain in the organization continue to look to the leader who seems to be doing the same things as before, but now even harder. Things just get worse. As a result, the organization remains managed, not in a manner that reliably provides services to clients, but in a manner that suits the personality of the increasingly frustrated founder.

Eventually, stakeholders confront the leader about the organization's recurring problems. Funders may confront the Chief Executive or Board. Without ongoing coaching and support, it is likely that the leader will be replaced, or even worse, the organization will fold. Founder's Syndrome is no one's fault – no leader sets out to intentionally damage the organization. Besides, the syndrome does not occur without members of the Board and staff blindly following the leader.

Leadership and Founder's Syndrome – the Good and Bad

Troublesome Traits Among Founders and Boards

Whether the founder is the CEO, someone on the Board or a group of people on the Board, founders are dynamic, driven and decisive. They carry clear vision of what their organization can be. They know their client's needs and are passionate about meeting those needs. Often these traits are strong assets for getting the new organization off the ground. However, other traits of founders too often become major liabilities. For example, founders often:

- Are highly skeptical about planning, policies and procedures. They claim "plans and procedures are overhead and just bog me down." They often believe they have found a new way to get things done.

- Make reactive, crisis-driven decisions with little input from others. They react to most problems with the lament "if only I had more money."

- Attend mostly to fundraising and generating new ideas for services.

- Handpick their Board members and staff. See these people as working for the founder as much as working for the organization's mission.

- Attract Board members through the founder's dynamic, often charismatic personality – not through focus on the organization's mission.

- Hold staff meetings primarily to report crises and rally the troops.

- Count on whomever seems most loyal and accessible, and motivate by fear and guilt, often without realizing it.

- See their Boards mostly as a source for fundraising, and work to remove Board members who disagree with the founder.

- Have a very difficult time letting go of the strategies that worked to quickly grow the organization, despite evidence that the organization can no longer absorb this rapid growth without major changes.

Ultimately, Founder's Syndrome sets in because the organization becomes dependent, not on the systems and structures of the organization, but on the unique style of the leader – whether the leader is consistently decisive or consistently indecisive.

Typical Traits of Well-Developed Leaders

The following traits are important for the Board members and Chief Executive to have if they are to effectively lead their nonprofits. They are in sharp contrast to leaders with Founder's Syndrome. Traits include:

- Appreciating plans and budgets as guidelines, and realize that these ultimately make the nonprofit more responsive to the needs of their customers.

- Making proactive decisions based on mission and affordability.

- Making staffing decisions based on staff's responsibilities, training and capabilities.

- Valuing Board and staff members for their strong expertise and feedback.

- Sustaining strong credibility among clients and service providers.

Basic Principles in Developing Leadership

Eventually, most founders realize they must change the way they operate. Many go on to evolve their leadership style to the next level. First, they realize they must change from within. They:

- Understand that the recurring problems are not their fault – they are doing the best they can.

- Are willing to ask for and accept help.

- Communicate often and honestly (this is often difficult for crisis-driven, "heroic" leaders).

- Engage in stress management, especially forms not related to their jobs.

- Are patient with themselves, their Boards and staff.

- Regularly take time to reflect and learn.

The following guidelines assume that the founder is the person who founded the organization and is also the Chief Executive. The Board model includes use of committees, as well. The CEO has staff reporting to him or her. However, as you read the following guidelines, adapt them to the particular model used by the Board and staff (if the nonprofit has staff) of your organization.

It will be extremely helpful now if you review the information in the previous sections about the context of restoring a Board on page 175 and a procedure for restoring a Board on page 183.

Actions Your Board Members Must Take

If the organization seems stuck in a highly reactive way of doing things, addressing the same problems over and over again, then it may be facing Founder's Syndrome. This requires a major change in the way that the Board and Chief Executive operate together. Making this change in leadership style is usually confusing, lonely and stressful for the founder, whether the founder is the CEO, someone on the Board or a group of people on the Board. The Board members can be the founder's greatest source of help if they:

1. **Understand and take full responsibility for the role of Board member.**
   Insist on highly condensed and focused Board training sessions on an annual basis in order to review the roles and responsibilities of a governing Board. Undertake a yearly self-evaluation of the Board to ensure it is operating effectively.

2. **Once a year, conduct a risk management exercise.**
   Pretend the founder suddenly left the organization. Who will/can quickly step in? Are you sure? What activities is the staff really doing to carry out programs? What grants does the organization have to perform against and when must you report on them? What is the cash flow situation? What stakeholders must be contacted? Where are the files/records?

3. **Know what is going on in the organization or how to quickly come up to speed.**
   Ensure job descriptions are up-to-date. Have staff complete weekly or biweekly written status reports. Ensure yearly written performance reviews are completed. Ensure regular staff meetings are held and actions are written. Is a staff member being cultivated as an assistant Chief Executive? Is this needed?

4. **Strategic planning is one of the best ways to engage the Board and take stock.**
   Conduct regular and realistic strategic planning with the Board and staff. Ensure the planning is carried out according to the nature of the organization, especially in a realistic and practical fashion. Focus on the top three or four issues facing the organization. Although most organizations scope plans to the coming three years, focus careful planning on the next six to 12 months. Establish clear goals and associated objectives, and work hard to responsibilities and timelines for each objective.

5. **Develop a highly participative Finance Committee or task force.**
   You might need to do the same with a Fundraising Committee or task force, too. Too often, Boards are extremely reluctant to face the founder by getting involved in finances. However, organizational problems are often revealed as financial problems. If a founder struggles or eventually leaves the organization, the finances are usually the first area to show major problems. Therefore, closely review the financial statements, especially cash flow.

6. **Do not be part of the problem!**
   Do not take on the traits of the crisis-driven founder and staff, or worse yet, just "numb out." Meet consistently and make decisions based on mission, planning and affordability, not on urgency. Avoid the notion of any quick fixes, such as hiring an associate director with "people skills." This does not address the problem and may make things even worse.

7. **Help Board members and staff to keep up their hopes.**
   Regularly communicate with each other (through appropriate channels). Remind each other that the recurring problems are the result of the organization's success and that current

changes are to best serve the needs of its clients. Staff members' morale will improve as they perceive stability, security and progress.

8. **Support the founder with ongoing coaching and affirmation.**
    The founder will change to the extent that he or she feels safe, understands the reasons for change, and accepts help along the way. Consider a Board Personnel Committee or task force to provide ongoing coaching to the founder (but not to replace his or her responsibilities and accountabilities). Include at least one or two experienced organizational leaders on this committee. Note that the founder is not changing roles, but priorities.

9. **Carefully monitor implementation and deviations from plans.**
    Do not hold the founder to always be doing what is in the plan or budget – but do hold the founder to be always explaining deviations and how they can be afforded.

10. **Implement development and evaluation plans for the founder.**
    Include the founder's input. Focus on the founder's accountability to implementing the plans or explaining deviations from them. Evaluate the founder as to how well he/she met his/her goals and objectives and the responsibilities in his/her job description.

11. **Consider policies to carefully solicit feedback from staff to the Board.**
    Consider having staff representatives on Board committees or task forces. Consider a 360-degree evaluation process for the Chief Executive, wherein staff provides feedback about the Chief Executive's performance. Establish a grievance procedure where staff can approach the Board about concerns if they can prove they have tried to work with the Chief Executive to resolve these issues.

12. **Closely monitor key indicators of successful change.**
    Ensure ongoing communications between Board members and the founder, sound financial management, implementation of plans and policies, and stable turnover of staff. Perhaps the most useful indicator is continued positive feedback from customers.

13. **If problems recur, take action.**
    If, after attempting to follow the above suggestions, the same major problems recur over the next six to nine months, then take major actions regarding the founder's position in the organization. The Board should have been highly involved in strategic planning, financial management, fundraising, authorizing policies, reviewing programs and evaluating the Chief Executive. If the founder's leaving would cause the organization to fold, then the Board has not been doing its job all along.

Actions Your Founder Must Take

The major actions mentioned below are intended to help the organization to retain focus and direction, and become more stable and proactive. Each nonprofit follows the practices according to its own nature and needs. The practices are not developed overnight and are never done perfectly. They should be followed to the extent that they are supportive, not restrictive. Start simple, but start! The following guidelines assume that the founder is the CEO, which, of course, is not always the case.

1. **Accept a mentor outside the organization and an advocate within.**
   Founder's Syndrome comes from doing what is natural for you. Changing your leadership style may be rather unnatural. Seek and accept help.

2. **Ensure a client-driven organization.**
   Always focus on the needs of clients. Regularly ask clients what they need and how the organization can meet their needs. Establish straightforward and realistic means to evaluate services. Start with basic questionnaires to gather clients' impressions. Interview some clients to get their "story."

3. **Set direction through planning.**
   Support the Board to carry out strategic planning. Ensure staff input as well. Conduct regular staff meetings to hear staff input. Cultivate a strong Finance Committee and Fundraising Committee (or task forces) and help them to fully understand the organization's finances and fundraising plans.

4. **Organize resources to meet goals.**
   Develop job descriptions with staff input to ensure mutual understanding of responsibilities. Develop staff-driven procedures for routine, but critical tasks.

5. **Motivate leadership and staff to meet goals.**
   Delegate to staff members by helping them understand the purpose of tasks. Get their input as to how the tasks can be completed. Give them the authority to complete the tasks. In regular staff meetings, celebrate successes! Bring in clients to tell staff how the organization helped meet their needs. Conduct regular performance reviews with staff to ensure organizational and staff needs are being met. In regular staff meetings, share status information and conduct day-to-day planning.

6. **Guide resources to meet goals.**
   Share management challenges with the Board and ask for policies to guide management. Work from the strategic plan and develop an associated budget to earmark funds.

7. **Think transition!**
   Help the Board to regularly undertake contingency planning, including thinking about what the organization will do if/when you are gone. Have the Board members pretend that, for some unknown reason, you were suddenly gone. What would they do? How?

Actions Your Staff Members Might Take

If the founder is on the Board or is the CEO, then other staff still might play a major role in helping the organization to recover. However, staff may be in somewhat of a high-risk situation because the founder (who often values loyalty at least as much as effectiveness) may perceive staff actions as hurting the organization, rather than helping it. Therefore, staff are advised to proceed with caution.

The syndrome can be quite stressful for staff. They can lose perspective amidst the continued confusion and anxiety in the workplace. If they have been in the organization long enough, they, too, become part of the problem. Therefore, it is important for staff to get perspective on the nature and extent of the problem.

1. **Get clear perspective by privately writing down a list of problems you perceive.**
   Privately record your concerns. In order to minimize your own biases, record only what you have seen with your eyeballs, not just felt with your heart. Document only those problems which seem to be persistent and/or which various people have tried to resolve.

2. **Work hard to identify an external mentor and an internal staff advocate.**
   Share your concerns and ideas with someone else whose judgment you highly respect.

3. **Match your list with previous section, "Some Troublesome Traits Among Founders."**
   How many of the symptoms match those recorded in your list? Consider sharing your list and results with someone whom you trust. Do they agree with your approach and results? It is up to you to conclude if the organization has the syndrome or not. Whether the organization has the syndrome or not, if there are enough other persistent problems, you may still want to take action.

4. **Assess if you want to stay in the organization and help it recover.**
   This requires that you carefully reflect on why you are in the organization, what you can do to help the organization recover, the likelihood of it recovering and how well you manage your own stress.

5. **If you stay in the organization and help it to recover, use the organization's structure.**
   That is, communicate your suggestions with peers and your immediate supervisor, whether that is the founder or not. Give them a chance to address your concerns. Promptly go to the Board if symptoms of the problem result in discrimination or harassment of you and if your personnel policies include a grievance procedure for you to go directly contact the Board. You might consider a letter to the Board if you resign, but this may hurt your career.

6. **Give suggestions from "Actions Board Must Take", "Actions Founders Must Take."**
   Do not provide all of the suggestions at once. Always associate your suggestions with a description of how they can constructively advance the mission of the organization. Do not personalize your descriptions of concerns by blaming them on someone. Make your suggestions in writing, for example, in status reports or in memos. Put a date on the suggestions so you can keep perspective on whether the suggestions are acted on or not.

7. **Monitor whether the organization is recovering or not.**
   Have you given the organization time to address concerns? Has the organization made substantial changes and symptoms have decreased? Or, do you see the same symptoms?

8.   **Update your resume and consider looking for another job.**
        Keeping your own health and happiness is the best thing you can do for yourself and
        ultimately the community. You will become ill if you stay in the organization. Your leaving
        may actually contribute to the organization's recovering if other staff members realize why
        you left. Even if you decide to stay, knowing that you can leave might shift your attitude
        enough to approach the situation with fresh energy or perspective.

9.   **Do not "burn bridges."**
        It is extremely compelling to write a blistering letter to all members of the Board and various
        staff members, explaining each and every problem in the organization. This may
        temporarily relieve you of your frustration, but it may also hurt your credibility with key
        members of the organization's community. If you communicate your concerns and reasons
        for leaving, be respectful and tactful.

APPENDICES:

Appendix A: Glossary

Accountability (in nonprofits)
> Board members continually making their nonprofits and themselves responsible to meet the expectations of stakeholders, and verifying with those stakeholders that their expectations are indeed being met. Also see **Stakeholders**.

Agenda (of Board meeting)
> Specification of the design of a planned Board meeting, including, for example: times to start and stop the meeting, major topics to be addressed in the meeting, along with the type of action sought for each topic (decision, resolution, etc.) and time to address each topic.

Articles of Incorporation
> The legal document used to describe and form a corporation, for example, a nonprofit corporation. Usually must be filed in the state or province in which the corporation prefers to be located.

Assessment
> Systematic collection of data, followed by analysis to generate findings and conclusions, for example, an organizational assessment to detect the strengths and weaknesses of all of the organization's most important operations.

Best practices
> Practices conducted by individuals, groups or organizations that are widely respected for some particular expertise or activity that involves those practices, for example: best practices in Board operations, personnel management and financial management. There can be wide disagreement about what constitutes a best practice, depending on the context of the practices and the values of those in observance of the practices.

Board development
> Raising the performance of the Board of Directors up another level, either to resolve major issues on the Board (restoring the Board) or to make sufficient performance even better. Can include a sequence of activities to enhance Board operations, for example, a Board self-evaluation, producing a Board development plan, orienting Board members, training Board members, coaching the Board Chair and re-assessing the Board's performance. Contrast to **Board orientation** and **Board training**. Also see **Restoring Boards**.

Board Manual
> Usually a manual, or handbook, provided to each Board member, containing the important information needed by the member in order to effectively conduct his/her role as a Board member. See **Board policies**.

Board model
> Structure by which Board members organize themselves and work together, including their level of involvement in management functions, if any. The model can be developed in a proactive, planful manner or emerge as Board members work together and with staff. There are a wide variety of models for governing Boards. See **Collective governing Board**, **Policy governing Board** and **Working governing Board**.

Board of Directors

Group of people legally charged to govern the corporation, whether for-profit or nonprofit. In a for-profit, Board members are responsible to ensure the business meets the needs of stockholders. In a nonprofit, members are responsible to ensure the nonprofit meets the needs of the community. See **Governance.**

Board orientation

Orienting Board members to the unique features of the organization, for example, to other members on the Board, where the Board meets, and the organization's programs and services. Contrast to **Board training** and **Board development**.

Board policies

General guidelines and sometimes specific procedures by which Board members choose to operate amongst themselves and sometimes with staff members, for example, policies to staff the Board, conflict-of-interest, attendance and evaluation of members.

Board training

Training Board members about the roles and responsibilities of a governing Board of Directors. Contrast to **Board orientation** and **Board development**.

Business planning

Activities to clarify the need for a product or service in the community, specific groups of people having that need, how the product or service meets each group's particular needs, resources needed to develop and provide the product or service, how the resources will be organized and managed, costs to obtain and support use of the resources, and how communications between the organization and community will be coordinated. Contrast to **Strategic planning**.

By Laws

Board members' comprehensive, primary policy that specifies how the Board members choose to operate among themselves and in the nonprofit, including, for example: Board structure, roles, committees, meetings, membership and attendance requirements. The contents of the By Laws is determined by statute in some states.

Capacity building (in nonprofits)

Activities to help a nonprofit enhance its effectiveness in working toward its mission.

CEO

See **Chief Executive Officer.**

Charitable nonprofit

See **Nonprofit (informal, formal, tax-exempt and charitable)**.

Charity (nonprofit)

See **Nonprofit (informal, formal, tax-exempt and charitable)**.

Chief Executive Officer (CEO, Executive Director)

Usually, the singular, organization-wide, staff position that is primarily responsible to carry out the strategic plans and policies established by the Board of Directors. The extent of authority and the scope and level of activities depends on the Board model preferred by the nonprofit. Not all nonprofits have staff members, including a CEO. Particularly in small or new nonprofits, the Board members and CEO often seem to work in partnership to oversee and manage the nonprofit's operations, even though the Board has the ultimate authority for governance and operations.

Collective governing Board

One model of a governing Board where Board and staff members work closely together in an egalitarian team to perform the functions of governance and management. Contrast to **Policy governing Board** and **Working governing Board**.

Committee (Board)

Subgroup of the overall Board members, often focused on overseeing and/or conducting a particular management function, for example, planning, personnel, marketing, fundraising and finances. Can be standing (or permanent) committees or ad hoc (temporary) committees. Also see **Task force (Board)**.

Consensus

Participatory decision-making method whereby all participants come to agreement on the desired outcome of a decision – even though some members might prefer a different outcome, those members go along with the majority's preference in their commitment to move forward on the decision and act as one unified body.

Corporate Board

Phrase used to refer to a Board of a for-profit corporation. This is a misnomer because the Board of a nonprofit corporation also is a corporate Board. Also see **Board of Directors**.

Corporation (for-profit or nonprofit)

Organization that is chartered (incorporated) by the appropriate governmental agency in order to exist as a legal entity separate from the members of the organization. Corporations require a Board of Directors to govern the corporation. Nonprofits often are chartered as corporations; thus, they must have a Board of Directors. There are certain advantages to chartering an organization as a corporation, including limited liability of organization members for the operations of the organization. Also, the corporation can own property, hold its own bank account, enter into contracts and conduct tax-exempt activities. Also see **Governance**.

Culture (of an organization)

The "personality" of an organization as defined by the aggregate of values, assumptions, opinions, behaviors, etc., by which members act in the organization.

Ethics

Simply put, ethics involves learning what is right or wrong, and then doing the right thing. Ethics includes the fundamental ground rules by which we live our lives, especially to treat others fairly and equitably. A code of ethics is an articulated set of values or principles by which a person or group should act.

Evaluation

Systematic collection and analysis of data to make a decision. Usually includes generation of findings and recommendations to address findings.

Ex officio (status)

Membership by virtue of the position, for example, a Board Chair having ex officio status on a Board committee. As to whether the person in the role has all of the rights of membership, such as qualifying as a member in the quorum count or voting, is up to the nonprofit.

Executive Director

See **Chief Executive Officer.**

Financial management

Activities to ensure the organization's finances are effectively accounted for, legally allocated, utilized in an optimum manner and at minimum risk. Includes operating according to fiscal policies and procedures, bookkeeping to monitor and record transactions, generating and analyzing financial statements, and actions to improve finances and management.

Founder's Syndrome

Exists when an overall organization operates more to the personality of one person in the organization than to its mission. Could be according to the founder or another prominent person in the organization.

Fundraising

Activities to solicit and report about funds from donors, including from individuals, foundations, corporations and/or government. Includes identifying fundraising targets (total monies to be raised during a certain period), researching prospective donors, soliciting each donor (via grants, events, etc.), recognition to donors, and managing grant documents and requirements.

Good faith (acts of Board member)

Board member acts sincerely and truthfully with the best of intentions to benefit the nonprofit.

Governance

Board of Director's activities to ensure that the nonprofit operates effectively and efficiently, according to its mission and strategic priorities, to meet the needs of the community. New perspectives consider governance to include stakeholders affiliated with the nonprofit.

Independent Board member

Board member with no direct personal and vested interest in the nonprofit, for example, is not a member of the staff or is not a very close friend of the CEO. Independent Board members might be more objective during deliberations and decisions and, thus, more inclined to challenge the CEO and staff members about their own opinions and decisions.

Leader

Person who sets direction and also directs or influences other individuals or groups to follow that direction. Person can be a leader by the nature of the authority in his/her role, expertise and/or personality.

Leadership

Nature of activities or the capacity to establish direction and influence another person or group to follow that direction. Can also refer to leadership traits or leadership roles.

Management (in organizations)

Traditionally, refers to the activities involved in the four overall, general practices: planning, organizing, leading and coordinating. The four functions recur throughout the organization and are highly integrated.

Management functions

Major types of recurring activities to implement top-level plans and policies, for example, program delivery, staffing, finances, fundraising, marketing and evaluations.

Marketing (inbound and outbound)

Wide range of activities involved in making sure that you are continuing to meet the needs of your clients and getting sufficient value in return. These activities include "inbound marketing", such as market research (for example, to find out what groups of potential clients exist, what their needs are, which of those needs you can meet, how you should meet them), analyzing the competition, positioning your new product or service (finding your market niche), and pricing your products and services. Activities also include "outbound" marketing, advertising, promotions, public relations and sales.

Members (general and corporate in nonprofits)

Nonprofits can be chartered as a membership organization in which case, corporate members have authority to add or modify terms of governance, structure and management. For example, changes in By Laws require approval of that membership. General members exist, for example, in associations in which members pay annual dues, receive a newsletter, attend an annual conference, etc. General members might not have corporate authority.

Micro-managing (by Board members)

When members are so involved in the details of management and staff that they damage operations because 1) staff are continually updating members with trivial information, and 2) members do not sufficiently attend to strategic matters of top-level policies and plans.

Minutes (of Board meeting)

Official documentation of the results and highlights of a Board meeting that has occurred. Are various formats of minutes. Often include, for example: the actual timing of start and stop of the meeting, listing of members in attendance and absent, major topics addressed in the meeting, along with the type of action that was taken for each topic (decision, resolution etc.), including who initiated the actions and who was assigned the actions. See **Agenda (of Board meeting)**.

Mission (nonprofit)

The overall purpose of the nonprofit in the community. A mission statement describes that mission, for example: what groups of clients the nonprofit serves, the results that the nonprofit aims to achieve among those clients, and the types of services/programs the nonprofit uses to achieve those results.

Nonprofit (informal, formal, tax-exempt and charitable)

Organization that exists primarily to meet a public need, rather than to make a profit. An informal nonprofit is a group of people who gather to work on usually a short-term need in the community, for example, to clean up the neighborhood streets. A "chartered," or incorporated, nonprofit has filed with the appropriate government agency to be a legal entity separate from the members of the organization. A tax-exempt nonprofit has attained status from the appropriate government agency that allows the nonprofit to refrain from paying certain federal, state (provincial in Canada) and/or local taxes. A tax-deductible (charitable) nonprofit (or charity) has attained status from the appropriate government agency enabling it to receive donations and allowing donors to reduce their tax liabilities based on the amount of their donations.

Policies (Board)

See **Board policies**.

Policy governing Board

One model of a governing Board where members attend primarily to developing and enforcing top-level plans and policies, usually delegating implementation of those plans and policies to staff. These Boards often use a variety of committees, some with staff members on them. Sometimes referred to as a "traditional" Board. Contrast to **Collective governing Board** and **Working governing Board**.

Program planning

Activities to carefully identify what community needs are to be met by a new program, what methods (or program activities) will indeed meet those needs, and what group(s) of clients will be served. Can also include identifying program's collaborators, competitors and pricing. Ineffective fundraising, program evaluations and promotions often are the result of ineffective program planning.

Programs (in nonprofits)

Highly integrated set of activities and resources to meet certain needs of a certain group of people (clients). Well-designed programs also include ongoing evaluations about the activities to deliver services (process evaluations) and about the actual results achieved by participants in the program (outcomes evaluations).

Restoring (Boards)

Carefully integrated set of activities designed to resolve major issues in Board operations in order to significantly improve the performance of the Board. See **Board development**.

Staff members

Personnel, other than the Board members, who have responsibility for operations of the nonprofit. Can be paid or volunteer. The CEO is a staff member.

Stakeholders

People or groups of people who "have a stake," or strong, vested interest in the operations of the organization, for example: Board members, staff members, clients, funders, collaborators, community leaders and government agencies.

Strategic planning

Activities to clarify the overall mission and most important priorities for the nonprofit to address, and how to address those. There are many different ways to conduct strategic planning, ranging from: 1) formal, explicit and systematic, including intentional and comprehensive analyses of external and internal environments, identification of critical priorities, and the goals, objectives, responsibilities and resource needs to address those priorities, to 2) informal, implicit and non-systematic, including ongoing and occasional clarification of priorities, along with what seems most reasonable to address the priorities for now. Also see **Business planning**.

Supervision

Activities by a supervisor to oversee the progress and productivity of people who report directly to the supervisor. Includes staffing analysis, specification of duties and responsibilities (job description), recruitment and selection of employees, assignment of goals, feedback on achievement of goals, rewarding achievement of goals and addressing performance problems.

Task force (Board)

Subgroup of the overall Board members, usually focused on overseeing and/or conducting a particular management function, for example, planning, personnel, marketing, fundraising and finances. Usually temporary in nature. Some nonprofits prefer not to utilize committees and might prefer instead to utilize task forces, focused on a particular function or event. Also see **Committees (Board)**.

Tax-deductible (charitable nonprofit) (charity)

See **Nonprofit (informal, formal, tax-exempt and charitable)**.

Tax-exempt (nonprofit)

See **Nonprofit (informal, formal, tax-exempt and charitable)**.

Team building

Activities to form and develop a small group of people to effectively work toward a common purpose and achieve specific goals. There are a wide variety of means to build teams, ranging from enhancing members' feelings about each other to improving structures (plans, roles and policies) in the teams.

Term limits

Specified amount of time that a Board member can serve on the Board. This is usually specified in the By Laws. The popularity of terms limits tends to come and go – now they are more popular again as people want new energy and perspectives on the Board and to avoid members "getting into a rut" in their governance.

Transparency (in nonprofits)

Board members always providing full disclosure and explanation of the nonprofit's governance, finances and affects on communities, and also willingly supporting stakeholders' efforts to understand that information.

Work plan (in Board committees or task forces)
> Specification of the goals, along with associated objectives, responsibilities and timing to achieve the objectives, in order to achieve the overall goal.

Working governing Board
> One model of a governing Board where members attend both to strategic and hands-on matters. Often used early in the life of a nonprofit when it has few or no staff members. Contrast to **Collective governing Board** and **Policy governing Board**.

Appendix B: Resources for Nonprofits

Free Management Library^{SM}

The Library includes extensive free materials about personal, professional and organization development. The Library includes over 675 topics that are organized into the following popular categories. The list of topics is located at http://www.managementhelp.org on the Web.

Advertising and Promotion	Benefits and Compensation	Boards of Directors
Career Development	Chief Executive Role	Communications (Interprsnl)
Communications (Writing)	Computers, Internet & Web	Consultants (using)
Coordinating Activities	Creativity and Innovation	Crisis Management
Customer Satisfaction	Customer Service	E-Commerce
Employee Performance	Employee Wellness Programs	Ethics - Practical Toolkit
Evaluations (many kinds)	Facilities Management	Finances (For-Profit)
Finances (Nonprofit)	Fundraising (Nonprofit)	General Resources
Group Performance	Group Skills	Guiding Skills
Human Resources Mgmnt	Insurance (Business)	Interpersonal Skills
Interviewing (all kinds)	Jobs	Leadership (Introduction)
Leadership Development	Legal Information	Management (Introduction)
Management Development	Marketing	Operations Management
Organizational Alliances	Organizational Change	Org'l Communications
Organizational Performance	Organizations (Introduction)	Organizing (many kinds)
Performance Management	Personal Development	Personal Productivity
Personal Wellness	Planning (many kinds)	Policies (Personnel)
Product Selection & Dev.	Program Management	Project Management
Public and Media Relations	Quality Management	Research Methods
Risk Management	Sales	Social Entrepreneurship
Staffing	Starting an Organization	Supervision (Introduction)
Supervisory Development	Systems Thinking	Taxation
Training Basics	Volunteers	----------------

Free Nonprofit Micro-eMBA^{SM}
Organization Development Program

This state-of-the-art, on-line training program includes 12 highly integrated courses that can be taken for free by anyone, anywhere at any time. At the end of the program, each learner will have all of the basic systems and processes needed to start and operate a nonprofit. Learners are encouraged to work with their Boards of Directors while going through the program. Participants going through the program together can share plans, policies and procedures.

Any of the 12 courses in the program can be taken separately. The courses and their learning objectives are located at http://www.managementhelp.org/np_progs/org_dev.htm on the Web, in the "Course Catalog." (Your organization may also have a wide range of materials around which you could organize courses.) Courses include the following:

1.   Preparatory Workshop (skills in reading, studying, getting help, etc.)

2.   Starting and Understanding the Nonprofit

3.   Overview of Role of Chief Executive

4.   Basic Skills in Management and Leadership

5.   Building and Maintaining an Effective Board of Directors

6.   Developing Your Strategic Plan

7.   Designing and Marketing Your Programs

8.   Managing Your Finances and Taxes

9.   Developing Your Fundraising Plan

10.   Staffing and Supervision of Employees and Volunteers

11.   Evaluating Your Programs

12.   Organizational "Fitness Test"

Organizations Assisting Nonprofits

In the USA

Contact your Secretary of State and/or state's Attorney General's office and ask for a list of resources.

1. Executive Service Corps (ESC) provides experienced consultation in the areas of technical and management (http://www.escus.org/).

2. National Council of Nonprofit Associations (NCNA) has chapters in almost all of the states. (http://www.ncna.org).

In Canada

1. The Voluntary Sector Knowledge Network provides information, assistance and tools regarding a wide range of functions in nonprofits (http://www.vskn.ca/).

2. United Way Canada provides information, publications and funding to Canada voluntary sector organizations (http://www.unitedway.ca/english/).

3. The Canadian Centre for Philanthropy provides programs, resources, tools and information for the benefit of Canadian communities (http://www.ccp.ca/).

General Resources

- Contact the local volunteer recruitment organization in your community and ask for assistance.

- Look in the Yellow Pages of your local telephone directory for professional associations. Look for networks or associations of organization development practitioners, facilitators or trainers.

- Look in the Yellow Pages of your local telephone directory under the categories "Consultant" and "Volunteering".

- Contact local large corporations. They often have community service programs and can provide a wide range of management and technical expertise. Speak to the head of the Human Resources Department.

- Call a local university or college and speak to someone in the college of Human Resources, Training and Development, or Business Administration.

- Ask other nonprofits (particularly those that have similar services and number of staff,) or current clients for ideas, contacts and references.

- Ask a retired business person (from a for-profit or nonprofit organization). Often, they have facilitated a wide variety of meetings.

Free, On-Line Newsletters and Forums

CharityChannel forums
CharityChannel provides a wide array of forums, including forums on Canada-specific topics. Go to http://www.charitychannel.com/ and scroll down until you see the topic "Forums" on the left-hand side. At the time of this writing, there is an annual fee of $37 to use CharityChannel forums.

PULSE
An on-line newsletter published by the Support Centers of America and the Nonprofit Management Association. To subscribe send an e-mail message to "sca@supportcenter.org" and in the body of the message type: "SUBSCRIBE PULSE!". You may also call (415) 541-7708.

Board Cafe
This is a free on-line newsletter for nonprofit Boards of Directors. To subscribe send an e-mail message to "msimpson@supportcenter.org" and in the body of the message type: "SUBSCRIBE BOARD CAFE". You may also call (415)-541-9000.

Additional newsletters and forums are listed in the Free Management Library under the topic "General Resources."

Board-Specific Resources

A-Z Directory for Board Governance
This directory offers an extensive range of guidelines and tools, from starting a Board all the way to fulfilling the mission, from Volunteer BC in Canada. Located on the Web at http://www.vcn.bc.ca/volbc/tools/governance.html .

Board Café (on-line newsletter)
A free on-line newsletter for nonprofit Boards of Directors. To subscribe, send an e-mail message to "msimpson@supportcenter.org" and in the body of the message type: "SUBSCRIBE BOARD CAFE". You may also call (415)-541-9000.

Board Match
Board Match Online helps place knowledgeable and enthusiastic volunteers on the Boards of Directors of registered charities within Canada. Located at http://www.boardmatch.org/ .

Boards (on-line discussion group)
A very active on-line discussion group regarding all aspects of Boards can be found at http://charitychannel.com/resources/Forums/All_Public_Forums/BOARDS/index.html .

BoardSource
Provides an extensive range of information, materials and publications about Boards of Directors in the USA. (Formerly National Center for Nonprofit Boards.) Located on the Web at http://www.ncnb.org/ .

Free, Complete Toolkit for Boards
An extensive range of step-by-step materials for Boards, and many links to others. Located on the Web at http://www.managementhelp.org/boards/boards.htm .

Institute on Governance
The Institute concentrates its work around specific knowledge areas, including aboriginal governance, accountability and performance measurement, Board governance, building policy capacity, technology and governance, and youth and governance. Located on the Web at http://www.iog.ca/ .

Sample By Laws
From the Institute on Governance in Canada. Find it on the Web at http://www.iog.ca/publications/sample_bylaws.pdf .

Voluntary Sector Roundtable's Board Development materials
Includes an extensive range and amount of practical information and materials about Boards of Directors within the Voluntary Sector in Canada. Located on the Web at http://www.boarddevelopment.org/ .

Some Mega-Websites About Boards

- Alliance for Nonprofit Management resources at http://www.allianceonline.org/ARC .

- Board Glossary at http://www.boardsource.org/Knowledge.asp?ID=1.1016 .

- BoardSource FAQ's at http://www.boardsource.org/Knowledge.asp?ID=3 .

- Canada Revenue Agency at http://www.cra-arc.gc.ca/tax/charities/menu-e.html .

- CharityChannel Governance Review articles at http://charitychannel.com/enewsletters/nbgr/ .

- Energize at http://www.energizeinc.com/art.html .

- Free Complete Toolkit for Boards at http://www.managementhelp.org/boards/boards.htm .

- Help4Nonprofits at http://www.help4nonprofits.com/H4NP.htm .

- Idealist at http://www.idealist.org/ .

- Internal Revenue Service (in USA) http://www.irs.gov/charities/topic/index.html .

- Learning Institute for Nonprofit Organizations at http://www.uwex.edu/li/learner/sites_board.htm .

- Nathan Garber's resources at http://garberconsulting.com/links.htm .

- National Study of Board Governance Practices in the Non-Profit and Voluntary Sector in Canada at http://www.strategicleveragepartners.com/bhg768kjmhgvxxyxzwq/National_Study_of_Boar d_Governance_Practices_in_the_Non-Profit_and_Voluntary_Sector_in_Canada.PDF .

- Nonprofit FAQ on Boards at http://www.nonprofits.org/if/idealist/en/FAQ/CategoryViewer/default?category-eid=3-1&sid=80627634-248-ewO .

- Nonprofit Good Resource Guide at http://www.npgoodpractice.org .

- Nonprofit Risk Management center at http://nonprofitrisk.org/library/articles/articles.shtml .

- Volunteer BC in Canada at http://www.vcn.bc.ca/volbc/tools/governance.html .

Appendix C: Guidelines to Form Your Advisory Board

Overall Benefit of an Advisory Board

Driving forces such as increased global telecommunications, public consciousness and diverse values are causing rapid change among organizations like never before. Consequently, the overall role of Board governance becomes very critical in guiding these organizations during rapid change. An Advisory Board can be a tremendous complement to the effectiveness of the governing Board of Directors as it works to carry out a specific, complex, major role (for example, financial analysis) or initiative (for example, construct a building). Advisory Boards are sometimes referred to as Advisory Councils or Advisory Committees.

What is an Advisory Board?

An Advisory Board is a collection of individuals who bring unique knowledge and skills which complement the knowledge and skills of the formal Board members in order to more effectively govern the organization. Also, Advisory Boards are sometimes used to maintain formal and visible relationships with people who have particular strong status, for example, people whose terms have expired on the governing Board, leaders in the community and people with highly respected skills in certain program areas.

The Advisory Board does not have formal authority to govern the organization, that is, the Advisory Board cannot issue directives that must be followed as in the case with a governing Board. Rather, the Advisory Board serves to make recommendations and/or provide key information and materials to the formal Board of Directors. Committees of governing Boards, for example, Fundraising Committees and Personnel Committees, are of the same capacity as Advisory Boards – their members only make recommendations to the full Board.

The Advisory Board can be standing (or ongoing) or ad hoc (one-time) in nature. It can have a "personality" like governing Boards. For example, members of the Advisory Board can be very hands-on like a working Board or attending only to high-level recommendations like a policy governing Board.

The amount of influence that Advisory Boards have in their recommendations to the governing Board or staff members depends on the charter, or formal description of the Advisory Board. For example, Advisory Boards that include members with highly technical skills often have significant influence. In contrast, Advisory Boards with members who bring status might have less influence.

How to Organize Your Advisory Board

The most useful Advisory Boards are organized almost as carefully as governing Boards.

1.   For ongoing, major activities (for example, which will last longer than a year) consider establishing a standing Advisory Board. For short-term activities (for example, one to nine months), consider establishing an ad hoc Advisory Board.

2. Carefully charter the role of the Advisory Board in the formal Board of Directors' By Laws. In the By Laws, specify the Advisory Board's purpose, duration, guidelines for membership, how it contributes knowledge and skills, and any structures/policies from which the Advisory Board interacts with the formal Board of Directors and organization members.

 To see a sample of a committee charter, see "Sample Board Committee Charter" on page 259.

3. An Advisory Board, like a governing Boards of Directors, should have a Chair who drives the operations of the Advisory Board. The Advisory Board's Chair might be the main point of contact between the Advisory Board and the formal Board of Directors. The Advisory Board might have members who also are on the governing Board of Directors.

4. Advisory Boards benefit from having policies similar to those of a governing Board, for example, job descriptions, calendar of activities, Board attendance, decision-making, conflict-of-interest and ethics policy. Members also deserve an orientation to these policies.

 See "Sample Board Policies" on page 249.

Appendix D: Guidelines to Working With Consultants

This section is included in this guide for Board members because members should be involved in the deliberations and decisions whenever a consultant is being considered for a project that would have a major impact on the organization. This is true especially for small nonprofits with very limited resources – resources that must be spent very judiciously. In addition, there is increasing scrutiny from government agencies, for example, the Internal Revenue Service in the USA, on the operations of organizations that regularly hire consultants. Those agencies want to be sure that the organizations are not resorting to hiring consultants, rather than employees, as a way to inappropriately avoid paying payroll taxes. Thus, Board members should be aware of the best practices in considering, hiring and using consultants.

Reasons You Might Need Consultants

Good Reasons to Hire an External Consultant

- The organization has limited or no expertise in the area of need, for example, to develop a new program for clients.

- The time of need is short-term, for example, less than a year, so it may not be worth hiring a full-time, permanent staff member.

- The organization's previous attempts to meet its own needs were not successful, for example, the nonprofit developed a Strategic Plan that was never implemented.

- Organization members continue to disagree about how to meet the need and, thus, bring in a consultant to provide expertise or facilitation skills to come to consensus.

- Leaders want an objective perspective from someone without strong biases about the organization's past and current issues.

- A consultant can do the work that no one else wants to do, for example, historical data entry. (Some would argue that this is not really a consulting project.)

- A funder or other key stakeholder demands that a consultant be brought in to help further develop the nonprofit organization.

Poor Reasons to Hire an External Consultant

The following reasons are likely open to disagreement – some people would argue that some or all of the following are good reasons to hire a consultant.

- The organization wants a consultant to lend credibility to a decision that has already been made, for example, the Board of Directors has decided to reorganize the nonprofit, but the Chief Executive Officer disagrees – so the Board hires a consultant to lend expert credibility to their decision. Many consultants might consider this to be an unethical reason to hire a consultant.

- A supervisor does not want to directly address a problem of poor performance with one of the employees, so the supervisor hires a consultant to do the job that the employee should be doing. This is an irresponsible action on the part of the supervisor.

- The organization does not want to pay benefits (vacation pay, holiday pay, pension, etc.) or go through the administrative processes to withhold payroll taxes (social security taxes, federal taxes, etc.), so the organization hires a consultant. This reason for hiring a consultant is likely to be illegal and could result in the organization paying fines and penalties to the appropriate government agency.

Major Types of Consultants to Nonprofits

1. **Technical consultants**
   They usually provide highly specialized content expertise regarding certain specific systems and processes in the organization, for example, computer systems, financial and accounting systems, market research, fundraising, lobbying and advocacy, or facilities management. Many nonprofits hire technical consultants. The types of services provided by these consultants are often referred to as technical assistance.

2. **Program consultants**
   They usually provide highly specialized "content" expertise that is unique to certain types of program services, for example, expertise about health care, education or childhood development. Their services might also be referred to as technical assistance, depending on how specific and focused their services are.

3. **Management consultants**
   They help leaders and managers be more productive at planning, organizing, leading and coordinating resources in the organization. Applications for their services might include leadership, management and supervisory development. The types of services provided by these consultants might be referred to as either technical assistance or organizational development activities (see the next paragraph).

4. **Organizational development consultants**
   This type of consultant helps organizations improve performance, often by focusing on changing a significant portion of the organization or the entire organization itself. These consultants often use a wide variety of approaches, tools and techniques to affect various systems and functions across the organization, for example, technical assistance, coaching, facilitation and training.

   There has been some confusion about the focus of organizational development consultants. Some people assert that these consultants focus mostly on "soft" skills regarding peoples' beliefs, feelings and perceptions, and less on "hard" skills regarding organizational structures, processes and operations. Other people assert that organizational development consultants focus on both the "soft" and "hard" skills. (This author follows the latter assertion.)

   Many people believe there is a difference between the phrases "organizational development consultants" and "Organization Development consultants." These people might use the latter phrase to refer to consultants who adhere to certain working assumptions and values commonly associated with the field of Organization Development.

Generalists and Specialists

Some people refer to specialists and generalists as overall, major types of consultants. They might refer to technical consultants as specialists. Many people would consider organizational development consultants to be generalists.

Whether program consultants and management consultants are generalists or specialists depends on the nature of their services. The more specific the nature of their services, the more likely they would be referred to as specialists.

Functional or Focused Services

Recently, the terms "functional" and "focused" have been used to refer to servicing a specific system, function or process, for example, marketing systems, financial systems or information technology. Functional and focused activities are considered similar or the same as technical assistance.

Types of Consulting Can Overlap

The distinctions among the types of consultants can be blurry. For example, a management consultant, program consultant or technical consultant might operate as an organizational development consultant if they work in a manner that affects a significant portion or all of the organization.

Also, each type of consultant might be needed at various times in a project. For example, if you are an organizational development consultant, you might work with a client to identify the most important problems in an organization. Later on, you might function as a management consultant to train and coach various leaders and managers during the change effort. You might also bring in various program and technical consultants to contribute their specific expertise to the change effort.

Where to Get Consultants

1. Contact professional associations, for example: networks of organization development practitioners, facilitators, trainers, fundraisers, accountants, lawyers, computer users, etc.

2. Contact local large corporations; they often have community service programs and can provide a wide range of management and technical expertise.

3. Consult the local telephone company's Yellow Pages under the category "Consultant" and "Volunteering."

4. Call a local university or college and speak to someone in the college of Human Resources, Training and Development, or Business Administration.

5. Ask other organizations for ideas, particularly those that have similar services and head-count size, for contacts and references.

Nonprofits can often get consultants to provide services on a pro bono basis. It is worth asking the consultant, especially if the consultant is in strong agreement with the community's need for the nonprofit's services.

How You Can Make Consultancies Productive as Possible

1. Know what you want before you get a consultant. Imagine what you would have if the consultancy worked out perfect. Keep that vision when you start to look for a consultant.

2. Get Board agreement on the hiring of the consultant. Ideally, (if your Board uses committees) appoint a committee such as the Personnel Committee or Project Committee to oversee the consultant progress.

3. Do not become dependent on a consultant. Be sure that the project has a start and stop point.

4. If possible, do not limit the consultant to recommending action. Get the consultant involved in implementing recommendations.

5. Fix causes, not symptoms. Do assessments, look closely at what you see and hear, then figure out the cause. It is often not what you see or hear that is the root cause of problems, rather it is the nonprofit's structures, roles, plans, etc., that cause the problems.

 See "Tools to Measure Health of Nonprofits" on page 227.

Getting and Hiring the Best Consultant

(This section includes advice graciously provided by Consultant, Barbara Davis, St. Paul, Minnesota.)

1. Give interested people the information they need to understand your needs by using a "request for proposal" (RFP) or "request for quote" (RFQ); direct conversation may work as well.

2. Get a written proposal from every interested party. Do not just talk to one consultant.

3. Get a bid on the fee and reimbursable expenses.

4. Look at more than one proposal and examine them all carefully.

5. Interview the best prospects and check their references. Consider their extent of expertise, listening skills, ability to adapt to the nature of your organization, ability to coach to ensure the organization can address the problem in the future, etc.

6. Do not pick someone based only on price.

7. Be sure there is no conflict of interest with the consultant that you want to hire. The consultant should not be faced with conflicting roles if working for your organization. For example, the consultant should not also be on your Board of Directors or be a member of your staff.

8.   Write a good contract including:

   a.   Start and stop date of the agreement.

   b.   List of specific, tangible "deliverables" that will be produced by the consultant.

   c.   Checkpoints at which you can evaluate programs, for example, have a Phase I, Phase II, etc.

   d.   Project completion date, including date for deliverables.

   e.   Payment schedule (consider making partial payments based on provision of each deliverable or project phase).

   f.   Agreement on reimbursable expenses.

   g.   Specification of the roles and responsibilities of the consultant and of your organization.

   h.   Name of person in your agency who has the authority to agree to expenditures or approve work.

   i.   A clear understanding of who will do the actual consulting.

   j.   "Bail-out" clause, ideally that you can immediately bail out by providing notice in writing.

   k.   Confidentiality about sharing any information regarding your organization and its activities.

   l.   Ownership of any materials used and/or produced during the project.

   m.   Scope of the agreement: that it supercedes any other agreements that you have with the consultant regarding that project

Additional Advice

Help Consultants Understand Your Organization

There are a few basic techniques which can greatly help the consultant to understand your organization, particularly if brought in to work organization-wide on non-technical issues.

1.   **Help them understand your service(s), market(s) and stakeholder(s).**
       Provide them with copies of your strategic plans, budgets, policies, most recent annual report, organization charts, and advertising/promotions/sales literature. If there is a full range of these types of documents, your organization probably values careful documentation when making important decisions, and will likely prefer the same from the consulting project. If these documents appear to be very comprehensive and include a great deal of graphs, figures, and numbers, your organization probably highly values careful research, analysis, and conclusions, and will prefer the same in the consultation project.

2.   **Give them a sense for the overall nature of your organization.**
       Are staff highly independent and work alone or do they prefer working in teams? Do you go

for consensus on decisions even if it takes a long time to get or do you want timely closure on decisions? Are there strong traditions you require based on the diversity of your workforce? How does the staff feel about using consultants?

3.   **Give them a sense for the overall priorities of your organization.**
     You might attempt to identify the general life stage of the nonprofit, such as start-up, developing/building, stabilizing, declining, etc. The stage will indicate your overall priorities as well, for example: getting any help you can get, grabbing more market share and/or more clients and/or more revenue, developing a wide range of careful documentation, divesting resources while ensuring client needs are met, etc.

Include Frequent Evaluations, Including Project Follow-Up

The extent of the consultant's and clients' participation in evaluating the project is often an indicator of how much they really see themselves responsible for the overall, long-term quality of the consulting project.

1.   **The consulting project should be evaluated regularly.**
     For example, include a brief evaluation at the end of each meeting (about the process used in that meeting), at mid-point in the planning effort and at its end. Specify in the contract that certain deliverables (tangible products, such as reports, presentations, project reviews, etc.) be delivered during the project. Ideally, the project is evaluated at three months and six months after completion. Be sure to focus on whether the consultant's recommendations were implemented or not and whether the project's goals were reached or not.

2.   **Establish criteria early on from which the consulting effort will be evaluated.**
     Establish criteria by having you and the consultant specify what constitutes a successful consulting project and process. Get descriptions to be as detailed as possible so that it will be easier to evaluate the project's success in the future.

3.   **Do not base evaluations mostly on feelings.**
     Avoid this mistake by specifying, as much as possible, behaviors that will reflect a successful consulting project.

Be Sure You Have "Independent Contractor" Relationship

A major, recent issue with some government agencies is the distinguishing between independent contractors and employees. Some organizations hire what they consider to be "independent contractors," but what the agencies conclude are really "employees." In these cases, the agencies demand that the organizations pay employees' taxes and also pay certain penalties. Consequently, a nonprofit must be very careful when entering into a relationship with a consultant in order to ensure that government agencies will not deem the relationship an "employee" relationship.

For example, in the USA, the Internal Revenue Service (IRS) is diligent about this matter and has issued guidelines about how to discern if a relationship is really more of an employee relationship than an independent contractor relationship. The IRS guidelines are similar to guidelines in Canada. Whether someone is deemed by the IRS to be an employee or an independent contractor depends primarily on the extent of control the nonprofit has over the person: the less control in the relationship, the less likely the IRS will deem the person to be an employee. Consider the following actions when attempting to define the relationship with an independent contractor:

1.   Carefully specify your relationship with the person in a written contract.

2.   The terms of the relationship (specific services, fees, project start and stop dates, etc.) should all be specified in the contract.

3.   Attempt to arrange fees to be based on results or tasks, rather than on time.

4.   In the contract, specify the relationship to be with an "independent contractor" who is responsible to pay his or her own taxes.

5.   The person doing the work should have all or considerable discretion in how services are carried out, including the process and scheduling.

6.   The person doing the work should be responsible to obtain and pay for his or her own training to carry out the services.

7.   The person should not be required to carry out his or her services at the offices of the client.

8.   The person should have or be making obvious efforts to advertise and retain business with other clients.

9.   The person should have his or her own place of business.

Note that the more a person appears as a manager in the organization (that is, makes operating decisions, supervises people, is responsible for resource allocations, etc.), the more likely that a government agency will deem the service provider an "employee," and not an independent contractor.

Currently, the Internal Revenue Service in the USA uses a set of questions to help determine which status (employee or independent contractors) best fits the role. To see these questions, go to http://www.irs.gov/govt/fslg/article/0,,id=110344,00.html .

Appendix E: Tools to Measure Health of Nonprofits

Board members are responsible to ensure that their nonprofit corporation provides programs and services that continue to meet the needs of the public in a highly effective and efficient manner. This means that Board members should know what is required to operate as a high-performing nonprofit organization. One of the most useful ways in which Board members can learn what is required to be high-performing – and one of the most useful ways to measure if the nonprofit is indeed high-performing – is through use of organizational assessment tools. There is a wide variety of free, useful tools on the Web now. This section lists many of those tools and includes one such tool (the Management Indicators Tool) in its entirely so that Board members can scan the types of questions asked by that comprehensive tool.

How to Select the Best Assessment Tool

Considerations When Selecting

Before you begin reviewing tools to use, be sure that you are aware of the major types of tools, the advantages and disadvantages of using each, and general guidelines for applying each type of tool.

1. **Focus**
   Does the tool focus on a broad range of nonprofit functions, including operations of the Board, strategic planning, programs, Chief Executive Officer, staff, marketing, finances, fundraising or evaluations?

2. **Purpose of the tool**
   For example, does it detect strengths and weaknesses of the organization, and compare them to certain "best practices?"

3. **Values and assumptions**
   For example, does the tool assume a specific Board model?

4. **Languages**
   English? Other(s)?

5. **Audiences for the tool**
   To whom will the tool be applied?

6. **Administrator of the tool**
   Who will guide the application of the tool? An outside person? Self-assessment? Will the data collection be participatory?

7. **User guide**
   Are there adequate descriptions of procedures for how to use the tool and analyze the results?

8. **Duration and frequency**
   How long will it take to use the tool? Is the tool to be applied at certain times? More than once?

9.   **Cost**
       What are any costs to obtain the tool? Use the tool?

10.   **Availability**
       How soon can the tool be made available?

11.   **Technical support for the tool**
       If you have questions or need guidance, can anyone help you?

12.   **Modification**
       You might need permission if you seek to modify the tool.

Available, Free Organizational Assessment Tools

The following list includes free, on-line tools, each of which assesses numerous aspects of a nonprofit organization. However, before selecting an already designed tool, be sure that you have addressed the considerations listed immediately above. Keep in mind that these types of tools include some inherent bias. To the author's knowledge, none of these tools has been tested for reliability or validity.

McKinsey Capacity Assessment Grid

 This is a comprehensive grid that suggests seven elements of organizational effectiveness, each with descriptions of four possible levels of performance for each element. Go to http://www.emcf.org/evaluation/mckinsey_assessment_tool.htm .

Minnesota Council of Nonprofits "Principles and Practices"

 This is a widely recognized, comprehensive, principles-based assessment tool that suggests principles for effectiveness in many of the major functions in nonprofits. Go to http://www.mncn.org/info_principles.htm .

Maryland Association of Nonprofit Organizations "Standards of Excellence"

 This is a widely recognized, principles-based assessment tool that suggests principles for effectiveness in many of the major functions in nonprofits. Go to http://www.marylandnonprofits.org/html/standards/04_02.asp .

Understanding Organizational Success: Self-Assessment Tool for Nonprofit Organizations

 This is a comprehensive, well-designed tool that nonprofits can use to assess their organizations. Directions to apply and analyze the tool are included. Go to http://smifoundation.org/NPAssessmentTool.pdf .

Self-Assessment Tool for United Way Agencies

This is a medium-sized, straightforward assessment tool regarding major functions in nonprofits. Go to http://www.uwac.org/uwac/repositories/Download/oat_uw.pdf .

United Way Management Indicators Organizational Assessment (includes best practices)

This is a well-designed, comprehensive, behaviors-based tool that also includes a suggested "best-practices" standard, as well. This tool, in its entirety, is included on the following pages of this Appendix.

One Example of a Very Good Assessment Tool

The following tool is available for free, online at
http://www.managementhelp.org/aboutfml/diagnostics.htm#anchor421212 .

Description

The following checklist is a resource developed by staff and volunteers of the Greater Twin Cities United Way for internal use by nonprofit organizations. Management can use the checklist to identify their organization's administrative strengths and weaknesses. It is believed that widespread use of the checklist ultimately results in a more effective and efficient nonprofit community. The checklist is not intended to be used as a tool for external evaluation, or by grantmakers in making funding decisions. This tool will be used to assist nonprofit organizations to gain a better understanding of their management needs and/or make improvements to management operations.

Note that the following checklist, or assessment tool, originally developed by the Greater Twin Cities United Way of Minnesota (USA), has been slightly modified by the author in order to make it relevant to organizations outside the United States.

This checklist includes the following sections:

- How To Use the Tool
- Disclaimers
- Legal Indicators
- Governance (Board) Indicators
- Human Resources Indicators
- Planning Indicators
- Financial Indicators
- Fundraising Indicators

How To Use the Tool

The checklist indicators represent what is needed to have a healthy, well-managed organization. Since it is a self-assessment tool, organizations should evaluate themselves honestly against each issue and use the response to change or strengthen its administrative operations.

Ratings

Each indicator is rated based on its importance to the operation and effectiveness of any nonprofit organization. The ratings are:
  E: Indicators with an "E" are essential or basic requirements to the operations of all nonprofit organizations. Organizations which do not meet the requirements of these indicators could place their organizations in jeopardy.
  R: An "R" rating signifies that these indicators are recommended as standard practice for effective nonprofit organizations.
  A: Additional indicators which organizations can implement to enhance and strengthen their management operations and activities are rated with an "A".

Checklist Responses

Organizations can respond in one of three ways to each indicator used:

Needs Work - An indicator that is marked as "Needs Work" implies that work has been done towards achieving this goal. The organization is aware of the need for this indicator, and is working towards attaining it.

Met - All indicators marked as "Met" demonstrate that the organization has fulfilled that essential management need. However, the organization should review these indicators in the future to be sure that its management remains healthy in view of the many internal and external changes that constantly occur in all organizations.

N/A - Indicators marked as "N/A" can mean several things, including:
- the indicator is not applicable to the management operations of this organization
- the organization is not sure of the need to meet the requirements of this indicator
- the organization has not met, nor is working on this indicator presently, but may address it in the future.

All Organizations Should Take Note

All responses to indicators should be reviewed carefully to see if they could improve management operations. Indicators checked "N/A" due to uncertain applicability to the organization must be further reviewed to determine if they should become a part of "doing business." If the assessors simply do not know what the indicator means, further information may be needed to accurately assess the feasibility of its application. Indicators may require immediate attention if they were marked "N/A" because they have not been met but still apply to the organization. Technical assistance, consulting, or training may be required to implement these indicators.

The indicators in this checklist should be informative and thought provoking. The checklist can be used to not only achieve a beginning level of good management, but also improve existing management to provide the organization with greater stability, reliability and success in the nonprofit community. If an organization is experiencing management problems, the checklist can be useful to help pinpoint any weaknesses where action can be taken or assistance sought to improve the organization's health. All organizations should use the checklist to re-assess themselves periodically to ensure compliance with established rules and regulations and to continue improving administrative health through the indicator's helpful suggestions.

Disclaimer

This checklist is designed to provide accurate and authoritative information regarding the topics covered. Legal requirements and non-legal administrative practice standards reflected herein are capable of change due to new legislation, regulatory and judicial pronouncements, and updated and evolving guidelines. The same are utilized with the understanding that the provision of this checklist does not constitute the rendering of legal, tax or other professional services.

If the organization requires professional assistance on these or other nonprofit tax, management, or accounting issues, please contact your own professional advisors.

Rating Best Practices in Legal Activities

Rating *	Indicator	Met	Needs Work	N/A
E	1. All relevant legal filings are current and have been made according to the laws and regulations of the nonprofit's country. (For example, in the USA, requirements might include: Annual Registration, Articles of Incorporation with all amendments, Change of Corporate Name or Address.)			
E	2. The organization is registered with and has filed its annual report with the appropriate governmental agency. (For example, in the USA, the report might be filed with the state's Attorney General's office.)			
E	3. For organizations operating on a tax-exempt basis, the organization has filed the necessary government form to obtain tax-exempt status. (For example, in the USA, IRS form 1023 was filed and the IRS provided a letter of determination. If the Form 1023 was filed after 7/15/87 or was in the nonprofit's possession on this date, it is available for public inspection.)			
E	4. Tax reports are filed on a regular basis. (For tax-exempt organizations in the USA, the IRS Form 990 and 990T for unrelated business income, if required, have been filed and copies of the 990 are available to the public.)			
E	5. Federal and state (or provincial) payroll taxes withholding payments are current. (This requirement applies to organizations with employees.)			
E	6. Quarterly and annual payroll report filings are current. (This requirement applies to organizations with employees.)			
E	7. If the organization has qualified employee health, welfare and/or retirement benefit plans, they meet with all the federal and state/provincial laws. (For example, in the USA: COBRA; initial IRS registration; plan documents; annuals filings of the 5500 C/R with copies available to employees.) This requirement applies to organizations with employees.			
E	8. Organization acknowledges and discloses to their Board and auditor any lawsuits or pending legislation which may have a significant impact on the organization's finances and/or operating effectiveness.			
E	9. When the Board of Directors makes decisions, a quorum is present and minutes are maintained.			
E	10. If the organization is subject to sales tax(es), then federal, state/provincial and/or city filings and payments are current.			
E	11. Organizations that participate in grassroots or direct lobbying have complied with all necessary filings and government regulations.			
E	12. Organizations that conduct charitable gambling have complied with government regulations.			
E	13. Organizations with employees represented by a union must have copies of the union contracts on file.			
E	14. Organizations that operate in a fiscal or host-organization relationship with another organization or group have a written agreement on file.			
Indicators ratings: E=essential; R=recommended; A=additional to strengthen organizational activities				

Rating Best Practices in Governance / Boards Operations

Rating *	Indicator	Met	Needs Work	N/A
E	1. The roles of the Board and the Chief Executive Officer (if applicable) are defined and respected, with the Chief Executive Officer delegated as the manager of the organization's operations and the Board focused on policy and planning.			
R	2. The Chief Executive Officer is recruited, selected, and employed by the Board of Directors. The Board provides clearly written expectations and qualifications for the position, as well as reasonable compensation.			
R	3. The Board of Directors acts as governing trustees of the organization, on behalf of the community at large and as contributors, while carrying out the organization's mission and goals. To fully meet this goal, the Board of Directors must actively participate in the planning process as outlined in planning sections of this checklist.			
R	4. The Board's nominating process ensures that the Board remains appropriately diverse with respect to gender, ethnicity, culture, economic status, disabilities, skills and/or expertise.			
E	5. The Board members receive regular training and information about their responsibilities.			
E	6. New Board members are oriented to the organization: the organization's mission, bylaws, policies and programs, as well as their roles and responsibilities as Board members.			
A	7. Board organization is documented with a description of the Board and Board committee (if applicable) responsibilities.			
A	8. Each Board member has a Board operations manual.			
E	9. If the organization has any related party transactions between Board members or their family, they are disclosed to the Board of Directors (the Internal Revenue Service in the USA) and the auditor.			
E	10. The organization has at least the minimum number of members on the Board of Directors as required by their bylaws, federal statute and/or state/provincial statute.			
R	11. If the organization has adopted bylaws, they conform to federal and/or state/provincial statutes and have been reviewed by legal counsel.			
R	12. The bylaws should describe: a) how and when notices for Board meetings are made; b) how members are elected/appointed by the Board; c) what the terms of office are for officers/members; d) how Board members are rotated; e) how ineffective Board members are removed from the Board; and f) a stated number of Board members to make up a quorum which is required for all policy decisions.			
R	13. The Board of Directors reviews the bylaws annually.			
A	14. The Board has a process for handling urgent matters between meetings.			
E	15. Board members serve without payment unless the agency has a policy identifying reimbursable out-of-pocket expenses.			

Indicators ratings: E=essential; R=recommended; A=additional to strengthen organizational activities

Rating Best Practices in Governance Operations (Cont.)

Rating *	Indicator	Met	Needs Work	N/A
R	16. The organization maintains a conflict-of-interest policy and all Board members and executive staff review and/or sign to acknowledge and comply with the policy.			
R	17. The Board has an annual calendar of meetings. The Board also has an attendance policy which requires that a quorum of the organization's Board meets at least quarterly.			
A	18. Each Board meeting has a written agenda and the materials relating to significant decisions are given to the Board members in advance of the meeting.			
A	19. The Board has a written policy prohibiting employees and members of employees' immediate families from serving as Board Chair or treasurer.			
Indicators ratings: E=essential; R=recommended; A=additional to strengthen organizational activities				

Rating Best Practices in Human Resources (Staff and Volunteers)

Staff

Rating *	Indicator	Met	Needs Work	N/A
E	1. The organization has a written personnel handbook/policy that is regularly reviewed, updated and approved by Board: a) to describe the recruitment, hiring, termination and standard work rules for all staff and b) to maintain compliance with government employment laws and regulations. (For example, in the USA, this includes: Fair Labor Standards Act, Equal Employment Opportunity Act, Americans with Disabilities Act, Occupational Health and Safety Act, Family Leave Act, Affirmative Action Plan if required, etc.)			
R	2. The organization follows nondiscriminatory hiring practices.			
R	3. The organization provides a copy of or access to the written personnel policies to all members of the Board, the Chief Executive Officer (if applicable) and all staff members. All staff members acknowledge in writing that they have read and have access to the personnel handbook/policies.			
R	4. The organization has job descriptions including qualifications, duties, reporting relationships and key indicators.			
R	5. The organization's Board of Directors conducts an annual review/evaluation of its Chief Executive Officer in relationship to a previously determined set of expectations.			
R	6. The Chief Executive Officer's salary is set by the Board of Directors in a reasonable process and is in compliance with the organization's compensation plan.			
R	7. The organization requires employee performance appraisals to be conducted and documented at least annually.			
A	8. The organization has a compensation plan and a periodic review of salary ranges and benefits is conducted.			
A	9. The organization has a timely process for filling vacant positions to prevent an interruption of program services or disruption to organization operations.			
A	10. The organization has a process for reviewing and responding to ideas, suggestions, comments and perceptions from all staff members.			
A	11. The organization provides opportunities for employees' professional development and training with their job skill area and also in such areas as cultural sensitivity and personal development.			
A	12. The organization maintains contemporaneous records documenting staff time in program allocations.			
Indicators ratings: E=essential; R=recommended; A=additional to strengthen organizational activities				

Rating Best Practices in Human Resources (Cont.)

Volunteer HR Management

Rating *	Indicator	Met	Needs Work	N/A
E	1. The organization has a clearly defined purpose of the role that volunteers have within the organization.			
E	2. Job descriptions exist for all volunteer positions in the organization.			
R	3. The organization has a well-defined and communicated volunteer management plan that includes a recruitment policy, description of all volunteer jobs, an application and interview process, possible stipend and reimbursement policies, statement of which staff has supervisory responsibilities over what volunteers, and any other volunteer personnel policy information.			
E	4. The organization follows a recruitment policy that does not discriminate, but respects, encourages and represents the diversity of the community.			
E	5. The organization provides appropriate training and orientation to the agency to assist the volunteer in the performance of their volunteer activities. Volunteers are offered training with staff in such areas as cultural sensitivity.			
R	6. The organization is respectful of the volunteer's abilities and time commitment and has various job duties to meet these needs. Jobs should not be given to volunteers simply because the jobs are considered inferior for paid staff.			
R	7. The organization does volunteer performance appraisals periodically and communicates to the volunteers how well they are doing, or where additional attention is needed. At the same time, volunteers are requested to review and evaluate their involvement in the organization and the people they work with and suggest areas for improvement.			
R	8. The organization does some type of volunteer recognition or commendation periodically and staff continuously demonstrates their appreciation towards the volunteers and their efforts.			
A	9. The organization has a process for reviewing and responding to ideas, suggestions, comments and perceptions from volunteers.			
A	10. The organization provides opportunities for program participants to volunteer.			
A	11. The organization maintains contemporaneous records documenting volunteer time in program allocations. Financial records can be maintained for the volunteer time spent on programs and recorded as in-kind contributions.			
Indicators ratings: E=essential; R=recommended; A=additional to strengthen organizational activities				

Rating Best Practices in Planning (Strategic and Programs)

Strategic Planning

Rating *	Indicator	Met	Needs Work	N/A
E	1. The organization's purpose and activities meet community needs.			
R	2. The organization frequently evaluates, by soliciting community input, whether its mission and activities provide benefit to the community.			
R	3. The organization has a value statement that is reflected in the agency's activities and is communicated by its constituents.			
A	4. The value statement includes standards of ethical behavior and respect for other's interests.			
E	5. The organization has a clear, meaningful written mission statement which reflects its purpose, values and people served.			
R	6. The Board and staff periodically review the mission statement and modify it to reflect changes in the environment.			
E	7. The Board and staff developed and adopted a written strategic plan to achieve its mission.			
A	8. Board, staff, service recipients, volunteers, key constituents and general members of the community participate in the planning process.			
E	9. The plan was developed by researching the internal and external environment.			
R	10. The plan identifies the changing community needs including the agency's strengths, weaknesses, opportunities and threats.			
R	11. The planning process identifies the critical issues facing the organization.			
R	12. The plan sets goals and measurable objectives that address these critical issues.			
E	13. The plan integrates all the organization's activities around a focused mission.			
R	14. The plan prioritizes the agency goals and develops timelines for their accomplishments.			
A	15. The plan establishes an evaluation process and performance indicators to measure the progress toward the achievement of goals and objectives.			
R	16. Through work plans, human and financial resources are allocated to insure the accomplishment of the goals in a timely fashion.			
A	17. The plan is communicated to all stakeholders of the agency – service recipients, Board, staff, volunteers and the general community.			
Indicators ratings: E=essential; R=recommended; A=additional to strengthen organizational activities				

Rating Best Practices in Planning (Cont.)

Planning Regarding the Organization's Programs

Rating *	Indicator	Met	Needs Work	N/A
E	1. Programs are congruent with the agency's mission and strategic plan.			
A	2. The organization actively informs the public about its programs and services.			
A	3. Clients and potential clients have the opportunity to participate in program development.			
R	4. Sufficient resources are allocated to ensure each program can achieve the established goals and objectives.			
R	5. Staff has sufficient training and skill levels to produce the program.			
A	6. Programs within the organization are integrated to provide more complete services to clients.			
R	7. Each program has performance indicators to insure that the program meets its goals and objectives.			
R	8. Performance indicators are reviewed annually.			
A	9. The agency networks and/or collaborates with other organizations to produce the most comprehensive and effective services to clients.			
Indicators ratings: E=essential; R=recommended; A=additional to strengthen organizational activities				

Planning Regarding the Organization's Evaluations

Rating *	Indicator	Met	Needs Work	N/A
R	1. Every year, the organization evaluates its activities to determine progress toward goal accomplishment.			
A	2. Stakeholders are involved in the evaluation process.			
R	3. The evaluation includes a review of organizational programs and systems to insure that they comply with the organization's mission, values and goals.			
R	4. The results of the evaluation are reflected in the revised plan.			
A	5. Periodically, the organization conducts a comprehensive evaluation of its programs. This evaluation measures program outcomes (impacts on clients).			
Indicators ratings: E=essential; R=recommended; A=additional to strengthen organizational activities				

Rating Best Practices in Financial Management

Rating *	Indicator	Met	Needs Work	N/A
E	1. The organization follows accounting practices which conform to generally accepted standards.			
E	2. The organization has systems in place to provide the appropriate information needed by staff and Board to make sound financial decisions and to fulfill government requirements (for example, the requirements of the Internal Revenue Service in the USA).			
R	3. The organization prepares timely financial statements including the balance sheet, income statement and cash flow statement which are clearly stated and useful for the Board and staff. (Note that these statements might be referred to by different names in various countries.)			
R	4. The organization prepares financial statements on a budget versus actual (comparative basis) to achieve a better understanding of their finances.			
E	5. The organization develops an annual comprehensive operating budget which includes costs for all programs, management and fundraising and all sources of funding. This budget is reviewed and approved by the Board.			
R	6. The organization monitors unit costs of programs and services through the documentation of staff time and direct expenses and using a process for allocation of management, general and fundraising expenses.			
E	7. The organization prepares cash flow projections.			
R	8. The organization periodically forecasts year-end revenues and expenses to assist in making sound management decisions during the year.			
E	9. The organization reconciles all cash accounts monthly.			
E	10. The organization has a review process to monitor that they are receiving appropriate and accurate financial information, whether from a contracted service or internal processing.			
E	11. If the organization has billable contracts or other service income, procedures are established for the periodic billing, follow-up and collection of all accounts, with documentation to substantiate all billings.			
E	12. Government contracts, purchase of service agreements and grant agreements are in writing and are reviewed by a staff member of the organization to monitor compliance with all stated conditions.			
E	13. Payroll is prepared following appropriate federal and state/provincial regulations and organizational policy.			
E	14. Persons employed on a contract basis meet all federal and state/provincial requirements for this form of employment. (In the USA, disbursement records are kept so 1099's can be issued at year end.)			
E	15. Organizations that purchase and sell merchandise take periodic inventories to monitor the inventory against theft, to reconcile general ledger inventory information and to maintain an adequate inventory level.			
R	16. The organization has a written fiscal policy and procedures manual and follows it.			

Indicators ratings: E=essential; R=recommended; A=additional to strengthen organizational activities

Rating Best Practices in Financial Management (Cont.)

Rating *	Indicator	Met	Needs Work	N/A
E	17. The organization has documented a set of internal controls, including handling of cash and deposits and approval over spending and disbursements.			
E	18. The organization has a policy identifying authorized check signers and the number of signatures required on checks in excess of specified dollar amounts.			
E	19. All expenses of the organization are approved by a designated person before payment is made.			
R	20. The organization has a written policy related to investments.			
R	21. Capital needs are reviewed annually and priorities established.			
R	22. The organization has established a plan identifying actions to take in the event of a reduction or loss in funding.			
R	23. The organization has established, or is actively trying to develop, a reserve of funds to cover at least three months of operating expenses.			
E	24. The organization has suitable insurance coverage which is periodically reviewed to ensure the appropriate levels and types of coverage are in place.			
E	25. Employees, Board members and volunteers who handle cash and investments are bonded to help assure the safeguarding of assets.			
E	26. The organization files forms in regard to tax-exempt and/or tax-deductible (charity) status in a timely basis within prescribed time lines.			
R	27. The organization reviews income annually to determine and report unrelated business income to the necessary government agency (for example, to the IRS in the USA).			
R	28. The organization has an annual, independent audit of their financial statements, prepared by a certified public accountant.			
R	29. In addition to the audit, the auditor prepares a management letter containing recommendations for improvements in the financial operations of the organization.			
R	30. The Board of Directors, or an appropriate committee, is responsible for soliciting bids, interviewing auditors and hiring an auditor for the organization.			
R	31. The Board of Directors, or an appropriate committee, reviews and approves the audit report and management letter and with staff input and support, institutes any necessary changes.			
E	32. The audit, or an organization-prepared annual report which includes financial statements, is made available to service recipients, volunteers, contributors, funders and other interested parties.			
A	33. Training is made available for Board and appropriate staff on relevant accounting topics and all appropriate persons are encouraged to participate in various training opportunities.			
Indicators ratings: E=essential; R=recommended; A=additional to strengthen organizational activities				

Rating Best Practices in Fundraising Activities

General Fundraising

Rating*	Indicator	Met	Needs Work	N/A
E	1. Funds are raised in an ethical manner for activities consistent with the organization's mission and plan.			
E	2. The Board of Directors and organization staff are knowledgeable about the fundraising process and the roles in the organization.			
E	3. The organization's Board of Directors has established a committee charged with developing, evaluating and reviewing fundraising policies, practices and goals.			
E	4. The committee is actively involved in the fundraising process and works to involve others in these activities.			
R	5. The Board of Directors, Chief Executive Officer (if applicable) and committees support and participate in the total fundraising process, including project identification, cultivation, solicitation and recognition.			
R	6. The fundraising program is staffed and funded at a level consistent with fundraising expectations.			
A	7. There are direct communications and relationships between information services or marketing, accounting and other administration support functions to assist in the fundraising needs and efforts.			
E	8. The organization is accountable to donors and other key constituencies and demonstrates its stewardship through annual reports.			
Indicators ratings: E=essential; R=recommended; A=additional to strengthen organizational activities				

Rating Best Practices in Fundraising Activities (Cont.)

Using an Outside Fundraiser

Rating *	Indicator	Met	Needs Work	N/A
A	1. The organization meets the nonprofit standards of the state/provincial charities review council, if one exists.			
R	2. If the organization chooses to use outside professional fundraisers, several competitive bids are solicited. Each prospective outside fundraiser's background and references are checked.			
E	3. The organization makes legal, mutual agreed upon, signed statements with outside professional fundraisers, outlining each parties' responsibilities and duties, specifying how the contributed funds will be physically handled, and to guarantee that the fees to be paid are reasonable and fair.			
E	4. The organization has verified that the contracted fundraiser is registered as a professional fundraiser with the appropriate government agency and all necessary filings have been made before the work commences.			
E	5. The Fundraising Committee or appropriate representatives from the Board of Directors reviews all prospective proposals with outside professional fundraiser and reviews and accepts all agreements before they are signed.			
R	6. If the outside professional fundraiser plans to contact potential donors directly, the organization must review the fundraising materials (e.g., public service announcements, print or broadcast advertisements, telemarketing scripts, pledge statements, brochures, letters, etc.) to verify their accuracy and to ensure that the public disclosure requirements have been met.			
E	7. The organization properly reports all required information regarding use of outside professional fundraisers, amount of funds raised and the related fundraising expenses as required by federal and state/provincial governments. The gross amount of funds raised by the contracted fundraiser is reported on the organization's financial statement. The fees and costs of the campaign must be reported on the statement of functional expenses.			
Indicators ratings: E=essential; R=recommended; A=additional to strengthen organizational activities				

Appendix F: Goals and Objectives for Board Development Committee

The following table depicts typical goals and objectives for a Board Development Committee.

Goal 1: Install/update new Board systems (three objectives for this goal are included below)	Start	Stop	Responsibility
1. Ensure development of committee work plans (objectives and time lines) for each Board committee.			Board Development Committee
2. Board approves Board Development Plan.			Board
3. Board approves new annual Board calendar.			Board
Goal 2. Ensure Board is fully resourced to govern.			
1. Review and update Board staffing policies to recruit and select new Board members with expertise to achieve the organization's goals.			Board Development Committee
2. Select new Board members.			Board Development Committee
3. Ensure all Board members receive Board orientation about our nonprofit's practices.			Board Development Committee
4. Ensure all Board members receive Board training about roles of a governing Board.			Board Development Committee
Goal 3. Ensure full participation and dedication of all Board members.			
1. Ensure all Board members are on at least one committee.			Board Development Committee
2. Approve and enact Board attendance policy.			Board
3. Approve conflict-of-interest policy.			Board
Goal 4. Ensure all Board meetings are highly focused and strategic.			
1. Propose a procedure for making Board decisions, such as consensus, then voting if necessary.			Board Development Committee
2. Ensure meeting materials are provided at least one week before full Board meetings.			Board Development Committee
3. Adopt a meeting evaluation procedure.			Board
Goal 5. Ensure Board leadership rigorously coordinates Board activities.			
1. Provide ongoing guidance and support to ensure an effective Board Chair position.			Board Development Committee
2. Analyze goals and timetables in work plan of each committee.			Executive Committee
3. Ensure each committee operates according to work plans in their charters.			Executive Committee
Goal 6. Ensure continuous improvement of the Board.			
1. Conduct Board self-evaluation once a year.			Board
2. Develop updated Board Development Plan based on self-evaluation results.			Board Development Committee
3. Conduct Board retreat focused on improving results.			Board

Appendix G: Typical Contents of Board Manual

Each member of the Board should have a Board Manual, or Handbook, that contains the types of contents listed below. Board members should be oriented to the contents, for example, during a Board orientation session. Contents of Board manuals may differ somewhat among different organizations, depending on the needs and nature of the organization, including the Board model preferred by the nonprofit. The contents of the Board Manual and activities to update it might be the responsibility of a Board Development Committee.

Legal Descriptions

Charter Documents

Articles of Incorporation
IRS letter of determination granting 501(c) status
Other evidence of exemptions from taxes
Licenses and Permits
Registration for Solicitation

Strategic Plan

Strategic Plan Document

Mission, Vision and Values Statements
Goals and Strategies
Action Planning (objectives, responsibilities, timelines, etc.)
Status Reports toward implementation of plan

Board Organization/Operations

By Laws and Policies

Board By Laws
Resolutions
Board Policies (some of which follow)
Code of Ethics and Code of Conduct
Board Meeting Attendance Policy
Board Staffing Procedure
Board Application Form
Board Member Contract
Board Conflict-of-Interest Policy

Board Organization and Membership

Organization Chart of Board
Roles and Responsibilities of Board
Job Descriptions of Board Officers and Other Members
Board Committees and Charters
List of Board Members (their organizations, contact information, etc.)
Board Member Biographies

Board Operations

Board Calendar
Work Plans ("to-do" list for each Board committee)
Board Meeting Agendas and Minutes
Committee Meeting Agendas and Minutes
Reports from Chief Executive

Programs/Products and Marketing

Program Planning for Each Program

Market Analyses
Descriptions
Service Objectives
Income Objectives
Evaluation Results

Marketing and Promotions for Each Program

Marketing and Promotions Plan
Positioning Statement
Brochures, articles, etc.

Finance/Fundraising

Financial Management, Policies and Procedures

Fiscal Policies and Procedures
Internal Control Policies (bookkeeping controls)
Collections for Accounts Past Due
Tracking In-Kind Donations
Tracking Volunteer Hours
Travel Reimbursements
Other Reimbursements

Financial Records/Data

Yearly Budget
Budget Narrative
Cash Flow Reports
Program Budgets
Financial Statements
Financial Analysis
Audit Reports

Fundraising

Fundraising Plan
Lists of Sources
Lists of Donors
Fundraising Reports

Community/Public Relations

Media Relations Policy
Interview Guidelines
Scripts (for reference during interviews)
Listing of Major Stakeholders and Contacts
Public Event Planning

Personnel Policies

Staff Organization and Data

Organization Chart
Job Descriptions
Staff Address List
Staff Information Form

Personnel (Staff) Policies and Procedures

Benefits and Compensation
Code of Ethics and Code of Conduct
Whistleblower Policy
Document Retention / Destruction Policy
Conference Room Layout / Reserving Rooms
Diversity Plan
Dress Code
During Chief Executive's Absence
In Case of Fire
Forms to Check Out Keys
Use of Kitchen Area
Large Mailings and Copy Lists
Office Forms
Office Supplies
Performance Management Policies (performance appraisal, firing, etc.)
Receptionist/Program Assistance Advance Notice
Snow Days
Special Recognitions
Telephone Coverage
Time Tracking
Vacations

Appendix H: Sample Board Policies

This section includes examples of common Board policies. The policies are in regard to how Board members prefer to operate when governing the nonprofit – they are not personnel policies about how to hire, manage and fire staff members, nor are they operational policies about how to conduct day-to-day activities in the organization. They are listed generally in the order in which they might be used when staffing and developing Board members. Note that By Laws is a type of Board policy, but is too large to include in this Appendix.

1. Sample Board Job Descriptions (Board member and major officers)
2. Sample Executive Director Job Description
3. Sample Annual Calendar of Board Activities
4. Sample Board and Staff Roles
5. Sample Board Committee Charter
6. Sample Board Staffing Checklist
7. Sample Board Member Recruitment Grid
8. Sample Board Member Application Form
9. Sample Board Member Ethics Policy
10. Sample Board Member Conflict-of-Interest Policy
11. Sample Board Member Contract
12. Sample Board Decision-Making Policy
13. Sample Executive Director Evaluation Form
14. Sample Board Self-Evaluation Form
15. Sample Board Member Self-Evaluation Form
16. Sample Board Member Attendance Policy
17. Sample Board Media Relations Policy
18. Sample Whistleblower Policy
19. Sample Document Destruction and Retention Policy

There are other documents or topics that could be considered Board policies, many of which typically are paragraphs in By Laws, for example, Board membership, Board elections, Annual Meeting, terms of quorum, terms of voting, and delegation to the CEO.

Board Policies Can Be Downloaded for Use by Owner of This Book

This guide includes various sample Board policies. The reader or organization that purchased this book has the right to download and use the policies within their organization. Each policy should be modified to suit the nature and needs of the organization, including its preferred Board model. Any other use is unlawful. The policies should not be modified for re-sale.

To download a copy of the policies, point your Web browser to http://www.authenticityconsulting.com/pubs/BD_gdes/board-policies.doc . Then save the document(s) to your computer's disk, for example, use the "Save As" command in your browser and name the file "policies".

Sample Board Job Descriptions

[Name of Agency]

Board of Directors Job Description

Title: **Board Member**

Term: Three years

Responsible to: Responsible to entire Board, reports to Board Chair

General Responsibilities:

1.   Overall governance of agency by establishing and monitoring policies and programs and supporting development and effectiveness of Board of Directors.

2.   Establish strategic purpose and direction for agency by participating in regular strategic planning and monitoring performance toward plan's results.

3.   Supervision of Chief Executive by hiring Chief Executive and monitoring performance toward Chief Executive's general responsibilities and yearly objectives.

4.   Fundraising by fundraising planning and participation to secure necessary resources to support operations, programs and services.

5.   Represent agency and its programs and services to stakeholders, including community, funders and clients.

6.   Ensure financial health of agency through conformance to up-to-date fiscal policies and procedures and through ongoing analysis of financial reports.

7.   Ensure effective performance of agency's programs through ongoing program planning and evaluation.

8.   Ensure conformance to federal, state, local and agency policies and procedures.

Specific Duties:

1.   Is a member of the Board.

2.   Builds collegial working relationship that contributes to consensus.

3.   Contributes financially to the nonprofit.

4.   Regularly attends Board meetings and important related meetings.

5.   Makes serious commitment to participate actively in Board and committee work.

6.   Volunteers for and willingly accepts assignments and completes them thoroughly and on time.

7.   Stays informed about Board policies and committee matters, prepares themselves well for meetings, and reviews and comments on minutes and reports.

[Name of Agency]

Board of Directors Job Description

Title:	**Board Chair**
Term:	Three years
Responsible to:	Board of Directors
Specific Duties:	(in addition to the "General Responsibilities" and "Specific Duties" listed in the job description of Board Member)

1. Provides leadership to the Board of Directors who sets policy and to whom the Chief Executive is accountable.

2. Chairs the meetings of the Board after developing the agenda with the Chief Executive.

3. Ensures Board's leading role in strategic planning.

4. Ensures ongoing financial planning and financial reports.

5. Along with other Board members, plays a leading role in fundraising activities.

6. Appoints the Chairpersons of committees, in consultation with other Board members.

7. Serves ex officio as a member of committees and attends their meetings when invited.

8. Leads discussions with the Chief Executive regarding any issues of concern to the Board.

9. Leads regular, formal evaluation of the performance of the Chief Executive and informally evaluates the effectiveness of the Board members.

10. Discusses issues confronting the organization with the Chief Executive, and shares recommendations with the Board.

11. Helps guide and mediate Board actions with respect to organizational priorities and governance concerns.

12. Leads evaluation annually of the performance of the organization in achieving its mission.

13. Performs other responsibilities assigned by the Board.

[Name of Agency]

Board of Directors Job Description

Title: **Vice Chair**

Term: Three years

Responsible to: Responsible to entire Board, reports to Board Chair

Specific Duties:

(in addition to the "General Responsibilities" and "Specific Duties" listed in the job description of Board Member)

1.   Serves as successor to the Chair position.

2.   Performs Chair responsibilities when the Chair cannot be available.

3.   Works closely with the Chair, Chief Executive and other staff.

4.   Participates closely with the Chair to develop and implement officer transition plans.

5.   Performs other responsibilities as assigned by the Board.

[Name of Agency]

Board of Directors Job Description

Title: **Committee Chair**

Term: Three years

Responsible to: Responsible to entire Board, reports to Board Chair

Specific Duties:

(in addition to the "General Responsibilities" and "Specific Duties" listed in the job description of Board Member)

1.   Ensure their committee has clear charge that is consistent with goals and preferences of Board and is fully understood by each committee member.

2.   Assigns work to the committee members, sets the committee agenda, facilitates the meetings, and ensures distribution of meeting minutes to full Board.

3.   Ensures committee members have the resources and information needed to do their jobs as committee members.

4.   Works closely with the Board Chair, Chief Executive and other staff as agreed to by the Board and Chief Executive.

5.   Sets the tone for committee work that is purposeful, complete and timely.

6.   Reports to the full Board on committee's decisions and recommendations.

7.   Initiates and leads the committee's annual evaluation for standing committees or final evaluation for ad hoc committees.

[Name of Agency]

Board of Directors Job Description

Title:	**Secretary**
Term:	Three years
Responsible to:	Responsible to entire Board, reports to Board Chair

Specific Duties:

(in addition to the "General Responsibilities" and "Specific Duties" listed in the job description of Board Member)

1. Maintains all major documents and records of the Board and ensures their effective management, retention and protection.

2. Is sufficiently familiar with major documents and records, for example, Articles of Incorporation, By Laws, Board Policies, Board Resolutions, etc. Reminds Board members of applicability of documents during Board operations.

3. Develops, manages and distributes written meeting minutes of Board meetings.

4. Ensures collection of meeting minutes from committee meetings.

5. Ensures review and approval of all meeting minutes.

[Name of Agency]

Board of Directors Job Description

Title: **Treasurer**

Term: Three years

Responsible to: Responsible to entire Board, reports to Board Chair

Specific Duties:

(in addition to the "General Responsibilities" and "Specific Duties" listed in the job description of Board Member)

1.   Oversees the management of the finances of the organization as approved and reviewed by the Board and managed by Chief Executive.

2.   Serves as Chair of the Finance Committee.

3.   With the Chief Executive, administrates fiscal matters of the organization.

4.   Provides annual budget to the Board for members' approval (often develops the budget with the Chief Executive and staff).

5.   Responds to annual audit, and ensures audit issues and recommendations are fully addressed.

6.   Ensures development and Board review of up-to-date financial policies and procedures.

7.   Ensures financial policies and procedures are adhered to by Board and staff.

8.   Ensures all Board members have sufficient understanding of analysis of finances in order to produce judicious decisions about finances and their effects.

Sample Executive Director Job Description

Job Description: Chief Executive Officer

Title: **Chief Executive**

Responsible to: Board of Directors

Functions:

1.   To implement the strategic goals and objectives of the organization.

2.   With the Chair, enable the Board to fulfill its governance function.

3.   To give direction and leadership toward the achievement of the organization's philosophy, mission, strategy, and its annual goals and objectives.

Major Functions/Accountabilities:

1.   Board Administration and Support – Supports operations and administration of Board by advising and informing Board members, interfacing between Board and staff, and supporting Board's evaluation of Chief Executive.

2.   Program, Product and Service Delivery – Oversees design, marketing, promotion, delivery and quality of programs, products and services, especially to ensure they are verified to be meet specific needs in the community.

3.   Financial, Tax, Risk and Facilities Management – Recommends yearly budget for Board approval and prudently manages organization's resources within those budget guidelines according to current laws and regulations.

4.   Human Resource Management – Effectively manages the human resources of the organization according to authorized personnel policies and procedures that fully conform to current laws and regulations.

5.   Community and Public Relations – Ensures that the organization and its mission, programs, and services are consistently presented in strong, positive image to relevant stakeholders; also ensures all major stakeholders have strong input to strategic and program planning.

6.   Fundraising – Supports the Board in its fundraising planning and implementation, including to identify resource requirements, research funding sources, establish strategies to approach funders, submit proposals, and administrate fundraising records and documentation.

Sample Annual Calendar of Board Activities

	Yearly Board Activity	**Suggested Timing**
1.	Fiscal year begins (assumes fiscal year beginning January 1)	January (fiscal-year timing is often specified in the By Laws and fiscal policies)
2.	Conduct Board Self-Evaluation (do once a year and in preparation for first Board retreat, might be twice per year)	March-April (do shortly before evaluating Chief Executive)
3.	Evaluate Chief Executive (reference his or her progress towards last fiscal year's goals and job description)	April-May (do shortly after completion of last fiscal year)
4.	Review and update By Laws, Board policies, insurances, personnel policies and Board staffing policies	April-June (do concurrent to Board and chief evaluations)
5.	Conduct first Board retreat (team building, address Board self-evaluation results, begin strategic planning, etc.)	April
6.	Begin recruiting new Board members	April-May (in time for June/July elections)
7.	Conduct strategic planning to produce organizational goals and resources need to reach goals	May-June-July (start planning in time for setting mission, vision, values, issues, goals, strategies, resource needs, funding needs, and getting funds before start of next fiscal year)
8.	Develop slate for potential new Board members	June-July (per By Laws)
9.	Establish Chief Executive's goals for next year (as produced from strategic planning)	August (as organizational goals are realized from planning)
10.	Hold annual meeting and elect new Board members	July (per By Laws)
11.	Draft next year's budget (based on resources needed to reach new strategic goals)	July-August-September
12.	Develop fundraising plan (with primary goals to get funds needed for budget)	July-August-September
13.	Conduct second Board retreat (address Board orientation/training, review Board/staff roles, re-organize or form new committees based on strategic goals, develop committee work plans, update Board operations calendar, review planning status, etc.)	August (in time to orient new Board members soon after they join the Board)
14.	Conduct fundraising plan (primarily to meet fundraising goals)	August-December
15.	Implement strategic plan, including to achieve goals and objectives according to deadlines in the action plans of the overall strategic plan	Ongoing

Sample Comparison of Board and Staff Roles

The following table is adapted from James M. Hardy, *Developing Dynamic Boards* (Essex Press, 1990). The nature of the extent of separation between Board and staff, if at all, depends very much on the particular Board model that members prefer. The primary responsibilities of Board and staff ultimately depend on the priorities, culture and life cycle of the nonprofit. The following suggestions might be useful to consider and change as needed.

Activities	Primary Responsibility
Organizational Planning	
Drive the process of strategic and organizational planning	Board
Provide input to mission and long range goals	Joint
Approve mission and long range, strategic goals	Board
Develop action plans (who does what and when) to achieve long-range goals	Staff
Approve action plans (e.g., in an annual Operating Plan)	Board
Implement action plans to achieve long-range goals (Board via committee work plans)	Joint
Follow-up to insure achievement of major goals and objectives	Board
Board of Directors	
Select new Board members	Board
Orient, train and organize members into committees	Board
Promote attendance at Board/committee meetings	Board
Plan agenda for Board meetings (joint with Board Chair and Exec. Dir.)	Joint
Take minutes at Board meetings (Board Secretary)	Board
Programs	
Assess stakeholder (customers, community, member, etc.) needs	Joint
Suggest program clients, outcomes, goals, etc.	Joint
Approve program outcomes and goals	Board
Ensure evaluation of products, services and programs	Board
Evaluate products, services and programs	Staff
Maintain program records; prepare program reports	Staff
Financial management	
Prepare preliminary annual budget	Staff
Finalize and approve annual budget	Board
Approve major expenditures outside authorized budget	Board
Ensure annual audit of organization accounts	Board
Ensure that expenditures are within budget during the year	Joint
Fundraising	
Establish fundraising goals (amounts / goals to be raised)	Board
Solicit contributions in fundraising campaigns	Joint
Organize fundraising campaigns	Joint
Manage grants (reporting, etc.)	Staff
Personnel Activities (staff and volunteers)	
Employ and supervise Chief Executive (Exec. Dir.)	Board
Decision to add general staff roles and / or volunteer roles	Staff
Select / train general staff and / or volunteers	Staff
Direct work of the general staff and /or volunteers	Staff
Public / Community Relations Activities	
Present / describe organization to community	Joint
Write descriptions of organization (newsletters, Web, etc.)	Staff

Sample Board Committee Charter (Board Development)

Purpose and Scope of Responsibility of Committee

Committee is a standing committee that provides guidance, oversight and support to ensure high-quality operations of the Board, including all officers, members and Committees. The Committee does not drive the car, that is, the Committee does not do the Board's job. Rather the Committee makes sure that car runs well and gets good maintenance, that is, the Committee makes sure that the Board gets good members, organizes active Committees, meetings are highly focused, etc.

Committee Organization and Reporting Structure

- Committee reports to the Board Chair.

- The Board Chair and Board Executive Committee will regularly monitor and ensure that the Board Development Committee achieves its goals and objectives.

- Committee makes recommendations to the full Board for Board's review and approval. (The Committee does not make final decisions for the Board.)

- A Committee Chair who is also a member of the Board leads Committee.

- Committee provides written reports about its meetings, recommendations and actions to the entire Board on a regular basis.

- Committee includes at least two members of the Board.

- Membership of the Committee is selected on an annual basis.

- Goals of the Committee are in accordance with the most recent Strategic Plan.

- Budget of resources for the Committee are allocated near the end of the fiscal year, soon after finalizing the organization's overall operating budget.

Goals of the Board Development Committee for 2009

The Committee's goals and objectives, along with start and stop dates for each objective, will comprise the Committee's "work plan," which will be approved by the full Board.

1. Ensure new Board systems (charters, job descriptions, etc.) incorporated into Board operations.

2. Ensure Board is fully resourced to govern the organization.

3. Ensure full participation and dedication of all Board members.

4. Ensure all Board meetings are highly-focused and strategic.

5. Ensure Board leadership rigorously coordinates Board activities.

6. Ensure continuous improvement of Board.

For an example of objectives associated with goals in a charter, see "Goals and Objectives for Board Development Committee" 243.

Sample Board Staffing Checklist (Board Renewal Cycle)

There are different perspectives and approaches to staffing a Board of Directors, that is, getting and developing members of the Board. Common perspectives are:

- Functional staffing: to gain expertise needed to establish and achieve current strategic goals.
- Diversification staffing: to achieve a wide diversity of values and perspectives.
- Representative staffing: to represent the major constituents of the organization.
- Passion-driven staffing: to gather members who have strong passion for the mission.

Board members also must have the time, energy and assignments to actively participate in the Board. To ensure that the staffing and engagement of their Board are conducted effectively, the Board of Directors of a nonprofit organization might use the following checklist.

Activity	Responsibility
❑ Based on approach to staffing (functional, representative and/or diversification), develop slate of new potential Board members during the year.	Board Development Cmte
❑ Distribute applications to each potential new Board member. Tell each person why you are interested in his/her expertise.	Board Development Cmte
❑ Receive applications from each potential Board member.	Board Development Cmte
❑ Board votes to select new Board members for open positions (or members are elected by general members, e.g., in an association).	Board
❑ Call the selected Board members to welcome them.	Board Chair
❑ Receive letter of acceptance from each elected Board member.	Board Development Cmte
❑ Provide Board manual (with Board policies, procedures, Bylaws, etc.) to each new member.	Board Development Cmte
❑ Conduct orientation about agency for new Board members, e.g., its programs, members, etc. (Review info in the Board manual.)	Board Development Cmte
❑ Conduct training about roles of any governing Board of Directors. (It is useful even for all Board members to attend.)	Board Development Cmte
❑ Appoint new Board officers. (Reflect this in the minutes.)	Board
❑ Organize new members into appropriate Board committee(s).	Board
❑ Ensure that each committee has an up-to-date Work Plan that includes objectives and deadlines. (The best way to keep good Board members is to give them something specific to do by a certain deadline – that is the best way to get rid of deadwood members you do not want, too! So use Work Plans!)	Board Development Cmte
❑ Issue new Board organization chart.	Board Development Cmte
❑ Executive Committee monitors implementation of Work Plans during the year. (Act like you deserve an active Board!)	Executive Committee

Sample Board Member Recruitment Grid

The following table might be useful to you to record features you need on your Board.

Features	Current Board Members								Candidates							
ID: (initials or code)																
Age:																
18-24																
25-39																
40-54																
55-69																
70+																
Gender:																
Male																
Female																
Geographic Location:																
Inner city																
Suburb North																
Suburb South																
Suburb East																
Suburb West																
Rural																
National																
International																
Other:																
Ethnicity:																
African American																
Asian American																
Caucasian																
Latino/Chicano																
Native American																
Other:																
Expertise:																
Boards																
Evaluation																
Financial																
Fundraising																
Human Resources																
Legal																
Marketing																
Planning																
Programs/Services																
Other:																

Sample Board Member Application Form

Thank you for your interest in our Board! We will help you carefully decide if you want to join, then we will orient you to our organization, train you about the roles and responsibilities of a member of a nonprofit Board of Directors, and organize you into the committee that most closely matches your skills and interests.

Please read the enclosed materials, fill out this application and return it to:

[insert Street address, City, State, Zip Code]

If you have any questions, you can call *[insert name of contact person]*. We will review your application and get back to you soon. Thank you!

Your name:_____

Your phone number: _____

Your address: _____

_____

Your email address (please write it carefully):

_____

Briefly describe why you would like to join our Board of Directors:

_____

_____

_____

_____

Your current organizational affiliations (names of the organization and your role(s):

1. _____

2. _____

3. _____

4. _____

Which of your skills would you like to utilize on the Board? Check those that apply:

❏ Board development   ❏ Financial management   ❏ Training

❏ Strategic planning   ❏ Fundraising   ❏ Marketing

❏ Staffing / HR   ❏ Evaluation   ❏ Volunteer management

❏ Program development   ❏ Community networking   ❏ Facilities management

Other skill(s) of yours that you would like to utilize? _____

_____

_____

What would you like to get for yourself out of your participation on the Board, e.g., what types of experiences, skills to develop, interests to cultivate for you, etc.?

_____

_____

_____

_____

_____

If you join the Board, you agree that you can provide at least 2-4 hours a month in attendance to Board and committee meetings, and that you do have any conflict of interest in participating on the Board.

Your signature: _____ Date:_____

If you are not selected as a member of the Board, or if you decide not to join, would you like to be a volunteer to assist our organization in various ways that match your skills and interests?

❏ Yes   ❏ No   ❏ Perhaps

Any other skill(s) of yours that you would like to utilize as a volunteer? _____

_____

_____

_____

Sample Board Conflict-of-Interest Policy

Members of the Board of Directors will perform their roles and responsibilities and arrange their personal and professional affairs in such a manner that 1) public confidence and trust in our nonprofit is always maintained; and 2) Board members' honesty, integrity, fairness and good faith are always apparent to themselves and others.

Purpose

1. Clarify concept of "conflict of interest"

2. Identify types of outside situations which might pose confict of interest

3. Provide disclosure and approval procedures to help Board members to report and deliberate about potential or actual conflict-of-interest situations

4. Provide guidelines for addressing actual conflict-of-interest situations

Definition of "Conflict of Interest"

One of the fiduciary responsibilities of a Board member is the duty of loyalty to the nonprofit organization that they serve. That duty requires that Board members disclose potential or actual conflict-of-interest situations. These are situations where a Board member might appear to be, or is actually, taking advantage of their role as a Board member for his/her own personal gain. These situations can compromise a Board member's best judgment for the nonprofit when carrying out his/her roles and responsibilities as a Board member.

General Types of Situations That Pose Potential, or Actual, Conflict of Interest

The following two general situations are the primary examples of these types of situations:

1. Where decision-making roles and responsibilities regarding oneself, other organizations or other persons, about products, services and/or markets that might, or actually do, conflict or compete with those of the nonprofit organization.

2. Where a Board member might appear to be, or actually is, taking advantage of their role as a Board member to make specific Board decisions, the result of which will enhance the member's personal financial situation.

Disclosure of Potential, or Actual, Conflict-of-Interest Situations

All Board members are responsible for disclosing potential, or actual, conflicts of interest. Disclosure shall include: the type of potential conflict, the nature of the activity or situation, description of major parties involved, potential financial interests and rewards for the Board member, any possible violations of laws and regulations and of our nonprofit's plans and policies, and any other information which the Board member feels necessary in order for our Board to evaluate the disclosure.

Commitments of Each Board Member

1.   Annually sign conflict-of-interest policy.

2.   Report any apparent or real conflict of interest.

3.   Excuse myself from any Board deliberations and decisions that might directly or indirectly benefit my family, my personal business or me.

4.   Annually disclose to members the nature of my current business services or employment, and a list of organizations with which I am directly affiliated and/or have a financially vested interest.

5.   Will not engage in a business relationship with another Board member or a staff member unless previously permitted by a majority of Board members.

Guidelines to Address Potential, or Actual, Conflict-of-Interest Situations

Upon full disclosure by the Board member:

1.   Board members decide if there is a potential, or actual, conflict-of-interest situation by reaching at least 2/3's majority vote of all Board members.

2.   The Board member associated with the potential, or actual, conflict-of-interest situation can first pose a suitable response to the situation. Suitable responses might include:

     a. Abstaining from Board decisions regarding the situation (for example, from a Board vote to hire a consultant for a project to which the Board member wants to apply).

     b. Removal of the Board member from the situation (for example, to quit the roles or association with another organization or person that shares products, services or markets with a conflicting or competing organization).

     c. To quit the Board of Directors of our nonprofit organization.

3.   Board members select suitable response by reaching at least 2/3's majority vote. It is ultimately up to the Board member to decide what he/she wants to do. However, inaction can be cause for dismissal from the Board.

4.   Board discussion and voting results are recorded in the Board meeting minutes.

Sample Board Member Contract

I _____ agree to serve as a member of the Board of Directors of [*insert name of nonprofit*]. I understand that my term of office begins _____ and last for three years, ending _____ .

As a member of the Board of Directors, I agree to:

1.   Be legally responsible for the governance, operations and effects of the nonprofit.

2.   Abide by the Articles of Incorporation, By Laws and Board policies.

3.   Make an annual financial contribution and participate in fundraising efforts.

4.   Attend 75% of all meetings of the Board, including special meetings, unless excused.

5.   Participate in deliberations, decisions and actions of the Board and its committees.

6.   Speak up when I disagree with any opinions or decisions of Board members.

7.   Support, not publicly disagree, with decisions made by a quorum of members.

8.   Report and avoid any apparent or real conflicts of interest.

9.   Participate in short- and long-range planning activities.

10.   Ensure effective fiscal controls and accountability.

11.   Approve the annual budget.

12.   Ensure our nonprofit's operations meets all legal and corporate requirements.

I agree that if, at any time, I am unable to fulfill the commitments of a member of the Board of Directors of [*insert name of nonprofit*], I will give appropriate notice of resignation to the Board Chair.

Printed name: _____

Signature: _____ Date: _____

Sample Board Ethics Policy

Purpose

This policy is intended to guide toward the highly ethical behavior of each Board member in his/her roles and responsibilities as a Board member in our organization. All Board members receive a copy of this official policy and agree to adhere to the policy. The policy is reviewed once a year and maintained in each member's Board Manual.

Adherence to Following Behaviors

As a Board member of [*insert name of nonprofit*], I will:

1. Know my roles and responsibilities as a member of the governing Board of Directors.

2. Do my best to be fully informed of the nonprofit's operations that can have significant effect on fellow Board members, staff members and other stakeholders of our organization.

3. Always strive to contribute my best judgment in carrying out my role, including provision of opinions and information during Board deliberations and decisions.

4. Avoid conflict of interest in appearance or in application – my actions as a Board member will always be first and foremost for the benefit of our nonprofit organization.

5. Adhere to all of the Board policies that are oriented to me during Board orientation. These will be included in my Board Manual.

6. Not directly assign tasks to staff members, rather I will coordinate my suggestions for those tasks through the Board as a body, which can, in turn, assign the CEO to carry out the tasks as he/she desires.

7. Maintain confidentiality about all Board information that is deemed by members to be confidential, including that are generated and decided during closed sessions of the Board.

8. Follow the ground rules for Board meetings as formally agreed upon by fellow Board members.

9. Respect the values and perspectives of fellow Board members and staff members with whom I interact.

10. Represent the nonprofit in the most positive image when I am dealing with stakeholders our nonprofit.

11. Adhere to the decisions made by the Board – I will avoid public disagreement with decisions, recognizing that all Board members must "speak from one voice."

Response to Unethical Behaviors

Determination of suspected or actual occurrence of any unethical behavior by a Board member will be decided by a simple majority (51%) vote of the Board. Any Board member can notify the Board of that type of behavior. Penalty for the behavior can be removal from the Board upon resolution passed by 2/3's of the voting members.

Sample Board Decision-Making Policy

Presenting New Topics for Board Decision

1. Staff and/or Board members suggest a new topic and its associated required action (for example, for Board approval, disavowal, resolution, etc.).

2. The Board Chair and Executive Director put the topic on the Board agenda for the next Board meeting.

    a. Otherwise, if the topic is suggested during a Board meeting and for that meeting's agenda, a majority vote of the Board members is required to change that agenda for the current meeting.

    b. Otherwise, the topic can be deferred to the next Board meeting, or assigned to a committee and/or staff member for further research before the next Board meeting, to prepare for a decision in that next meeting.

3. Background materials for the decision are provided to all Board members at least one week before the full Board meeting.

Procedure to Make Formal Board Decisions

1. The type of decision required from Board members about a topic is articulated on the Board agenda, for example, Board approval, Board disavowal, generate resolution, etc.

2. The amount of time to address the topic is associated with that time on the agenda.

3. Discussion and/or debate occurs in Board meeting.

4. Consensus is attempted within the time allotted for the topic.

5. If consensus cannot be achieved in a timely manner, then a simple majority vote is conducted among Board members. Decision outcome goes to the majority vote, as long as at least a quorum of the Board members participated in the vote.

6. The decision is documented in Board minutes for that Board meeting.

7. In the future, all Board members support the decision – they speak from "one voice."

Sample Executive Director Evaluation Form

Sample Schedule to Evaluate Chief Executive

Activity	Approx. # of months before start of next fiscal year
Conduct Board self-evaluation	10
Evaluate the Chief Executive, by referencing his or her progress towards last fiscal year's organizational goals and responsibilities on their job description	9
Hold Board retreat to address results of Board self-evaluation, conduct any team building and begin strategic planning	8
Conduct strategic planning to produce organizational goals and identify resources needed to accomplish the goals	7
Establish Chief Executive's goals for the next fiscal year, by referencing goals produced from strategic planning	6
Establish next year's fundraising goals and budget by referencing resources needed to reach strategic goals	6
Conduct fundraising to meet fundraising goals	6
Fiscal year begins	0

General Guidelines When Evaluating Chief Executive

1. Be sure the process is fully documented in a procedure so the process is well understood and carried out consistently year-to-year. The procedure should be in conformance with up-to-date, Board-approved personnel policies and procedures.

2. If staff members are involved in evaluation of the Chief Executive, be sure this procedure is clearly specified and understood by the Chief Executive.

3. The evaluation should be administered by a Board committee, not by one Board member. Committees might be the Executive Committee, a Personnel Committee or an ad hoc committee.

4. All Board members should have input to the evaluation of the Chief Executive.

5. If the Board perceives the Chief Executive to have performance issues, then Board members can initiate an evaluation. However, do not initiate evaluations only when there are perceived issues – this is abusive. Be sure that conclusions about performance issues are based on observed behaviors of the Chief Executive, rather than on interpretations or speculations about the Chief Executive's character or personality.

Sample Form to Evaluate Chief Executive: Guidelines

The following is one sample set of guidelines and a form that might be used by the Board to evaluate the Chief Executive. This sample should be customized to the particular culture and purpose of the nonprofit by modifying the performance criteria (in the following table) as appropriate for the organization, inserting those criteria in the table below, and conducting the evaluation using the updated table.

1. The Board should establish a policy for evaluating the Chief Executive and establish a current or ad hoc committee to carry out the evaluation.

2. The Board, working with the Chief Executive, should establish performance criteria and insert them in the following evaluation form. Criteria should come from the Chief Executive's job description and any strategic goals from the most current strategic plan.

3. The Board then assigns specific weighting factors for each of the major categories below. Factors depend on what the Board believes should be priorities for the Chief Executive during the evaluation period. The factors should total 100%. Example weightings might be finances 15%, revenue 20%, human resources 15%, products/programs 20%, facilities 10%, planning and governance 20%.

4. Each Board member and the Chief Executive complete the evaluation form about the Chief Executive's performance during the evaluation period. Each criteria is ranked from 1-5, with 1=unsatisfactory, 2 = partially within expectations, 3=meets expectations, 4=exceeds expectations, and 5= far exceeds expectations. This numerical ranking system tends to give clear perspective more than commentary. Rankings with commentary are ideal.

5. Multiply each ranking by the category's weighting factor. Put the answer in the score column.

6. On a separate sheet of paper, provide any commentary that addresses rankings lower than 3. Consider adding commentary for high ratings as well.

7. Provide evaluation sheets and commentary to the Board member who is assigned to collate the sheets (usually the Board Chair).

8. The Board may decide to provide the Chief Executive an average ranking for each category. Similarly, commentary can be summarized or each comment provided to the Chief Executive.

9. The evaluation committee provides the evaluation report to the Chief Executive and schedules a meeting with him or her shortly thereafter.

10. Ensure the meeting ends on a positive note.

11. Ensure plans are made to address ratings below 3, including specific actions by specific dates.

Sample Form to Evaluate Chief Executive

Name of Preparer	Ratings	Weight Factor	= Score
Planning and support of governance, consider: ▪ Provides relevant and meaningful information to support Board plans and policies ▪ Establishes appropriate plans and priorities, which are clearly described to staff members ▪ Ensure implementation of plans in a timely manner Comments:			
Finances, consider: ▪ Stays within budgets and/or gets approval for deviations ▪ Maintains needed cash flow to pay bills on time ▪ Receives a "clean" financial audit ▪ No loss of operating funds ▪ No prolonged legal difficulties Comments:			
Revenue, consider: ▪ Raises enough revenue through fundraising and fees for services to accomplish significant program goals ▪ Maintains a financial balance in keeping with organizational policy Comments:			
Programs and services, consider: ▪ Ensures high-quality operations in programs ▪ Verifies that each program is achieving its program goals and the desired outcomes among clients Comments:			
Human resources, consider: ▪ Maintains or increases productivity of staff ▪ Maintains sufficient and effective volunteer corps ▪ No undue staff turnover ▪ No ongoing personnel complaints Comments:			

Sample Board Member Self-Evaluation Form

This form can be used by a Board member to evaluate how well he/she is doing as a Board member. The best time for a member to complete this form is when all Board members are also conducting a self-evaluation of the quality of operations of the overall Board. (That self-evaluation involves each member sharing opinions about the overall Board activities, rather than his/her own activities as a Board member.) Results of the member's own self-evaluation can be confidential to that person or shared with all members. The more open and honest that each member can be to all other members, the more learning and improvement that can come from the overall Board self-evaluation and each member's individual self-evaluation.

Board member name _____ Date _____

Current position on Board _____ Length of time as a Board member ___

Use the following scale in your answers:

    1 – strongly disagree;   2 – disagree;   3 – no opinion;   4 – agree;   5 – strongly agree

1. I fully understand my duties and responsibilities as a member of a governing Board, e.g., I've undergone a formal training to be sure about my role. ____

2. I fully understand and comply with the Board's bylaws and Board policies. ____

3. I am aware of each of our nonprofit's programs, including who is served, how they are served and the results achieved from the program. ____

4. I am verifying/measuring that our nonprofit is meeting a specific community need. ____

5. I attend all Board meetings and/or am excused beforehand for my absences. ____

6. I read all materials provided to me before each Board meeting. ____

7. I know how to analyze and make decisions about the financial information that I get. ____

8. I fully participate in members' deliberations and decisions. ____

9. I speak up when I disagree with an opinion, conclusion or decision. ____

10. Even though I might disagree with a decision of a quorum, I support the decision to our stakeholders. ____

11. I complete my Board assignments on time, e.g., in actions in my Committee. ____

12. I am fulfilled from my Board activities. (On separate paper, describe what's fulfilling and what would make it even more so.) ____

13. I was completely honest and accurate in completing this evaluation. ____

What other questions should be added to this questionnaire? Write the question and your answer:

_____

_____

_____

What am I going to do to improve my performance as a Board member? _____

_____

_____

_____

What could Board members to do become more effective, overall? _____

_____

_____

_____

Sample Board Self-Evaluation Form

Use the following scale in your answers:
 1 – strongly disagree;   2 – disagree;   3 – no opinion;   4 – agree;   5 – strongly agree

	Name: (optional)	5	4	3	2	1
1.	Board members clearly understand the roles and responsibilities of a nonprofit governing Board.					
2.	Board members understand the nonprofit's mission and *each* of its products / programs.					
3.	Nonprofit has clear organizational structure (Board, officers – and CEO/staff if used).					
4.	Board ensures relevant and realistic strategic planning annually, producing approved Plan.					
5.	Board has clear goals and actions (who is going to what by when) resulting from relevant and realistic strategic planning.					
6.	Meeting materials are provided well in advance so members come prepared to meetings.					
7.	Board meeting agenda includes strategic topics and specific time to address each topic.					
8.	Board meetings are facilitated to the agenda topics and timing (if topics need more time, then a Board and/or staff is delegated to get more info).					
9.	Board attends to policy-related decisions, and decisions are monitored for implementation.					
10.	Each Board committee (if the nonprofit uses committees) has specific goals and deadlines.					
11.	Board receives and understands regular reports on finances/budgets, and make suitable decisions.					
12.	Board regularly monitors and evaluates progress toward strategic goals and program performance.					
13.	Board verifies/measures that the nonprofit is indeed meeting a specific need in the community.					
14.	Board helps set specific fundraising goals and is actively involved in fundraising.					
15.	Board effectively represents the organization to the community, e.g., meeting with stakeholders.					
16.	Board regularly evaluates CEO, if a CEO is used.					
17.	Board has approved comprehensive personnel policies, reviewed by a qualified professional.					
18.	Board members are aware of all Board policies (e.g., conflict-of-interest, attendance, etc.) and conform to those policies.					
19.	All Board members actively participate in Board deliberations and decisions.					
20.	Board formally evaluates itself at least once a year.					

Please list themost important three to five priorities on which you believe the Board should focus its attention in the next year. Be as specific as possible in identifying the priorities. *(You can provide your name, if you prefer.)*

1.

2.

3.

4.

5.

Sample Board Attendance Policy

Purpose

This policy is intended to support the full participation and contribution of all Board members. All Board members receive a copy of this official policy. The policy is reviewed once a year and maintained in each member's Board Manual. The terms for attendance and associated termination of Board members are in accordance between this policy and the By Laws.

Definition of a Board Attendance Problem

A Board attendance problem occurs if any of the following conditions exists in regard to a Board member's attendance to Board meetings:

1. The member has two un-notified absences in a row ("un-notified" means the member did not call ahead to a reasonable contact in the organization before the upcoming meeting to indicate he/she was unable to attend).

2. The member has three notified absences in a row.

3. The member misses one third of the total number of Board meetings in a twelve-month period.

Response to a Board Attendance Problem

1. If the Board notices a Board attendance problem with a member, the Board Chair will contact the member within one week to discuss the problem.

2. The Chair will share the member's response with the entire Board within one week.

3. In the next Board meeting, the Board will decide what actions to take regarding the Board member's future membership on the Board.

4. If the Board decides to terminate the Board member's membership, termination will be conducted per this policy.

5. The Board will promptly initiate a process to begin recruiting a new Board member according to the Board Staffing Policy.

Sample Board Media Relations Policy

Board members have a fiduciary duty of loyalty to our nonprofit corporation, including that members present favorable information about our operations, programs and services. Members also have a responsibility to favorably represent our nonprofit to its stakeholders. The intents of this policy are to: a) consistently present unified and accurate information to the media, including, but not limited to reporters, free-lance writers, funders and members of collaborating organizations; b) ensure that the most qualified personnel present the information to the media; and c) cultivate courteous and respectful relationships with media personnel.

There are a wide variety of occasions where organizational personnel might interact with members of the media. It is not practical to define guidelines for each and every occasion and contingency. However, the following are the principle guidelines that address the vast majority of occasions.

1.   The Board Chair and Chief Executive Officer will approve content of press/media kits, standard talking points and other communications (pictures, videotapes, etc.) before it is conveyed to external stakeholders. Content will be generated by the Marketing Committee and approved by the Board in accordance with strategic priorities included in the most recent strategic plan.

2.   Information about our stakeholders (for example, Board members, staff members, clients, funders, collaborators, etc.) will not be shared with media without the expressed consent of each of the individuals involved.

3.   Content will always be in reference, in wording and in nature, to our branding, including our preferred image and our logo, and to our mission, visions, values. Additional points in reference to the organization's current operations or events will be approved by the CEO for staff members and by the Board Chair for Board members.

4.   The Board Chair and/or CEO will be the only designated spokesperson(s) for the organization, unless either of these two personnel explicitly permits other organizational personnel to communicate with media. Other organizational personnel who are contacted by media personnel will promptly refer media personnel to the Board Chair and/or the CEO. Organizational personnel will report the referrals to the Board Chair and/or the CEO.

5.   Organizational personnel interacting with media with always be in their best appearance and language, for example: in dress, communications style and positive attitude about the organization.

6.   In occasions where media personnel are persistent and referrals to the Board Chair and/or CEO are not immediately practical, for example, in the event of a health or facility emergency, organizational personnel will always be respectful, and consistently and concisely focused on the most obvious and verifiable facts. Do not conjecture or engage in communications not based on the most obvious facts.

Sample Whistleblower Policy

This policy is intended to encourage Board members, staff (paid and volunteer) and others to report suspected or actual occurrence(s) of illegal, unethical or inappropriate events (behaviors or practices) without retribution.

1. The Whistleblower should promptly report the suspected or actual event to his/her supervisor.

2. If the Whistleblower would be uncomfortable or otherwise reluctant to report to his/her supervisor, then the Whistleblower could report the event to the next highest or another level of management, including to an appropriate Board committee or member.

3. The Whistleblower can report the event with his/her identity or anonymously.

4. The Whistle blower shall receive no retaliation or retribution for a report that was provided in good faith – that was not done primarily with malice to damage another or the organization.

5. A Whistleblower who makes a report that is not done in good faith is subject to discipline, including termination of the Board or employee relationship, or other legal means to protect the reputation of the organization and members of its Board and staff.

6. Anyone who retaliates against the Whistleblower (who reported an event in good faith) will be subject to discipline, including termination of Board or employee status.

7. Crimes against person or property, such as assault, rape, burglary, etc., should immediately be reported to local law enforcement personnel.

8. Supervisors, managers and/or Board members who receive the reports must promptly act to investigate and/or resolve the issue.

9. The Whistleblower shall receive a report within five business days of the initial report, regarding the investigation, disposition or resolution of the issue.

10. If the investigation of a report, that was done in good faith and investigated by internal personnel, is not to the Whistleblower's satisfaction, then he/she has the right to report the event to the appropriate legal or investigative agency.

11. The identity of the Whistleblower, if known, shall remain confidential to those persons directly involved in applying this policy, unless the issue requires investigation by law enforcement, in which case members of the organization are subject to subpoena.

Sample Document Retention/Destruction Policy

This policy specifies how important documents (hardcopy, online or other media) should be retained, protected and eligible for destruction. The policy also ensures that documents are promptly provided to authorities in the course of legal investigations or lawsuits.

Document Retention Schedule

The following types of documents will be retained for the following periods of time. At least one copy of each document will be retained according to the following schedule.

Corporate Records

Article of Incorporation to apply for corporate status	Permanent
IRS Form 1023 (in the USA) to file for tax-exempt and/or charitable status	Permanent
Letter of Determination (for example, from the IRS in the USA) granting tax-exempt and/or charitable status	Permanent
By Laws	Permanent
Board policies	Permanent
Resolutions	Permanent
Board meeting minutes	Permanent
Sales tax exemption documents	Permanent
Tax or employee identification number designation	Permanent
Annual corporate filings	Permanent

Financial Records

Chart of Accounts	Permanent
Fiscal Policies and Procedures	Permanent
Audits	Permanent
Financial statements	Permanent
General Ledger	Permanent
Check registers/books	7 years
Business expenses documents	7 years
Bank deposit slips	7 years
Cancelled checks	7 years
Invoices	7 years
Investment records (deposits, earnings, withdrawals)	7 years
Property/asset inventories	7 years
Petty cash receipts/documents	3 years
Credit card receipts	3 years

Tax Records

Annual tax filing for the organization (IRS Form 990 in the USA)	Permanent
Payroll registers	Permanent
Filings of fees paid to professionals (IRS Form 1099 in the USA)	7 years
Payroll tax withholdings	7 years
Earnings records	7 years
Payroll tax returns	7 years
W-2 statements	7 years

Personnel Records

Employee offer letters	Permanent
Confirmation of employment letters	Permanent
Benefits descriptions per employee	Permanent
Pension records	Permanent
Employee applications and resumes	7 years after termination
Promotions, demotions, letter of reprimand, termination	7 years after termination
Job descriptions, performance goals	7 years after termination
Workers' Compensation records	5 years
Salary ranges per job description	5 years
I-9 Forms	5 years after termination
Time reports	3 years after termination

Insurance Records

Property Insurance policy	Permanent
Directors and Officers Insurance policy	Permanent
Workers' Compensation Insurance policy	Permanent
General Liability Insurance policy	Permanent
Insurance claims applications	Permanent
Insurance dispersements / denials	Permanent

Contracts

All insurance contracts	Permanent
Employee contracts	Permanent
Construction contracts	Permanent
Legal correspondence	Permanent
Loan / mortgage contracts	Permanent
Leases / deeds	Permanent
Vendor contracts	7 years
Warranties	7 years

Donations / Funder Records

Grant dispersal contract	Permanent
Donor lists	7 years
Grant applications	7 years
Donor acknowledgements	7 years

Management Plans and Procedures

Strategic Plans	7 years
Staffing, programs, marketing, finance, fundraising and evaluation plans	7 years
Vendor contacts	7 years
Disaster Recovery Plan	7 years

Document Protection

Documents (hardcopy, online or other media) will be stored in a protected environment for the duration of the Document Retention Schedule. Computer backup media will be included.

Document Destruction

Hardcopy of documents will be destroyed by shredding after they have been retained until the end of the Document Retention Schedule. Online copies will be destroyed by fire or other proven means to destroy such media after they have been retained until the end of the Document Retention Schedule.

Provision of Documentation for Investigations or Litigation

Documents requested and subpoenaed by legally authorized personnel will be provided within 5 business days. The Board Chair and CEO will authorize provision. No documents will be concealed, altered or destroyed with the intent to obstruct the investigation or litigation.

Bibliography

Various categories of readings are included below. The following readings are by no means all of the important works in each category. However, the listed works will provide you a strong start to understanding information in that particular category. Bibliographies of many of the works listed below will help you to find related works from which you can continue to develop your knowledge about the particular category.

Boards of Directors

Building Better Boards, David A. Nadler (Editor), Jossey-Bass, 2005.

> This book describes how Boards can become high-performing teams. Lists the influences that have the greatest effects on Board success and principles to improve Boards. Although the book is based on research with organizations that have many resources, the principles still apply to small- and medium-sized nonprofits.

Exploring the Puzzle of Board Design: What's Your Type, David Renz, Nonprofit Quarterly, Winter 2004, Vol 11, Issue 4. (Also available free online at http://www.nonprofitquarterly.org/section/655.html)

> The article reminds consultants that there is no one right design for Boards. The article clearly conveys the wide range of types, or personalities, of Board of Directors and how to categorize them. Includes a well-designed graph for discerning the type of any governing Board.

Governing for Results: A Director's Guide to Good Governance, Mel D. Gill, Trafford Publishing, 2005.

> Well-researched guide to a practical understanding of the roles of a governing Board and the wide range of different Board structures actually used by Boards (one of the best books for understanding the different structures). Explains the practices and structures to achieve good governance, and suggests the extent of governance versus management for each structure.

Governance Models: What's Right for Your Board?, Nathan Garber & Associates, available free online at http://garberconsulting.com/governance%20models%20what's%20right.htm .

> Describes Board models, including: Advisory, Cooperative, Patron, Management Team and Policy, and includes guidelines for how to pick the best model.

Quick Overview of Governance Models/Board Types, Mel Gill, Synergy Associates, at http://www.synergyassociates.ca/publications/OverviewGovernanceModels.htm .

> Overviews of Board models, including: Operational, Management, Collective, Constituent Representational, Traditional, Results-Based, Policy Governance, Fundraising and Advisory.

The Strategic Board: The Step-by-Step Guide to High-Impact Governance, Mark Light, Wiley, 2001.

> Includes broad guidelines for achieving effective governance, such as establishing clear vision and values for strong leadership, effective delegation through clarity of roles and responsibilities, and translating Board decisions throughout the organization via clear management plans and measures.

Capacity Building

Building Capacity in Nonprofit Organizations, edited by Carol J. De Vita, Urban Institute Press, 2001.

> Written especially for foundations considering capacity building programs, but relevant to all providers. Depicts overall framework for nonprofit capacity building. Suggests eight aspects of effective capacity building programs and describes continuum of capacity building services. Free at http://www.urban.org/UploadedPDF/building_capacity.PDF .

Building for Impact: The Future of Effectiveness for Nonprofits and Foundations, Grantmakers for Effective Organizations, 2002.

> Report on the 2002 National Conference of grantmakers that highlights expected trends in philanthropy, suggesting more priority on nonprofit performance. Offers four possible scenarios that grantmakers might follow in the future. Challenges grantmakers to focus on their own organizational effectiveness for capacity building. Free at http://www.geofunders.org/_uploads/documents/live/conference%20report.pdf .

Building the Capacity of Capacity Builders, Conservation Company, June 2003.

> Provides overview of nonprofit capacity builders, suggests four key capacities for effective nonprofit organizations: leadership, adaptive, managerial and technical. Includes recommendations for capacity builders to improve services. Free at http: //www.tccgrp.com/pdfs/buildingthecapacityofcapacitybuilders.pdf

Echoes from the Field: Proven Capacity Building Principles for Nonprofits, Environmental Support Center and Innovation Network, Inc., 2002.

> Suggests nine principles of effective capacity building. An excellent read for those who want to understand the broad context of capacity building and the realities of providing capacity building programs. Free at http://www.envsc.org/bestpractices.pdf .

Effective Capacity Building in Nonprofit Organizations, Venture Philanthropy Partners, 2001.

> Suggests seven overall elements of nonprofit capacity building. Describes lessons-learned from nonprofits that have engaged in successful capacity building efforts. Provides comprehensive assessment instrument to assess organizational effectiveness according to the seven elements. Free at http://vppartners.org/learning/reports/capacity/capacity.html .

Lessons from the Street: Capacity Building and Replication, Milton S. Eisenhower Foundation.

> Based on street-level experience from 1990 to 2000 in offering technical assistance and training for capacity building, especially with grassroots organizations in inner cities. Offers top ten lessons and recommendations for funders regarding assistance and replication of programs. Free at http://www.eisenhowerfoundation.org/aboutus/publications/lessons_intro.html .

Mapping Nonprofit Capacity Builders: A Study by LaSalle University's Nonprofit Center, Kathryn Szabat and Laura Otten (1999).

> Overview of research to identify "the universe of capacity builders ..." Mentions capacity builders by general characteristics and reports results of research, with percentage of capacity builders in various categories. This is an interesting perusal for those wanting a

quick impression of the world of capacity builders. Free at
http://www.np-org-dev.com/survey.doc .

Reflections on Capacity Building, The California Wellness Foundation.

Lists numerous lessons-learned from TCWF's implementation of capacity building services.
Reflections and lessons-learned are numerous and meaningful for funders providing capacity
building services. Free at
http://www.tcwf.org/reflections/2001/april/index.htm .

Results of an Inquiry into Capacity Building Programs for Nonprofits, by Susan Doherty and
Stephen Meyer of Communities for Action.

Describes organizational capacity and why it is important. Explains why capacity building
does not happen naturally and offers seven overall elements that work for capacity building
efforts. Brief overviews of major areas of capacity building. Free at
http://www.effectivecommunities.com/ECP_CapacityBuildingInquiry.pdf .

Strengthening Nonprofit Organizations: A Funder's Guide to Capacity Building, by Carol Lukas,
Amherst H. Wilder Foundation.

Describes types of capacity building services. Provides straightforward explanation of
process for funders to consider offering capacity building programs, and adds general
strategic process for funders to identify which capacity building services to offer.

Consulting

Consultants Calling, Geoffrey M., Jossey-Bass, 1990.

Does an excellent job helping readers closely examine why they want to be a consultant.
Includes numerous guidelines to set up a practice, understand organizations and clients,
maintain balance and boundaries, and more.

Consulting for Dummies, Bob Nelson and Peter Economy, IDG Books, 1997.

Highly readable resource that touches on the most important aspects of setting up and
marketing a consulting business. The *Dummies* series is well-known for being easy to
reference and well-designed.

Consulting With Nonprofits: A Practitioners Guide, Carol Lukas, Amherst H. Wilder
Foundation, 1998.

Easy-to-read, general overview of one perspective on stages of consulting to nonprofits,
including the "artistry" of working with others and the business and marketing of consulting
with nonprofits.

Flawless Consulting: Guide to Getting Your Expertise Used, Second Edition, Peter Block,
Jossey-Bass Publishers, 2000.

Block's break-through book first heralded in the innovative approach of collaborative
consulting. His book is probably the most referenced general resource when first training
consultants to conduct collaborative and effective consulting projects.

How to Succeed as an Independent Consultant, Herman Holtz, Third Edition, Wiley, 1993.

This well-known resource goes into more depth than most other consulting books about the
roles of a consultant, starting a business, writing proposals and contracts and reports, etc.

Jumping the Job Track, Peter C. Brown, Crown, 1994.

Comprehensive guidelines for considering the job change to consulting, including conducting a skills inventory, thinking about your markets, setting up shop, etc. Includes many real-life examples.

Facilitation and Groups (General)

Facilitation, T. Bentley, McGraw-Hill, 1994.

Provides a somewhat philosophical overview of facilitating, particularly about indirect facilitation. Readers would be best to review this book after having first reviewed more basic books on facilitation, such as Clarke's book listed later on below.

Process Consultation: Its Role in Organization Development, E. Schein, Addison Wesley Publishing Company, 1969.

This is a seminal work in group dynamics and facilitation. Process consultation is widely considered to be the foundation for group dynamics and effective facilitation. This is a must-read for facilitators for organizational change.

Technology of Participation: Group Facilitation Methods, Institute of Cultural Affairs, 1994.

Provided in the Institute for Cultural Affairs' ToP facilitation workshop. Provides a straightforward overview of facilitating discussions, workshops and action planning techniques, especially for multi-cultural organizations.

The Skilled Facilitator: Practical Wisdom for Developing Effective Groups, R. M. Schwartz, Jossey-Bass Publishers, 1994.

Provides a comprehensive and useful overview of facilitation. It is somewhat academic, that is, research-oriented with theories, models and concepts. Readers might read this after reading a more basic, straightforward book, such as Clarke's, below.

Who, Me Lead a Group?, J. I. Clarke, Winston Press, Inc, 1984.

Beginning facilitators might read this straightforward book first to get an understanding of different types of meetings and then how to lead them.

Financial Management

Bookkeeping Basics: What Every Nonprofit Bookkeeper Needs to Know, Debra L. Ruegg and Lisa M. Venkatrathnam, Amherst H. Wilder Foundation, 2003.

The book explains important practices and procedures in bookkeeping and the overall bookkeeping cycle, generating the most important nonprofit financial statements, and how to establish the most important financial controls in a nonprofit organization.

Streetsmart Financial Basics for Nonprofit Managers, Thomas A. McLaughlin, John Wiley and Sons, 1995.

The book describes how to make management decisions based on financial information. The book includes numerous, easy-to-reference diagrams, along with numerous examples. Includes on-line copies of useful checklists and worksheets.

Bibliography

Fundraising

Fundraising Basics: A Complete Guide, Second Edition, Barbara L. Ciconte and Jeanne Jacob, Jones and Bartlett, 2001.

This book explains the basics of fundraising, including critical foundations for successful fundraising, types of fundraising, how to plan your fundraising activities, and trends in fundraising. Includes fundraising on the Internet. Includes case studies and real-life examples.

Fundraising for Dummies, Second Edition, John Mutz and Katherine Murray, Jossey-Bass, 2000.

This book describes the most important basic considerations and activities to plan and conduct your fundraising. Includes how to get the Board engaged in fundraising, and how to research major donors and write grants. Similar to other *Dummies* books, this book includes a lot of handy tips and conventional wisdom.

Raise More Money: The Best of the Grassroots Fundraising Journal, Kim Klein and Stephanie Roth, Jossey-Bass, 2001.

This book combines the best advice from Klein's seminal publications on grassroots fundraising. The advice is always specific and easy to apply. This is a must-read for anyone working with small- to medium-sized nonprofit organizations. The advice still applies to nonprofits of any size.

Leadership and Supervision (includes staffing and volunteers)

Executive Director's Survival Guide, Mim Carlson and Margaret Donohoe, Jossey-Bass, 2003.

This book was written for the Chief Executive Officer who wants to understand all aspects of the role and develop into a wise and effective leader. Includes guidelines to avoid burnout, identify organizational effectiveness, lead organizational change and work effectively with the Board.

Executive Leadership in Nonprofit Organizations: New Strategies for Shaping Executive-Board Dynamics, Robert D. Herman and Richard D. Heimovics, Jossey-Bass, 1991.

The is one of the first publications to suggest that, although theory and law assert that the Board governs the organization, the quality of the working relationship between the Board and Chief Executive Officer is one of the most important determinants of the effectiveness of the organization.

Field Guide to Leadership and Supervision for Nonprofit Staff, Carter McNamara, Authenticity Consulting, LLC, Minneapolis, MN, 2002.

This guidebook provides complete, step-by-step guidelines to conduct the most essential activities in successful leadership and supervision in a nonprofit organization. Includes Board and staff roles, leading yourself, analyzing staff roles, recruiting and selecting staff, training and organizing staff, meeting management, performance management and how to avoid Founder's Syndrome.

Marketing (including advertising and promotions)

Field Guide to Nonprofit Program Design, Marketing and Evaluation, Carter McNamara, Authenticity Consulting, LLC, Minneapolis, MN, 2003.

There are few resources about program planning, so this book is unique. It addresses the activities of program design, marketing and evaluation as they should be – as activities that are highly integrated with each other. This guidebook includes complete step-by-step guidelines and on-line worksheets to successfully conduct activities on an ongoing basis.

Successful Marketing Strategies For Nonprofit Organizations, Barry J. McLeish, Wiley, 1995.

The author argues that marketing is not just an activity, but should be an orientation among all management. Guidelines describe how to develop a strategic marketing plan from analyzing the external and internal environments of the nonprofit, and then producing a plan that best fits both environments.

Workbook for Nonprofit Organizations: Volume 1 Develop the Plan, Gary J. Stern, Amherst H. Wilder Foundation, 1990

This book explains the theory and importance of marketing in nonprofits. It describes a five-step process to develop a marketing plan: establishing goals, positioning the nonprofit, doing a marketing audit, developing the plan, and associating a promotions campaign. Includes worksheets.

Organizational Development and Change

Appreciative Inquiry: Change at the Speed of Imagination, Jane M. Watkins and Bernhard J. Mohr, Jossey-Bass, 2001.

Appreciative Inquiry (AI) has become a prominent movement in organizational change and development. It offers a truly new paradigm in how we see organizations and its members, and as a result, how we plan and change organizations. There are numerous resources on AI, but this book is one of the most well-organized and understandable, replete with various models to apply AI and how to explain AI to other people.

Changing the Essence, Richard Beckhard and Wendy Pritchard, Jossey-Bass, Inc., 1992.

This is one of the seminal works on organizational change and written by the "father" of the field of Organization Development. It includes a comprehensive and strategic overview of key considerations in achieving successful organizational change.

Making Sense of Life's Changes, William Bridges, Addison Wesley, 1980.

Bridge's book provides an excellent overview of the psychological and sociological aspects and considerations for successful organizational change. His book, combined with Block's (in the "Consulting" section in this Appendix) and Beckhard's (above), comprise a comprehensive "toolkit" for conducting successful organizational change.

Organizational Culture and Leadership, 3rd Edition, Edgar H. Schein, Jossey-Bass, 2004.

Seminal work on the subject. Defines culture, levels and dimensions, key issues to manage during change, relationship between leadership and culture, and how leaders create organizational cultures.

Organization Development and Change, Seventh Edition, Thomas G. Cummings and Christopher G. Worley, South-Western Educational Publishing, 2000.

This is a classic, up-to-date text on the field and practices of Organization Development (OD). Includes history, movements and major research findings. It is a must-read for the reader serious about becoming a professional in the field of Organization Development.

Power of Appreciative Inquiry: Practical Guide to Positive Change, Diana Whitney and Amanda Trosten-Bloom, Berrett Koehler, 2002.

This is a comprehensive, yet practical, book about AI. It provides numerous approaches to AI across a wide variety of organizations, and includes case studies for the approaches, as well.

Practicing Organization Development: A Guide for Consultants, William J. Rothwell, Roland Sullivan and Gary N. McLean, Jossey-Bass, 1995.

This book is focused on guidelines and other advice for the practitioners who seek "how to" resources to conduct successful organizational development projects.

Reframing Organizations, Lee Bolman and Terrence Deal, Jossey-Bass, 1991.

This book has been a wonderful gift to organizational consultants because it reminds them that different people can have quite different perspectives on the same organization. Those different perspectives can result in widely varying interpretations and suggestions about organizational change.

The 5 Life Stages of Nonprofit Organizations, Judith Sharken Simon, Amherst H. Wilder Foundation, 2001.

Provides a highly understandable and meaningful overview of life stages of nonprofits and includes a comprehensive, yet practical, life-stage assessment tool with examples, analysis and advice.

Program Evaluation

Evaluation of Capacity Building: Lessons from the Field, Deborah Linnell, Alliance for Nonprofit Management, 2003.

Describes results of research among a variety of capacity builders, along with descriptions of the general activities of each builder and what they are doing to evaluate their particular programs. Numerous lessons-learned are conveyed, as well as suggestions for further research.

Field Guide to Nonprofit Program Design, Marketing and Evaluation, Carter McNamara, Authenticity Consulting, LLC, Minneapolis, MN, 2003.

There are few resources about program planning, so this book is unique. It addresses the activities of program design, marketing and evaluation as they should be – as activities that are highly integrated with each other. This guidebook includes complete step-by-step guidelines and on-line worksheets to successfully conduct activities on an ongoing basis.

Qualitative Evaluation and Research Methods, Michael Quinn Patton, Sage Publications, 1990.

Provides comprehensive overview of qualitative research and data collection methods, many of which can be used in practical approaches to market research and program evaluation.

Program Planning and Design

Field Guide to Nonprofit Program Design, Marketing and Evaluation, Carter McNamara, Authenticity Consulting, LLC, Minneapolis, MN, 2003.

> There are few resources about program planning, so this book is unique. It addresses the activities of program design, marketing and evaluation as they should be – as activities that are highly integrated with each other. This guidebook includes complete step-by-step guidelines and on-line worksheets to successfully conduct activities on an ongoing basis.

Designing and Planning Programs for Nonprofit and Government Organizations, Edward J. Pawlak, Robert D. Vinter, Jossey-Bass, 2004.

> Books focuses on nonprofit and government organizations. Suggests step-by-step activities for major phases, including planning, implementation and program operations. Ideally suited to large organizations with complex programs and systems.

Strategic Planning

Field Guide to Nonprofit Strategic Planning and Facilitation, Carter McNamara, Authenticity Consulting, LLC, Minneapolis, Minnesota, 2003.

> Comprehensive, step-by-step guidebook to facilitate a Strategic Plan that is relevant, realistic and flexible. Includes a variety of planning models that can be used and guidelines to select which model is best. Also includes on-line tools that can be downloaded for each planner.

Five Most Important Questions You Will Ever Ask About Your Nonprofit Organization: Participant's Workbook, Peter F. Drucker Foundation, Jossey-Bass Publishers, 1993.

> Top-level workbook guides organizations through answering five key strategic questions: What is our business (mission)? Who is our customer? What does the customer consider value? What have been our results? What is our Plan?

Strategic Management: Formulation, Implementation, and Control, Fourth Edition, John A. Pearce II and Richard B. Robinson, Jr., Irwin Publishing, 1991.

> Explains the strategic planning process in the overall context of strategic management. Explains complete strategic management cycle, primarily for large for-profit corporations. Much of the information applies to nonprofits, including processes that nonprofits tend not to do, but should.

Strategic Planning for Public and Nonprofit Organizations, John Bryson, Jossey-Bass Publishers, 1995.

> Provides an extensive, well-organized and in-depth explanation of a 10-step strategic planning cycle that can be used in planning with organizations ranging from small to large. This book is often referred to as the seminal source of strategic planning expertise for nonprofit organizations.

Strategic Planning Workbook for Nonprofit Organizations, Revised and Updated, Bryan Barry, Wilder Foundation, St. Paul, MN, 1997.

> Well-organized and readable, top-level workbook provides guidelines and worksheets to conduct strategic planning for a variety of types, sizes and designs of nonprofit and public organizations.

Index

Notes

Authenticity Consulting Titles Specific to Nonprofits

Field Guide to Developing, Operating and Restoring Your Nonprofit Board

This guide will help your Board to be highly effectively in all of the most important aspects of governance, including strategic planning, programs, marketing, staffing, finances, fundraising, evaluations, transparency, sustainability and lobbying. It includes guidelines to detect and fix broken Boards; select the best Board model for the nonprofit to implement; define how much the Board members should be involved in management, depending on the Board model; decide whether to use committees or not, and if so, which ones; establish specific, appropriate goals for Board committees; conduct comprehensive succession planning of the CEO position; ensure legal compliance to the Sarbanes-Oxley act; and ensure highly ethical behavior of Board members. Comprehensive guidelines and materials are written in an easy-to-implement style, resulting in a highly practical resource that can be referenced at any time during the life of a Board and organization.

296 pp, softcover, revised 2008   Item #7110, ISBN 978-1-933719-05-4 / 1-933719-05-2 $32

Field Guide to Nonprofit Strategic Planning and Facilitation

The guide provides step-by-step instructions and worksheets to customize and implement a comprehensive nonprofit strategic plan – that is relevant, realistic and flexible for the nonprofit organization. The guide describes the most useful traditional and holistic approaches to strategic planning. It also includes the most important tools and techniques to facilitate strategic planning in an approach that ensures strong participation and ownership among all of the planners. Emphasis is as much on implementation and follow-through of the plan as on developing the plan document. Hardcopy and online worksheets help you to collect and organize all of the results of their planning process.

284 pp, softcover, revised 2007   Item #7120, ISBN 978-1-933719-06-1 / 1-933179-06-0 $32

Field Guide to Leadership and Supervision for Nonprofit Staff

Top-level executives, middle managers and entry-level supervisors in nonprofit organizations need the "nuts and bolts" for carrying out effective leadership and supervision, particularly in organizations with limited resources. This guide includes topics often forgotten in nonprofit publications, including: time and stress management, staffing, organizing, team building, setting goals, giving feedback, avoiding Founder's Syndrome, and much more. It also includes guidelines to ensure a strong working relationship between the Chief Executive Officer and the Board.

303 pp, softcover, revised 2008   Item #7130, ISBN 978-1-933719-07-8 / 1-933179-07-9 $32

Field Guide to Nonprofit Program Design, Marketing and Evaluation

Nonprofits have long needed a clear, concise – and completely practical – guidebook about all aspects of designing, marketing and evaluating nonprofit programs. Now they have such a resource. This guide can be used to evolve strategic goals into well-designed programs that are guaranteed to meet the needs of clients, develop credible nonprofit business plans and fundraising proposals, ensure focused and effective marketing, evaluate the effectiveness and efficiencies of current programs in delivery of services to clients, evaluate program performance against goals and outcomes, and understand how a program really works in order to improve or duplicate the program.

252 pp, softcover, revised 2006   Item #7170, ISBN 978-1-933719-08-5 / 1-933719-08-7 $32

Field Guide to Consulting and Organizational Development With Nonprofits

This highly practical book combines the tools and techniques of the field of Organization Development with the power of systems thinking and principles for successful change in nonprofits. The book also addresses many of the problems with traditional approaches to consulting and leading. The result is a proven, time-tested roadmap for consultants and leaders to accomplish significant change in nonprofits. You can use this book to accomplish change in small or large nonprofit organizations, for instance organizations that
>   1) have a variety of complex issues,
>   2) must ensure a strong foundation from which to develop further,
>   3) must evolve to the next life cycle,
>   4) need a complete "turnaround,"
>   5) must address Founder's Syndrome or
>   6) want to achieve an exciting grand goal.

517 pp, softcover, 2005   Item #7180, ISBN 978-1-933719-00-9 / 1-933719-00-1 $58

Additional Titles for Business, Government and General Use

Field Guide to Leadership and Supervision in Business

Top-level executives, middle managers and entry-level supervisors in organizations need the "nuts and bolts" for carrying out effective leadership and supervision, particularly in organizations with limited resources. This guide includes topics often forgotten in trendy publications, including: time and stress management, staffing, organizing, team building, setting goals, giving feedback, and much more. It also provides guidance for Boards and business leaders to work together effectively.

262 pp, softcover, revised 2010   Item #7430, ISBN 1-933719-27-3 / 978-1-933719-27-6 $32

Field Guide to Consulting and Organizational Development

This highly practical book combines the tools and techniques of the field of Organization Development with the power of systems thinking and principles for successful change in for-profits and government agencies. The book also addresses many of the problems with traditional approaches to consulting and leading. The result is a proven, time-tested roadmap for consultants and leaders to accomplish significant change. You can use this book to accomplish change in small or large organizations, whether the organization is dealing with a variety of complex issues or striving to achieve goals for the future.

499 pp, softcover, 2006   Item #7480, ISBN 978-1-933719-20-7 / 1-933719-20-6 $58

Additional Titles About Action Learning and Peer Coaching Groups

Authenticity Circles Program Developer's Guide

Step-by-step guidelines to design, build, manage and troubleshoot an Action Learning-based, peer coaching group program. The program can be used by consultants or an organization's leaders for training enrichment, problem solving, support and networking among peers.

127 pp, comb-bound, 2002   Item #7730, ISBN 978-1-933719-10-8 / 1-933719-10-9 $26

Authenticity Circles Facilitator's Guide

This Guide describes how to organize, facilitate and evaluate peer coaching groups. Groups can be facilitated by an external facilitator or groups can self-facilitate themselves. It can also be used to recruit, develop and support facilitators of peer coaching groups. The Guide includes appendices with worksheets for the facilitator's use and a handy Circles Quick Reference tool.

114 pp, comb-bound, 2002   Item #7720, ISBN 978-1-933719-11-5 / 1-933719-11-7 $22

Authenticity Circles Member's Guide and Journal

This Guide provides step-by-step guidelines for group members to get the most out of their Action Learning-based, peer coaching groups, including how to select goals to be coached on, how to get coached and how to coach others. The Guide includes a journal of worksheets to capture the learning of the group members and a handy Circles Quick Reference tool.

110 pp, comb-bound, 2004   Item #7710, ISBN 978-1-933719-12-2 / 1-933719-12-5 $16

Coming in 2010 – Watch our website for news!

Field Guide to Strategic Planning and Facilitation - *For business now too!*

To order

To get your copies of these and other useful publications, contact us:

Online: www.authenticityconsulting.com/pubs.htm

Phone: 800.971.2250 toll-free in North America or 1.763.971.8890 direct

Mail: Authenticity Consulting, LLC
4008 Lake Drive Avenue North
Minneapolis, MN 55422-1508 USA